Some of the questions asked—and answered—
in this book:

What are the Jews? What is Judaism? What is Zionism?

What is the significance of the various Jewish holidays?

What is the origin of Jewish dietary laws?

What is the origin of the Sermon on the Mount? The
   Golden Rule? The "non-resistance" doctrine?

What is the difference between *Passover* and *Easter*?

What is the origin of baptism?

What is a Christian? How did Christianity begin?

What are the basic differences between Judaism and
   Christianity? What are the basic similarities?

What do Jews and Christians mean by salvation and
   original sin?

RAPHAEL H. LEVINE

RABBI, TEMPLE DE HIRSCH, SEATTLE

TWO PATHS

JUDAISM AND

TO ONE GOD:
CHRISTIANITY

With an Introduction by the

RT. REV. STEPHEN F. BAYNE, JR.

Executive Officer of the Anglican Communion

COLLIER BOOKS
NEW YORK, N.Y.

Two Paths to One God originally appeared under the title *Holy Mountain*

This Collier Books edition is published by arrangement with the author

Collier Books is a division of The Crowell-Collier Publishing Company

First Collier Books Edition 1962

Library of Congress Catalog Card Number: 62-18370

*To a better and fairer understanding between Christians and
Jews, recognizing our basic oneness implicit in our unyielding faith in God, which has inspired us, Jew
and Christian alike, to climb the holy mountain where both can work together to
glorify God in the eyes of all the
family of man, this book is humbly dedicated.*

Acknowledgments

THERE ARE MORE people than I can name to whom I owe a debt for the information, inspiration, and encouragement which made *Holy Mountain* and this revised version possible. There are some, however, whose assistance in so many ways helped me in the preparation of the manuscript that the least I can do is to express here my grateful thanks to them—to my Board of Trustees, the members of our Religious School Committee and our Religious School teachers, whose encouragement started me on the project; to the University Printing Company, who, at great sacrifice to themselves, printed the original manuscript in June, 1952; to our Temple Sisterhood; to Professor W. M. Read and Mr. W. H. James of the University of Washington Press; to Professor Harry Bauer, former director of libraries and professor of librarianship, University of Washington; to Edwin H. Adams, director of radio-television, University of Washington; and to the late Dr. Samuel S. Cohon, professor of theology at the Hebrew Union College, who read the manuscript and offered valuable suggestions for its improvement.

I am also grateful to the Union of American Hebrew Congregations; the National Federation of Temple Brotherhoods; the Central Conference of American Rabbis; the National Conference of Christians and Jews for permission to use material published by them; to Mrs. Nora Cuse, my secretary, who helped so much in preparing this manuscript; and to Binfords & Mort who published the original book.

To the Anti-Defamation League of the B'nai B'rith, I owe a very great debt for their interest in the book as a contribution to their fine program of education for democracy and their labors over many years to promote better understanding between all religious and racial groups in our country.

Finally, and with gratitude I can hardly express in words, I want to say thank you to the Right Reverend Stephen F. Bayne, Jr., former Bishop of Olympia, now Executive Officer of the Anglican Communion, London, England, to Mr. James

Stevens, author of *Big Jim Turner*, *Paul Bunyan*, and other books, and to Dr. Miriam Reinhart of Bridgewater Teachers' College, Massachusetts, for their constant help, guidance, and advice.

For this quality paperback edition I am greatly indebted to Rabbi Michael Robinson, Croton-on-Hudson, whose interest in the original *Holy Mountain* brought it to the attention of Mr. Bruno Fischer, senior editor at Collier Books, leading to its present publication.

Most of all I am indebted to my dear wife, Reeva, who did the art work for the inside cover of the original *Holy Mountain*, and whose encouragement and understanding has always been a source of strength and inspiration.

RAPHAEL H. LEVINE

Foreword

And the mountain of the Lord's house
Shall be established as the top of the mountains,
And shall be exalted above the hills;
And all nations shall flow unto it,
And many peoples shall go and say:
"Come ye, and let us go up to the mountain of the Lord,
To the house of the God of Jacob;
And He will teach us His ways,
And we will walk in His paths. . . ."

—Isaiah 2:2-3

THIS IS A BOOK for Christians and Jews and for all others who
may be interested in understanding two great religions and the
peoples who profess them. Its basic purpose is to foster a
better and fairer understanding of the Jew and his religion on
the part of Christians, and of Christianity on the part of Jews.
My experience during thirty years as a rabbi both in England,
where I spent the first ten years of my ministry, and in this
country, where I have been since my return in 1941, has made
me painfully aware that the misconceptions of Christians
about the Jew and his religion is equaled only by those of
Jews about Christianity. There are some in both groups who,
because of their uncharitable attitudes towards each other's
faiths and practices, have created a wide gulf of misunderstanding and even hatred which is only now beginning to be
bridged. I want to help strengthen and support that bridge
with one more girder.

I am not interested in mere tolerance for each other's faith.
That we already have largely accomplished—a tolerance en-
forced by the Constitution of the United States and by a long
American tradition of "live and let live" in religious matters.
My purpose in writing this book, and my hope in placing it
before the reader, is to achieve something more than tolerance
—something akin to respect, indeed even reverence—which

9

I feel needs to be cultivated by all of us for the faiths and traditions of our fellow men.

I am a Jew. I shall live and die a Jew. But I cannot believe that because I am a Jew I must look with disdain at the aspirations toward God which differ from mine in creed and ritual and worship. On the contrary, my Judaism, if I interpret its spirit rightly, enjoins me to regard my non-Jewish brother's religious aspirations with respect and even reverence. The prayerbook which I use at my Sabbath services tells me to fulfill my mission as a Jew *with zeal tempered by wisdom and guided by regard for other men's faith* (italics mine). I take very seriously the plea of the prophet Malachi: "Have we not all one Father; hath not one God created us?" I am equally convinced that God in His infinite wisdom has created us with the capacity to be different one from the other, even to be different in our quest for and in our worship of Him. How else can I explain the great diversity of races, cultures, languages, religions, and points of view if not that God in His wisdom had willed it so?

I do understand something of the geographical, sociological and psychological factors that created, through the ages, the multicolored pattern of our human family and society. But I believe that the whole pattern of human development has been governed by a power greater than ourselves— the power of God using what we call natural forces and laws and the ever-changing human conditions to achieve the great diversity that characterizes the family of man. And this diversity, although it has brought its problems and its difficulties, has also given us a power for growth, enrichment, and fulfillment such as no generation before us, less diverse and less complex than ours, could ever dream of attaining.

In one way or another this is the thesis of this book. It is a plea for unity in the midst of our diversities; for seeking the common ground upon which we can stand, Jew and Christian alike, as children of God, and from which we can rise together toward God's holy mountain—not necessarily by the same path. That is neither possible nor desirable; but at least we may rise with the same zeal and devotion in our striving to build God's kingdom on earth where in His infinite wisdom and goodness He has placed us for a time. The first step in

this difficult ascent is to dispel ignorance and to bring understanding. That I have tried to do.

I have used the question-and-answer method because of its
simplicity. I have tried to avoid all technicalities of theology
and language; for I want the general reader, not only the
student of religion, to be helped toward the goal and perhaps
even to enjoy the effort of the climb. Because of this question-
and-answer style there may be occasions in which material
is repeated in dealing with problems of a related nature. That
I did not avoid, for I desired to make each question and answer separate and independent—thus enabling the reader to
understand a single question of interest to him without his
having to read a chapter or more to clarify the answer.

I am aware of the literary limitations of this method, but I
hope that greater ease in acquiring the desired information
may compensate for these limitations. It is with a prayerful
hope that this book may be helpful to those who seek a better
understanding and a more fruitful cooperation between Christians and Jews, indeed among all the children of God, that I
present this book for your consideration.

RAPHAEL H. LEVINE

Seattle, Washington

Introduction

ONE OF the first things I heard about Jews (I regret to say from a kinsman) was that they customarily had machine guns in their cellars with which to attack their Christian neighbors. At the time, this struck me as simply one more picturesque and imaginative detail about life in the picturesque and imaginative New York of my childhood. Fortunately, by the time I had reached the age when such rumors might have settled into convictions, I had heard also that Jews believed that Christians boiled babies and ate them, and, by a process of comparison of idiocies, I had reached a little perspective in such things.

But I very soon came to see that for us in our bewilderingly rich and various city, a choice had to be made between two paths. Either we were to settle down, like our cats and sparrows, to an endless vigilance and hostility based on ignorance, or else we would follow the way of light and knowledge. I think I was too inquisitive to bear the first solution. The mysteries of Friday suppertimes in our Jewish neighbor's apartment, where candles burned behind a closed door; the curious appearance of the Ten Commandments in the little stationery store where we bought our licorice sticks; the fact that the "old clothes man" in our neighborhood looked exactly like Moses who apparently was one of "them" as well as one of "us"—these and a multitude more were simply too much for my blood. I had to know; although I was innocent of the fact that such knowledge might be also a virtue, I could not endure not knowing.

And, inevitably, with the knowledge of my neighbors came a knowledge of myself. I discovered that the mysterious biblical people about whom I learned in Sunday School still lived, and lived indeed no further away than next door. I discovered that the cup which, week by week, I raised to my lips in Holy Communion was not very different from the cup which my neighbor shared with his family. Granted that my Lord had set a new and infinitely precious meaning on it, still it had

13

come from them, and for a great part of the way it was a cup which Jewish and Christian hands held together. I discovered that the great commandment by which I was trying to guide my life was not very different from the *Sh'mah,* which our grocery boy had taught me how to say one lazy afternoon.

And when, long afterward, I came to the mature study of Christian theology, I was immeasureably enriched to be able to bring to it even what little I had learned of this strange people from whose life my Lord and my saints and I myself had come. Even more, after that, when I left the practice world of school to begin my life in the real world, I brought with me a measure of understanding and comradeship which was a better cargo, by far, than the stupid callousness which I might otherwise have had.

I do not mean to write an autobiography. I mean simply to say to the man or woman who picks up this book what I firmly believe: that there is no excuse nor place in our American life for deliberate ignorance, that for Christians it is a double sin not to know our common heritage with Jews, and that Rabbi Levine has done a very great service to us all in entering into this difficult field with an ardent and eager willingness to bring light where there is, too often, darkness.

Rabbi Levine is writing for Christians as well as Jews, crossing a frontier where men of good will may meet. It is not an easy thing to do, for one is assailed by temptations on both sides—either to soften and sentimentalize the differences in belief between the two great groups, or to apply a harsh judgment on the tensions which exist, and reopen old wounds. But I honestly feel that this book has escaped both dangers and opened for many readers a new and fairer and more thoughtful common knowledge than they have had before.

A great Pope said, speaking to Christians, that we must remember that "we are spiritually Semites." By which he meant, no doubt, many things; but certainly this: that Christians share a common inheritance with their Jewish brothers which is a determining and commanding element in Christianity. A passionate loyalty to the God whose will is known and to be obeyed; a certainty that history is a sure theater of God's provident action; an assurance that God takes and keeps the initiative in human affairs, that He reigns on earth as in heaven; a granite faith in the reality of human freedom under God and of human responsibility to God for one's brother man—these are some of the imperative elements in our blood, Jew and Christian together, and they are ties which bind us together far more deeply than we realize.

This is not to say that there are no fundamental differences; nor does Rabbi Levine say so. Christian and Jew alike have too great respect for one another's faith and freedom to be careless or sophisticated about honest convictions, and Rabbi Levine is too sensitive and intelligent a man to smudge or blur differences. He knows as well as I do that there are clear and often radical differences in our beliefs and that those differences reflect themselves practically in our lives. He understands, also, something of the deeper mystery of the dark wrestle of the two faiths over nineteen centuries and of the scars those years have brought. For that reason he has opened through his book a way into Judaism for many Christians, and an understanding of Christianity for many Jews; and I am sincerely hopeful that his words will be as widely read as I am sure they will be helpful.

There are times when I think he makes the problem a bit too easy. When that is so, it is not because he is beguiled into sentimentality; it is because he is a kind and thoughtful man whose certainty about the ultimate truth of brotherhood leads him inescapably to think men are better than they really are. That is a good fault in times like these. As a Christian, I would far rather have Rabbi Levine take me for what I might some day know and be, than for what my ancestors have been.

The differences are real enough; but even the differences, where they are clearly seen and stated in a common tongue and against a common background, can serve to bind together rather than divide. This, I think, has been excellently done, in a way which will open a door to many readers. So may it be.

STEPHEN F. BAYNE, JR.

Contents

17

Two Paths to One God: Judaism and Christianity

WHAT IS A JEW?

But thou, Israel, My servant,
Jacob whom I have chosen,
The seed of Abraham, My friend;
Thou whom I have taken hold of
From the ends of the earth,
And called thee from the uttermost parts thereof,
And said unto thee, "Thou art My servant, . . ."

Behold, all they that were incensed against thee
Shall be ashamed and confounded;
They that strove with thee
Shall be ashamed and confounded;

For I the Lord thy God hold thy right hand,
Who say unto thee, "Fear not, I help thee."
                                        —Isaiah 41:8-13

Across Four Thousand Years

Now THEREFORE, if ye will hearken unto My voice indeed,
and keep My covenant, then ye shall be Mine own treasure
from among the peoples; for the earth is Mine; and ye shall
be unto me a kingdom of priests and a holy nation.
                                        —Exodus 19:5-6

In the book of Genesis, Chapter 12, the Bible tells us:

Now the Lord said unto Abram [later changed to Abraham,
which means "Father of the people"], "Get thee out of thy
country, and from thy kindred and from thy father's house
unto the land that I will show thee. And I will make of thee
a great nation, and I will bless thee and make thy name
great; and be thou a blessing. And I will bless them that
bless thee, and him that curseth thee I will curse; and in
thee shall all the families of the earth be blessed."
                                        —Genesis 12:1-3

25

With this summons from God the first Jewish ancestor, tradition tells us, left his native Ur in the Chaldees about four thousand years ago and started a career in the fulfillment of God's will which his descendants have been carrying on since then in every corner of the earth.

It has been a career at times wondrously glorious, at times incredibly tragic. Count Leo Tolstoy, the great Russian novelist and philosopher of the 19th century, wrote a letter in which he tried to evaluate the Jew's place in the history of civilization:

> What is a Jew? This question is not at all so odd as it seems. Let us see what kind of peculiar creature the Jew is, which all the rulers and all nations have together and separately abused and molested, oppressed and persecuted, trampled and butchered, burned and hanged—and in spite of all this is yet alive! What is a Jew, who has never allowed himself to be led astray by all the earthly possessions which his oppressors and persecutors constantly offered him in order that he should change his faith and forsake his own Jewish religion?
>
> The Jew is that sacred being who has brought down from heaven the everlasting fire, and has illuminated with it the entire world. He is the religious source, spring, and fountain out of which all the rest of the peoples have drawn their beliefs and their religions. . . .
>
> The Jew is the emblem of eternity. He whom neither slaughter nor torture of thousands of years could destroy, he who was the first to produce the oracles of God, he who has been for so long the guardian of prophecy, and who transmitted it to the rest of the world—such a people cannot be destroyed. The Jew is everlasting as is eternity itself.
>
> —Hertz, Book of Jewish Thoughts, p. 130

Allowing for the flights of fancy and extravagant poetry permitted to an imaginative writer like Tolstoy, his observations, nonetheless, reveal deep insight into the spirit of Jewish history, struggle, and achievement through the centuries. These observations are all the more noteworthy because they are voiced by a great Christian.

When Abraham began his mission to follow the invisible

God Whose dictates he felt in his innermost soul, he was all alone in a pagan world. For nearly two thousand years after him his descendants endeavoring to fulfill the mission he entrusted to them were a people unique in a world still pagan. During these two thousand years their career was chequered by external wars and internal dissensions.

They were often conquered and enslaved. Their cities were laid waste and their sacred shrines were ground into the dust. Their years of tranquility during these two millenia were few. But their very tragedies served to temper their souls and to harden their will to live, as fine steel is hardened and tempered by the fire. Mighty spirits rose from among them to lead, to guide, and to inspire them with an unyielding faith which has become the miracle of the ages. Their survival across four thousand years was a veritable fulfillment of God's promise voiced by the unknown prophet of the Babylonian exile:

When thou passest through the waters, I will be with thee,
And through the rivers they shall not overflow thee;
When thou walkest through the fire thou shalt not be burned
Neither shall the flame kindle upon thee,
For I am the Lord thy God
    The Holy One of Israel, thy Savior.

—Isaiah 43:2

This tremendous faith in God and in Israel's ultimate vindication was nurtured and fostered by many men. Moses, of whom the poet Heine said, "How small Sinai appears when Moses stands upon it," was one of them. The immortal galaxy of God-inspired men, the Hebrew prophets, who for more than four hundred years served as the conscience of Israel helping to keep their feet steadfast on the road to the God of Abraham, Isaac, and Jacob, were others. The rabbis of the Talmud carried on the heritage of the lawgivers and prophets with their ideal that "the world depends for its existence and survival upon three things—truth, justice, and peace."

Buttressed by this faith in God and in a glorious future for mankind, the Jews found in their Judaism inexhaustible reservoirs of spiritual power to survive the tragic centuries. Indeed, the more they were persecuted the stronger they became, outlasting every one of their persecutors. The mighty empires of ancient Egypt, Assyria, Babylonia, Persia, Greece, and Rome, who in turn conquered, enslaved, and dominated them, are now buried beneath the dust of the ages. Their once magnificent pagan civilizations are known today only to the historian and to the archeologist digging among their ruins. The Jews live on, still playing their unique role in the changing career of mankind.

Although the Jews at the height of their numerical greatness never exceeded perhaps sixteen million, the Jewish religion with its concept of one God ruling the universe through law and love has become the spiritual fountainhead whence more than half the world's people today draw their spiritual sustenance and inspiration. Through Christianity, born of the spirit of Judaism and embodied in the personality of Christianity's master teacher, Jesus, the Jew of Nazareth, and through Mohammedanism, founded about six centuries later, the truths which Judaism first conceived and proclaimed have become the heritage of mankind. The Jewish Bible has become the cornerstone of much of the world's faith.

Walt Whitman, writing of the Bible's influence, says:

How many ages and generations have brooded and wept and agonized over this book! What untellable joys and ecstasies, what support to martyrs at the stake, from it! To what myriads has it been the shore and the rock of safety —the refuge from driving tempest and wreck! Translated into all languages how it has united this diverse world! Of its thousands there is not a verse, not a word, but is thick studded with human emotion.

—Hertz, Book of Jewish Thoughts, p. 137

Matthew Arnold, the incisive English thinker of the nineteenth century, speaking of the foundations of our Western civilization, said with deep insight that perhaps one third of our heritage came from ancient Greece and Rome and the other two thirds are the heritage of the Hebraic tradition which in our day we call the Judeo-Christian tradition. The Greeks and Romans gave us our ideals of beauty, of speculative thought, and statecraft. The Hebrews gave us our faith in God and in the moral law. They gave us the eternal ethical ideals and the moral and spiritual values which undergird the structure of our civilization, of which the beauty and philosophy of Greece and the statecraft of Rome are but transient facets in the changing pattern of our human society. The Ten Commandments are eternal whatever form our civilization may assume. The injunction to love our neighbor as ourselves applies equally to European, Asian, American, and African. The Golden Rule makes for abundant and creative living whether it is practiced in America, or Europe, or in the wilds of darkest Africa. God is one, His moral law is universally valid. The brotherhood of man is the hope of all the world. It is these things which the Judeo-Christian tradition proclaims as the chief cornerstone of the kingdom of God on earth which the ages are building.

> Israel is a Nation by reason only of his religion—by his possession of the Torah.
>
> —Saadia Gaon, 933 C.E.

What Are The Jews? A Race, Nationality, or Religious Community?

In the answers to this question there is great diversity of opinion among Jews, as among non-Jews, and much confused thinking. The reason is that people often ignore the fact that the character of Jewish life and the nature of the Jewish community have changed during the past four thousand years.

1. *Are the Jews a race?* Not in any sense in which most anthropologists use the term. There are only three races of mankind recognized by anthropologists: the Caucasoid (white), the Negroid (black), and the Mongoloid (various colors from yellow to red). The Jews at most can be regarded as members of the Semitic branch of the Caucasian race, and the word Semitic refers to a group of languages spoken by a number of peoples who developed in the Middle East, including the Arabs, Syrians, and some peoples no longer existing,

like the Assyrians, Babylonians, Phoenicians, Canaanites, and others mentioned in the Bible.

With many of these ancient Semitic peoples the Hebrews intermingled throughout their early history, and there has been intermixture between their Jewish decendants and the people of almost every nation in Europe since then, either voluntarily or through force. So the belief in a pure Jewish group today is untenable.

The Jews are sometimes erroneously referred to as a race, but the term is used very loosely and inaccurately—as, for example, when speaking of the French "race," the German "race," and so on, we mean a national, cultural, or historical group of people.

At one time in their history the Jews were such a people, and many Jews and non-Jews think they are still. That is why the answer to the next question is so difficult to state in terms acceptable to all Jews and non-Jews.

2. *Are the Jews a nation or religious community?* The answer to this question is exceedingly complicated. When the ancient Hebrew clans or tribes were united by King Saul, and later by David about 1000 B.C.E. (Before the Christian Era), they started their national career in ancient Palestine. They were a nation among the nations of the world with a land, a language, a culture, and a developing history of their own. They continued as a nation for a thousand years thereafter with several important breaks in their independence through conquests by Assyria, Babylonia, Persia, Greece, and Rome. Their independent national existence in a land of their own was finally terminated by the Romans when the second Temple was destroyed and the Jews were scattered in 70 C.E. (Christian Era).

During this thousand-year period of national existence the Jewish religion was developing to maturity with its beliefs, institutions, customs, and traditions. In the last two hundred years of this period the influence of the sages and rabbis grew to such an extent that at the time of the final destruction of the Jewish State in 70 C.E., they were ready to take over the remnants of the people's shattered life. The synagogue became the substitute for the temple and the state; the Torah (the

Bible) and the religious discipline it developed became the government and the law by which they lived; prayer and right-doing became the language and the technique of communion with and relation to God. In the eyes of the rabbis, who were now the undisputed leaders of the people, the Jews had become essentially a religious community, though the religion was identified with a distinct people which had been a nation and was still a nation exiled from its homeland.

This national-religious character continued through the centuries, both by the will of the Jews and because of the hostile attitudes of the Christian Church which tried to segregate and to subordinate Jews throughout Christian Europe. A radical change in the status of the Jews came in the early nineteenth century with the growth of modern nationalism ushered in by the French Revolution. The Jews of Western Europe were, for the first time in many centuries, permitted to become part of the political, civic, economic, and national life of the peoples among whom they lived. The theory of this new nationalism was that any person, whatever his race or religion, could become a citizen of the nation in which he was born or lived and to which he pledged his undivided loyalty and allegiance.

With the rise of this modern nationalism the Jews, in countries where they were granted such privileges, began to emphasize the religious character of their Jewishness and to play down the national. However, these privileges and rights of citizenship were not granted to all Jews. In Russia and Eastern Europe, where the vast majority of the European Jews lived, they were still treated as aliens though they had lived in those countries for centuries. Thus the Western European and American Jews, who were granted civil and political rights and freedoms, began to think of themselves as members of the nations to which they belonged by birth or adoption, differing from their fellow citizens only in their religious traditions and practices. The Jews of Eastern Europe, forced into an alien status, continued to think of themselves as a nation exiled from their homeland, Palestine. Thus arose the confusion that divides Jews today on whether they are a national group or simply a religious community.

The problem as to what the Jews are has become even more

confused in recent times because of the growth of a racial kind of anti-Semitism diabolically perfected by Hitler and Nazism. As a result of such anti-Semitism both Jews and non-Jews have come to think of Jews as distinguished from non-Jews by much more than their religious beliefs and practices, culture, and history, almost as if they were a different racial group. That is why it is so difficult today to give any answer as to what the Jews are that will be universally accepted.

Today, with the establishment of the state of Israel, the issue is both simplified and complicated. It is simplified because it is obvious that politically Jews must and do regard themselves as nationals of the land of their birth or adoption. It is complicated because there is an Israeli nation developing in the state of Israel, the majority of whose people are Jews. Israel is, therefore, often referred to as "the Jewish State," and the Israeli as "the Jewish people." Because of this loose thinking many people—Jews and non-Jews alike—are beginning to think again in terms of a Jewish nation, although they really mean an Israeli nation in which there are citizens of the Mohammedan faith and Christians as well as Jews, just as the American nation is composed of all kinds of religious and cultural groups and people of diverse national origins who are Americans by birth or by naturalization. Only in the sense that Italy is sometimes called a Catholic nation or America a Christian country can Israel be called Jewish—Jewish in the sense that the majority of its citizens are of the Jewish faith.

Another source of confusion about the relation of the state of Israel to world Jewry is the fact that the name *Israel* is used in Jewish worship. The *Sh'Mah*—the great affirmation of God's unity, "Hear, O Israel, the Lord our God, the Lord is One"—refers to the ancient Jewish community and calls upon them to adhere to the one and only God. Through the centuries the Jewish people were called the children of Israel, a reference to the descendants of Jacob, called Israel, the man who wrestled with God (Genesis 32:29). Because the state of Israel chose that ancient biblical name some confusion has arisen in the relation between the Israeli State and the Jewish religious community. When in Jewish worship the word Israel is used, it refers to the Jewish religious community *not to the modern state of Israel*.

So the controversy goes on. The best answer as to what is a Jew must be given in terms of the various positions and attitudes that are held today.

1. There are those who say that a Jew is anybody who regards himself as a Jew or is so regarded by the non-Jewish world.

2. There are those who think of the Jews as a distinctive cultural, historical people whose national homeland is the present state of Israel, but who, politically and culturally, are nationals of the countries of their birth or adoption.

3. There are those who contend that the Jews may have been a national-religious group at one time, but that they are now essentially a religious community with perhaps cultural and historical overtones. The protagonists of this thesis point to the fact that religion has always been the hallmark of the Jew; that non-Jews who adopted Judaism as their faith were always welcomed into the Jewish community; that there are Jews of all races and languages—black Jews from Abyssinia, yellow Jews from China, brown Jews from India, and white Jews from almost every Caucasian land on earth. It is their common religious heritage and perhaps a common memory of their life in ancient Palestine, and in more recent times the common danger from anti-Semitism, that establishes the kinship between the diverse peoples who regard themselves as, or are considered by others to be, Jews.

And so the controversy goes on, and it will continue; for the answers to this question among Jews cannot be resolved by argument, logic, or reason, not even by evidence. They are largely emotional. Those who feel at home in a non-Jewish environment are inclined to minimize the cultural, historical, and sociological differences which distinguish Jews from their non-Jewish neighbors. They tend to emphasize only the religious aspects of their Jewish heritage, those beliefs, customs, and religious traditions which distinguish Judaism from other religions. In all other respects they feel that they are part of the national and cultural life of the countries in which they live. In America they feel as Americans of Jewish faith, even as Catholics and Protestants are Americans of their respective faiths.

There are other Jews, however, who do not have this sense of complete at-homeness in non-Jewish countries because of the various aspects of anti-Semitism which subject them to prejudices and various kinds of discrimination. The restricted hotels and residential districts, the social clubs which exclude the Jew regardless of his individual worth and fitness, discrimination in employment, quotas in colleges, and numberless crude and subtle reminders that he is a member of a tolerated minority—all these experiences tend to make some Jews feel that they are not fully accepted as equal members of the society in which they live. Therefore, they are made to feel that the things that distinguish the Jew from his non-Jewish neighbors go much deeper than religious differences. Feeling thus, no rational arguments, no logic, and no evidence can convince them otherwise.

That is why the discussion of this question among Jews sometimes becomes heated. It is a question that calm reason cannot resolve. It is a matter of feeling, of attitude, of desire. So the controversy will go on.

Why Are Jews Sometimes Called Hebrews or Israelites?

Perhaps the most ancient name by which the ancestors of the Jews were known is Hebrew from the word *ever* (across, or the other side), and tradition ascribes the name to Abraham who came from Ur in the Chaldees, in the Tigris and Euphrates Valley. Therefore, the people in Palestine, those living west of the Euphrates called him and his group "the people from the other side"—*Ivrim* (Hebrews).

The name Israelite comes from the biblical account of how Jacob had his name changed to Israel. In Genesis 32:23-30, the story is told how Jacob wrestled with a mysterious being at night. As morning approached this being tried to get away but Jacob would not let him go until the mysterious person blessed him. Whereupon this person or angel said, "Thy name shall be called no more Jacob, but Israel." Israel means the man who wrestled with God. Since tradition makes Jacob the progenitor of the twelve tribes, descended from his twelve sons, they were called the children of Israel, or Israelites.

The name Jew is derived from the tribe of Judah. After the death of Solomon the twelve tribes, which had been welded into a nation by Kind David, broke up into two kingdoms— the kingdom of Israel containing ten tribes in the north of Palestine, and the kingdom of Judah with its satellite tribe of Benjamin in the south. In 722 B.C.E., the kingdom of Israel was conquered by the Assyrians and many of the people were deported from Palestine into Assyria, thus giving rise to the story of the ten lost tribes, for the kingdom of Israel never recovered from that conquest. Only the kingdom of Judah remained in the south, and it is from Judah that most of the Jews of today are descended. The people of the Judean kingdom were known as Judeans, or Jews for short.

What Happened to the Ten Lost Tribes?

It was the custom of the ancient conquerors to deport the artisans, skilled workers, priests, and nobles from the conquered land to prevent any future uprisings. An important segment of the ten Israelite tribes, who were conquered by Assyria in 722 B.C.E., was thus deported and perhaps ultimately assimilated with the Assyrians. The vast majority of the population, consisting of the peasants and poorer artisans, remained in the land and in time were assimilated with many foreigners who were either imported by the Assyrians or infiltrated and settled in the land. These foreigners adopted many of the Israelite religious beliefs and practices. The hybrid people came to be known as Samaritans from the name of the capital city of the former kingdom of Israel, Samaria. The phrase "good Samaritan" in the New Testament parable refers to a member of this group.

In modern Palestine in the town of Nablus on the site of the ancient city of Shekhem there is a small community of those who call themselves Samaritans and claim to be direct descendants of the ancient Samaritans. This small group, perhaps two hundred in all, still carries on religious practices reminiscent of the Israelite religion of twenty-seven hundred years ago. If their claims are true, then they are the last remnant of the so-called ten lost tribes.

The theories relating the ten lost tribes to American Indians, to the British, or to other peoples are fanciful and not accepted by most reputable scholars.

Why Are Some Jews Called Sephardim and Some Ashkenazim?

The word Sephardim comes from the Hebrew word *Sepharad* (Spain, the Iberian peninsula) and refers to Jews who came from Spain and Portugal. In 1492 the Jews of Spain and later the Jews of Portugal were given the choice of conversion to Christianity or expulsion. Most of them chose to leave and they migrated to Holland, Italy, and Turkey, where asylum was given them.

The descendants of these Jews are known as Sephardim. They live mostly in and around Israel, Turkey, North Africa, India, with some large Sephardic communities in London, Manchester, New York, Cincinnati, Los Angeles, Seattle, Philadelphia, and Chicago.

The word Ashkenazim comes from the Hebrew for German and refers to Jews who lived in the Rhineland district and to the north from about the third century C.E. During the Middle Ages many of these Jews either were forced to migrate or migrated voluntarily to Eastern Europe, especially to Poland and Russia. Most of the Jews in the world today are descended from these Ashkenazi Jews.

The Sephardic Jews are mostly Orthodox and differ from other Orthodox Jews in minor rituals and customs which grew up locally. They also differ in their pronunciation of the Hebrew, which the Jews of the state of Israel have adopted.

The Hebrew Language

Hebrew is one of the Semitic languages used by a group of peoples living in the Middle East in biblical times. They were called Semites because Bible tradition described them as descendants of Shem, one of Noah's three sons. The languages of the Semitic group still extant are Aramaic, Syriac, and Ethiopic, as well as Hebrew and Arabic.

The Jewish Bible (Old Testament) was originally written in the Hebrew language from which it was later translated into Greek and Latin and subsequently into all the languages spoken by man. By the third or fourth pre-Christian centuries Hebrew had ceased to be a spoken language among Jews. It continued to be the language of the Bible, of worship, and of scholarship, but was replaced by Aramaic as the vernacular. In the time of Jesus only the scholars could converse in Hebrew. Jesus used the Aramaic when he spoke to the people, and when he uttered his last words on the cross it was in Aramaic that he cried, "O Lord my God, why hast Thou forsaken me?"

Among the Jews of Europe during the past thousand years and more the vernacular was either Yiddish—a German type language, spoken by the Jews of Poland and Eastern Europe —or Ladino—a Spanish vernacular spoken by the Jews who came from Spain and Portugal (see Yiddish and Hebrew). Hebrew was regarded as the holy tongue, used only in worship and in the study of the scriptures. It was not until the early nineteenth century, stirred by the enlightenment which was spreading throughout Europe, that some Jewish scholars tried to revive Hebrew as a spoken language. The movement had a powerful upsurge with the beginnings of Zionism and the colonization of Palestine. Many scholars labored to create a modern Hebrew which would be adequate to meet the needs of twentieth-century Jews. Among the greatest and most zealous of these was Eliezer Ben Yehudah who dedicated his life to the creation of a modern Hebrew dictionary, thus laying the foundation for the modern Hebrew language now spoken in the state of Israel.

The Hebrew Alphabet

The Hebrew alphabet contains twenty-two letters with several of them having two sounds under certain conditions. The letters are as follows:

א Aleph—A

ב Beth or Base—B (also Vase—V, among Ashkenazi Jews)

ג Gimel—G (hard)

ד Daled (dah-led)—D

ה Hay—H

ו Vav—V

ז Za-in—Z

ח Heth (Hess)—gutteral H (*kh*, or German *ch*)

ט Teth—T (Tess, among Ashkenazi Jews)

י Yode—Y

כ Kaf—C (hard) also Khaf

ל La-med—L

מ Mem—M

נ Noon—N

ס Samekh—S

ע Ayin—Ng (or silent)

פ Pay—P (with a dot inside; without a dot, it is Fay—F)

צ Tsa-de—Ts (sometimes erroneously pronounced as Z)

ק Koof—K

ר Resh—R

ש Shin—Sh (also S)

ת Tav—T (also Sav—S, among Ashkenazi Jews)

Originally Hebrew was written almost entirely with consonants, the vowels being left to the reader's understanding. During the period of the second Temple, beginning perhaps about twenty-four hundred years ago, it became customary to supply certain aids in the reading and understanding of the Hebrew scriptures by supplying the letters Vav, Aleph, Hay, and Yode to symbolize certain vowel sounds. As Hebrew ceased to be a spoken language it became necessary to supply more and more vowel assistance until by the sixth or seventh century C.E. the creation of a whole system of vowel signs became imperative. Two schools of Jewish learning worked out such a system, one in Babylonia and one in Tiberias, Palestine. The Tiberian system was universally adopted. Both systems consist of a series of dots and dashes placed over or under the letters. The Tiberian system placed the vowel signs under the letters, and that is how most Hebrew books are printed today. However the Torah scroll is still without vowel signs.

Hebrew Letters as Numerals

The Hebrew letters were also used as numerals by the ancient Jews and are still used in Hebrew religious writings. The following is the numerical equivalent of the Hebrew letters:

Aleph—1	Za-in—7
Beth—2	Heth—8
Gimel—3	Teth—9
Daled—4	Yode—10
Hay—5	Yode Alep—11
Vav—6	

Yode Beth is 12, and so on, until the number 20 is reached, except for 15 and 16 which normally would be Yode Hay and Yode Vav. These combinations are considered to resemble the abbreviated word for God too closely, hence 15 and 16 are written Teth Vav and Teth Za-in (9 and 6, and 9 and 7).

From 20 onward the letters after Yode are used. Thus:

20—Kaf	200—Resh
30—La-med	300—Shin
40—Mem	400—Tav
50—Noon	500—Tav Koof
60—Samekh	600—Tav Resh
70—Ayin	700—Tav Shin
80—Pay	800—Tav Tav
90—Tsa-de	900—Tav Tav Koof
100—Koof	

Thousands are indicated by starting again with Aleph and placing two dots over it. Thus, our present year 1962 would be written in Hebrew: Aleph (two dots on top) Tav Tav Koof Sameka Beth.

What Is the Difference between Yiddish and Hebrew?

Hebrew is the original language of the Bible and ceased to be a spoken language among the ordinary people in the third pre-Christian century, perhaps even earlier. In the time of Jesus the language of the street and marketplace was Aramaic, a language as similar to Hebrew as Spanish is to Italian. Classical Hebrew became the language of worship and scholarship.

In the middle nineteenth century there was an attempt to revive Hebrew as a spoken language. These efforts were given impetus by the growth of the Zionist movement (the movement whose purpose was to establish a Jewish homeland in Palestine) during the past sixty years. Today modern Hebrew is the official language of the state of Israel.

Yiddish is derived from the German language which the Jews of Germany used during the Middle Ages. It was originally Medieval German with many Hebrew words and phrases added. When the Jews of Germany migrated to Poland and Eastern Europe in the fourteenth and fifteenth centuries, they took with them their German-Jewish language. This language in the course of time accumulated a number of Polish and Russian words and phrases and became the Yiddish, the vernacular of most East European Jews until our own time. A rich literature developed in this Yiddish language which is still cherished by many Jews who are trying to preserve it; but they are fighting a losing battle against the process of linguistic acculturation and assimilation which is going on everywhere, especially in the Western Hemisphere.

Among Sephardim (descendants of Spanish and Portuguese Jews), the vernacular corresponding to Yiddish is Ladino. It is a mixture of Spanish, Portuguese, and some Hebrew words and phrases. Later Italian, Turkish, and Greek words were included among Sephardim who found asylum in those countries.

Do Jews Regard Themselves as the "Chosen People"?

In early biblical times it was the belief of all ancient peoples that they were the chosen people of their gods. Every people, including the ancient Hebrews, believed that each nation had its own god or gods who were sovereign over the territory occupied by that nation. Thus the Babylonians had their gods, the Phoenicians theirs, the Assyrians theirs, and the Hebrews their one God. Among the Hebrews in early times the belief was common that Yhvh (Jehovah) was their special God and that He had nothing to do with the other nations.

It was not until the coming of the great Hebrew prophets beginning with Amos about 750 B.C.E.—who taught that Yhvh was not merely the God of the Hebrews but the one, universal God, creator of the world and Father of all men—that the concept of a tribal or national god among the Hebrews was changed to the one eternal Creator and Ruler of the universe. Amos challenged the tribal concepts of his time in these immortal words:

> Are ye not as the children of the Ethiopians unto Me,
> O Children of Israel? saith Yhvh.
> Have I not brought up Israel out of the land of Egypt,
> And the Philistines from Caphtor, and Aram from Kir?
> —Amos 9:7

It was probably with Amos that the concept of the chosen people changed. Until then the Israelites believed that their God, Yhvh, was interested only in them; that He had chosen them from among the nations and had made a special covenant with their forefathers, which placed them in a specially privileged position in relation to Him. Amos challenged the idea of special privilege. If the people thought they had a special relation to God they were right, he said; but that relation imposed upon them special responsibilities and services, not special privileges.

> You only have I known of all the families of the earth;
> Therefore I will visit upon you all your iniquities.
> —Amos 3:2

Because Israel had known God longer than other people, because they had been given the Ten Commandments and moral laws to guide and govern their lives, their wrongdoing was especially blameworthy and deserving of punishment.

This new concept of the chosen people was carried on by the other prophets and especially by the great unknown prophet of the Babylonian exile, Deutero-Isaiah (second Isaiah), who told the people that they were the servants of God whose lives and deeds must bear witness to His truth and greatness among the peoples of the earth.

> But thou, Israel my servant,
> Jacob whom I have chosen;
> The seed of Abraham my friend. . . .
> —Isaiah 41:8

and later:

> Ye are My witnesses, saith Yhvh,
> And My servant whom I have chosen. . . .
> —Isaiah 43:10

The concept of the chosen people, where it is held by Jews today, is accepted as a mission from God to bear witness to His truth by word and deed. The *Union Prayerbook,* used by all Reform congregations in this country, puts the present-day concept in these words:

> Almighty and merciful God, Thou has called Israel to Thy service and found him worthy to bear witness to Thy truth among the peoples of the earth. *Give us grace to fulfill this mission with zeal tempered by wisdom and guided by regard for other men's faith.* [Italics mine]. May our life prove the strength of our own belief in the truths we proclaim. May our bearing toward our neighbors, our faithfulness in every sphere of duty, our compassion for the suffering and our patience under trial show that He whose law we obey is indeed the God of all goodness, the Father of all men. . . .
> —*Union Prayerbook,* Vol. I, newly revised edition, p. 34

But even in ancient times, as early as two thousand years ago and perhaps earlier, the rabbis of the Talmud anticipated our modern concepts by speaking of Israel not only as a chosen but as a choosing people. In a meaningful legend describing God's revelation on Mount Sinai, the rabbis tell us that before God offered the Torah (the Ten Commandments and the disciplines which are the basis of the covenant between Him and Israel) He first offered it to each of the other nations of the world, and each of them in turn refused it for one reason or another. Finally the Torah was offered to Israel, and when the people heard what it contained they replied with one accord: "All that the Lord hath commanded we will do and heed."

Among Liberal Jews the words "chosen people" are merely a metaphor describing the responsibility that the Jews feel as descendants of the original Hebrews to whom God first revealed Himself. Because of their heritage they feel a special obligation to fulfill the will of God as commanded in the Torah and in its moral, ethical, and spiritual disciplines. They feel deeply the sense of Israel's mission as outlined by the Hebrew prophets, especially Deutero-Isaiah in his description of Israel as the "servant of God." In a very real sense every people is "chosen by God" if it accepts the responsibilities implicit in the concept "chosen by God"—if it makes its contribution to the welfare of mankind.

Do Jews Accept Converts?

Yes; Jews welcome proselytes who come to Judaism out of sincere conviction and the desire to live by the religious disciplines of the Jewish faith and tradition. But Jews do not go out to seek converts.

Judaism, unlike Christianity, is not a missionary religion. And the reason is that Jews do not believe that people have to become Jews in order to be "saved." "The righteous of all peoples shall have a share in the world to come," said an ancient rabbi. It was his way of saying that all good people are acceptable to God. So long as people live by His moral law they are acceptable to Him equally with Jews who do the same.

Judaism does not claim to possess the only way to God. Judaism recognizes that there may be many ways of approaching God in creed and worship; *but all roads must follow the path of righteous living if they are to lead ultimately to the one living God*. That is why Jews do not feel the same compulsion to seek converts that most Christians do who believe that the way to God through Christ is the only way.

What Are the Requirements for Conversion to Judaism?

A non-Jew who sincerely wishes to become a Jew may do so by consulting any rabbi. The rabbi must point out to the prospective convert the difficulties involved in accepting the Jewish faith and discipline and in identifying himself with a minority religious group so often persecuted and martyred. He must also explain that according to Jewish belief one does not have to become a Jew in order to attain salvation; that the "righteous among all peoples shall have a share in the world to come," that is, are acceptable to God.

If in spite of these warnings and assurances the non-Jew still desires to become a Jew, the rabbi will outline for him a course of study in Judaism, its beliefs, customs, and traditions. Upon a satisfactory completion of these studies and upon the rabbi being convinced of the sincerity of the proselyte, a simple ceremony of conversion will be arranged in which the convert will be formally inducted into the Jewish faith. The ceremony consists in the convert's declaration of his sincere intention to live by the principles of Judaism and to rear his or her children in that faith. Three rabbis are usually required to form a tribunal to examine and to accept the proselyte. In Reform congregations one rabbi with two Temple officers may accept the proselyte where three rabbis are not available.

What Is the Jewish Attitude toward Mixed Marriage and Intermarriage?

Jews, like most religious groups, do not look with favor upon mixed marriage, that is, a marriage between members of different faiths where the parties to the marriage retain their respective faiths.

The reasons are both religious and practical. It is generally agreed that the strength of any religious group derives from the religious training the individual receives in his home and church. A religiously divided home can only become a source of confusion, tension, and conflict, especially to the children in their most impressionable years. Few religious groups, therefore, would willingly and knowingly encourage or sanction such conditions.

Judaism does not, however, object to intermarriage where the non-Jewish person adopts the Jewish faith. Through such conversion the proselyte becomes a Jew in every sense that Judaism understands the term. Whatever objections may arise from individual families to intermarriage are grounded in the practical social and psychological difficulties of a marriage where the backgrounds of the two people and their families are widely dissimilar. Rabbi Barnet Brickner, in answer to the argument that "opposites attract," wisely said, "The only attraction of opposites in a successful marriage should be the opposites in sex." In everything else there should be as much similarity of social, cultural, and spiritual background as possible.

What Is Zionism?

The word Zionism comes from the Hebrew *Tziyon*, the name of the Temple hill in ancient Jerusalem, Mount Zion, and refers today to the movement begun in 1896 by Theodore Herzl for the restoration of Palestine as the national home of the Jewish people.

Ever since the destruction of the second Temple by the Romans in 70 c.e., which put an end to the second Judean Commonwealth, Jews have looked for a restoration of their ancient homeland. They believed that the destruction of their Temple and state was a punishment from God for their sins, and they hoped that in God's own good time He would forgive them and send His Messiah to redeem them from exile and restore them to Judea. For this messianic redemption and restoration, pious Jews prayed three times every day in their three daily worship services.

About the middle of the nineteenth century Russian Jewish intellectuals, inspired by this hope and impelled by Russian persecution of the Jews, began a movement for the peaceful penetration of the Holy Land which then was under the domination of Turkey. They called themselves *Ho-vee-vay Tzi-yon* (lovers of Zion). With tremendous zeal and inspired idealism, hundreds treked across the Russian steppes to Palestine. It was an heroic but futile adventure.

It was not until 1896 that modern Zionism really began as an effective movement. The inspiration was given by a Viennese Jewish journalist, Theodore Herzl, foreign correspondent of an important Viennese newspaper. Herzl was in Paris covering the infamous trial of Alfred Dreyfus, a Jewish army captain falsely accused of selling French military information to a foreign power. The trial aroused outbreaks of anti-Semitism throughout France. Herzl, a product of nineteenth-century liberalism, was horrified by this outbreak of prejudice, bigotry, and intolerance in liberal France. In the heat of his disillusionment he wrote an impassioned phamphlet, which he called "The Jewish State," in which he argued that there was no hope for the Jews to live as a free people anywhere except in a legally secured and publicly recognized home of their own.

This was the beginning of the modern Zionist movement. Herzl became obsessed with his idea of a Jewish State as the solution to the Jewish problems and devoted all his great talents and energies to its propagation among Jews and non-Jews. In 1897 he called upon the Jews of the world to send representatives to a world congress to discuss his proposition. Delegates from many countries answered his call, and they met at Basle, Switzerland. This gathering of Jews became the first World Zionist Congress which has met periodically ever since.

Herzl himself died at the age of forty-four, worn out by his labors and heartbroken because of the feeble response to his efforts by the statesmen of the world upon whose good will he had depended, and by the antagonism of Jews who were opposed to the whole concept of a sovereign Jewish State.

However, the spark that his dream ignited caught fire as the years went by and the lot of the Jews of Europe progressively deteriorated. His magic words, "If we will it, it is not a dream," became the battle cry of the Zionist movement. A powerful impetus was given to Zionism by the Balfour Declaration of 1917. Lord Balfour, foreign minister of Great Britain during World War I, sent a letter to Lord Rothschild in which he stated that "His majesty's government views with favor the establishment in Palestine of a national home for the Jewish people." For the first time a great power had declared itself officially in favor of Zionist aspirations in Palestine. The spark of Zionist enthusiasms was fanned into a flame.

Inspired by this declaration and stimulated by the unparalleled tragedy that had overtaken the Jews of Europe with the advent of Hitler and Nazism, Jews all over the world forgot their diverse ideologies in relation to the status of Palestine. They poured their energies and millions of dollars to rescue the victims of Nazi persecution and to save the pitiful remnant of a once great European Jewish community. Thus was Palestine built up, until in 1948 part of it became the state of Israel with the blessings of our own government and the United Nations.

With the establishment of the state of Israel the Zionist movement lost much of its original *raison d'etre* and with it much of its influence, especially among American Jews. It still exists, but its chief function today is that of "friend of Israel" helping to raise funds for the settlement of Jews still in need of a home, selling Israel bonds, and helping to develop interest in and sympathy for the new Hebraic culture which the Israeli people are creating.

> Have we not all one Father;
> Hath not one God created us;
> Why do we deal treacherously
> Every man against his brother . . . ?
>
> —Malachi 2:10

Why Are Jews Called Semites?

The word Semite comes from the Hebrew *Shem,* the name of one of Noah's sons, from whom the Jews were supposed to be descended. The Bible tells us (Genesis 10) that Noah had three sons, Shem, Ham, and Japheth. Ham was supposed to be the progenitor of the colored races, and Japheth, the ancestor of the Greeks and other Europeans.

As the word Semite is used today, and has been used since about the middle of the nineteenth century, it refers to a group of peoples in the Middle East and North Africa whose languages stem from a common source, and includes such peoples as the Arabs and Jews. The Nazis used the word Semite as a racial term to distinguish Jews from Aryans, which their distorted science also regarded as a racial term. In fact the term Aryan is merely a description of peoples whose languages stem from Indo-European sources. Thus both Semitic and Aryan are merely designations of different language groups.

What Are the Reasons for Anti-Semitism?

Anti-Semitism is a term coined about the middle of the nineteenth century and tragically dramatized by Hitler and Nazism to describe prejudices and hatred against the Jews. The reasons for anti-Semitism are many and varied, but fundamentally they stem from the same causes that have created and fostered prejudices and hatreds between human groups since history began.

Among these causes, perhaps the most fundamental is xenophobia, the dislike for the unlike. Since the dawn of history, groups of humans more or less organized in clans, tribes, nations, and religions regarded one another with suspicion and distrust either as actual or potential enemies. It was a struggle of the in-group against the out-group, the native against the stranger.

In that conflict each group tried in every way to strengthen its own forces and fighting potential. One of the ways was to ascribe to itself all the human virtues and to the out-group all the human vices. In this way, unfavorable mental images and attitudes toward all members of the out-group were developed so that members of the in-group felt no compunction about hating and destroying them as enemies. Such tactics have been used in every war, each warring faction claiming for itself all righteousness while ascribing to the enemy all vicious and diabolical motivations and characteristics.

Through centuries of such indoctrination a whole pattern of unwholesome stereotypes and images has been developed among the nations, cultures, and religions of the world toward one another, which are the basis of most of the prejudices among them today.

In the case of anti-Semitism, prejudice against Jews, all these factors causing general group prejudice operated, and, in addition, certain special factors arising from the conflict between Christianity and Judaism.

When the followers of Jesus broke away from the Jewish religion, especially after Saul of Tarsus (Saint Paul) began to preach to the Gentiles, the conflict between Judaism and its daughter, Christianity, became increasingly bitter. Christianity was accepted by the Roman Emperor Constantine and started on its triumphant career as a world religion. It now had the opportunity and power to wreak vengeance upon its rival, Judaism, by degrading it in the eyes of the world it dominated. Judaism and the Jew became the symbol of everything that was vile and hateful, so that the Christian world was reared with mental attitudes about Jews which pictured them as utterly wicked and depraved members of the human family, whose only hope of redemption was the acceptance of the true faith. Since most of the Jews of the world live in countries dominated by the Christian tradition, these hateful images of the Jew have kept prejudice against Jews alive and active.

Added to this religious prejudice were economic, social, political, and psychological factors making for anti-Semitism. In times of economic prosperity, when there was enough for everybody, the economic successes of some Jews were more or less tolerated. But when depression set in and unemployment and hunger stalked the land, the resentment of people turned first against those they regarded as strangers within their gates, the Jews, against whom they aready had prejudices as the alleged enemies of Christ and Christianity.

These religious and economic resentments made the Jews everywhere convenient scapegoats for demagogues and politicians to use to further their selfish ambitions. It is common knowledge how Hitler and Nazism rose to power in Germany by blaming the Jews for all of Germany's misfortunes—for their defeat in World War I, for the severe economic depression that followed, for the misery, frustrations, and insecurities from which Germans suffered as individuals and as a nation. All minority groups are sometimes used as such scapegoats, but rarely with such tragic consequences as the Jews of Germany and Europe suffered during the period from 1939 to 1945 when more than six million were killed in concentration camps, gas chambers, and crematoria.

There are also psychological factors operating to foster an active prejudice between groups, especially against Jews. All of us seek an outlet for our aggressive tendencies arising out of our personal and social maladjustment; and these aggressions are most often turned against some defenseless minority—colored peoples, minority religious groups, and the like. Much modern anti-Semitism can be explained in terms of these aggressions of people seeking compensation for inferiorities, frustrations, and mental and emotional tensions.

The reason sometimes advanced that anti-Semitism results from bad Jewish behavior is specious and untenable. The bad behavior of individual members of a minority group may aggravate the prejudice against the group, but in no case is it a cause. The prejudice was always there for the reasons enumerated before. The bad behavior of an individual Jew merely corroborates in the mind of the prejudiced person the unpleasant mental picture already held. To such a person, good behavior by Jews is always regarded as an exception, bad behavior as natural and normal. For the prejudice is in the mind of the prejudiced. It is always irrational.

A. J. Murrow in his book, *Living without Hate* (Harper & Bros., New York, 1951), reports the following story by Gordon W. Allport, professor of sociology at Harvard, who told how a person holding strong prejudices against Jews can and does evade and misinterpret facts which tend to destroy his prejudiced attitudes. This prejudiced person asserted that during World War II Jews were slackers. When informed that their percentage of voluntary enlistment was greater than that of Gentiles, the bigot retorted that if it were true it was only to escape the draft. When told that Jewish boys were drafted in greater proportion to the population than Gentiles, he insisted that this was another Jewish trick to get in early so that they might have a better chance to become officers. When he was further told that in proportion to other groups Jewish draftees showed a higher percentage in the enlisted ranks, the bigot replied that it was only because they wanted to get the soft jobs in the Quartermaster Corps. When informed that the Jews were in the toughest outfits—infantry, artillery, engineers, and so on, the bigot seemed disturbed but remained unconvinced. "Well," he retorted, "that's because the Jews don't want to risk criticism and they are going all out to look good."

One of the most ludicrous distortions of reason and logic in this connection which the present writer himself heard was a statement by a Nazi propagandist in Liverpool, England, in 1934. He was trying to explain why the Nazis were persecuting the Jews of Germany. "Jews are hated in Germany," he said, "because the international Jewish financiers are conspiring to spread Communism in Germany and throughout the world."

True indeed, prejudice is in the mind of the bigot, defying reason and common sense because it is utterly irrational.

WHAT IS JUDAISM?

For this commandment which I command thee this day is not too hard for thee, neither is it far off. It is not in heaven that thou shouldest say: "Who shall go up for us to heaven and bring it unto us, and make us to hear it that we may do it?" Neither is it beyond the sea that thou shouldest say: "Who shall go over the sea for us and bring it unto us, and make us to hear it that we may do it?" But the word is very nigh unto thee, in thy mouth and in thy heart that thou mayest do it.

—Deuteronomy 30:11-14

I BELIEVE that Jewish wisdom is more all-human and universal than any other; and this not only because it is firstborn, but also because of the powerful humaneness that saturates it, because of its high estimate of man.

—Maxim Gorki, 1916

What Is Judaism?

Judaism is the religion of the Jews. Unlike Buddhism, Mohammedanism, Confucianism, and Christianity which derive their names from a single founder, Buddha, Mohammed, Confucius, or Christ, Judaism is named after no individual. It is the religion of the Jews developed through 4,000 years of the Jews' quest for God and the good life. Although Abraham and Moses are regarded as the traditional founders of the Jewish faith, their names are merely two among many prophets and teachers who shaped the character of Judaism through the centuries.

Is There More than One Kind of Judaism?

Yes; there are three major divisions or interpretations of Judaism: Orthodox, Conservative, and Reform or Liberal. A fourth, Reconstructionism, is of recent origin. It is supported by members of both Conservative and Reform groups. It is yet hardly another denomination in Judaism. A variation of Orthodoxy is Hasidism (*see* Hasidism).

Reform and Conservative Judaism were an outgrowth of the new spirit of liberalism brought into Western civilization by the French Revolution with its ideals of liberty, equality and fraternity. Since these ideals could have no meaning if they were restricted to Christians only, Jews, too, for the first time in more than fifteen hundred years, were granted human rights and freedoms in some parts of Western Europe. They were allowed to emerge from the ghettoes (segregated Jewish quarters) to which they had been confined, and were permitted to become citizens wherever the influence of the French Revolution extended. This emancipation affected their outlook on life and also their religion.

The religious customs, manner of worship, and practices congenial in the ghetto environment were out of place in the freer environment which the Jews now enjoyed. Therefore, two German Jewish businessmen, Israel Jacobson and David Friedlander, organized a modernized service in Berlin in 1814 with a sermon in German and a few prayers in the German language added to the Hebrew ritual. This was the beginning of Reform Judaism.

It began as a laymen's movement to modify the ritual. It was soon taken over by rabbis and scholars like Abraham Geiger and Leopold Zunz who evolved a theology and a philosophy of Judaism justifying the changes in ritual and forms of worship which the laymen instituted. From their study of Jewish tradition they discovered that Judaism had always been a growing and evolving interpretation of God's will as the Jews' knowledge of God and his experience of life broadened and deepened.

The Bible itself, they showed by their exhaustive scientific studies, revealed God's progressive revelation of His will across fifteen hundred years of growing religious insights. Judaism had always responded to the deepening insights of Jews in every age, they said. There are beliefs and values in Judaism which are eternal and unalterable, but there are also numerous man made traditions and institutions, developed to meet conditions in different ages and places, which had been changed, abolished, or new ones instituted as circumstances required. That had always been the pattern, said the Reform scholars.)

Unfortunately, for more than a thousand years the free flow of the Jewish spirit was stopped and the pattern of its growth frozen by the unhappy conditions in which Jews were forced to live in a hostile Christian world. Now all this was changed; Jews had human rights and freedoms like their fellow citizens of other faiths, they said. Their religion, too, could now throw off the shackles of centuries of ghetto life. They therefore developed a new interpretation of Judaism, which is the basis of present Reform Jewish faith and practice, a Judaism responsive to the changing needs of Jewish life.

Conservative Judaism began as a compromise between the rigid and unyielding Orthodoxy and the radical interpretations of Reform. The main exponent of this philosophy was Zacharaiah Frankel, a great scholar of the mid-nineteenth century. Although he agreed in principle with the advocates of Reform, he objected to making changes in Jewish customs and practices unless these changes grew "historically" out of the spirit of Judaism. Frankel's view came to be known as "Historical Judaism," and in America the movement he started came to be known as Conservative Judaism.

What Is the Difference between the Three Major Divisions of Judaism?

The Orthodox believe that Judaism is a religious tradition containing laws and commandments, festivals and holydays, customs and ceremonies, all of which were revealed and ordained by God originally in the first five books of the Bible, known as the Torah (also called the law of Moses). This Torah has been interpreted by the rabbis in the Talmud and its commentaries, and extended by them to regulate the whole of Jewish life. Thus Orthodox Jews believe that everything of significance in Judaism which has come down to us from the past are divine commandments which they must obey without question and without change. Only an authorized body of rabbis recognized by all the Jews as authoritative can make any changes in the interpretation of this tradition.

Conservative and Reform or Liberal Jews both believe that

the Jewish tradition is not a fixed and unchangeable system of divine commandments. (They hold that although there are eternal and unchangeable moral and spiritual principles, many of the customs, ceremonies, and practices in Jewish life are human institutions created by Jews to meet certain needs at certain times in their history; that these may be changed as the conditions of Jews change in different times and places.)

The difference between Conservative and Reform Judaism lies chiefly in their attitudes toward changes in the "tradition." Conservative Jews want to conserve as much of the tradition as possible, hence their name "Conservative." They are very slow to make any changes, and some among them are almost Orthodox in their veneration of the past. (Reform Judaism is much more ready to make Judaism responsive to the changing needs of Jews, believing that only in that way can Judaism become a dynamic influence in Jewish life.)

A few examples will help to illustrate these differences. Conservative Jews still observe two days of each holyday, like the Orthodox, following the ancient tradition. Reform Jews observe only one day, following the modern fixed calendar. Conservative Jews, like Orthodox, still wear hats in their synagogues following the ancient custom of showing respect. Reform Jews worship with heads uncovered, responsive to our modern way of showing respect. (For other differences between the three divisions in Judaism, see the other questions in this book.)

Reconstructionism is a movement begun by Rabbi Mordecai Kaplan about 1925. It grew out of his thesis propounded in his monumental work, "*Judaism as Civilization*," in which he argues that Judaism is not merely a religion in the conventional sense of the term but a religious civilization encompassing the whole of Jewish life. That is how it developed in Palestine and that is how it must continue if it is to give the Jew the maximum opportunity for Jewish living, says Rabbi Kaplan. His book gave the impetus to the organization of the Society for the Advancement of Judaism, which he founded.

The Reconstructionist movement stresses the need for intensive Hebrew education, the cultivation of Hebrew art, literature, and drama, and the preservation of historic Jewish folkways. In a word, Reconstructionists view Judaism as a culture of which religion is only one, though a very important, part.

What Is Hasidism?

Hasidism is an Orthodox religious movement with mystical overtones which began among the Jews of Eastern Europe about the middle of the eighteenth century. The name is derived from the Hebrew *hasid* (pious, saint). The founder of the movement was a man called Israel, known as *Baal Shem Tov* (master of the good name), abbreviated into the word *Besht*. Israel Baal Shem Tov (1700-1760) was a man of little learning but of great soul. Deeply sensitive, highly emotional, and with a love for all people, Israel felt that the intellectual approach to religion which characterized the rabbis of Poland was totally inadequate to meet the needs of the unlearned, ordinary folk who needed a religion of warmth and emotional experience, a religion of joy and ecstasy, to help them endure their tragic lot as Jews in a non-Jewish world which persecuted and degraded them.

Toward that end he emphasized spontaneous prayer, rich in emotional content and expressed in joy with ecstatic enthusiasm. His teaching and preaching caught the imagination of the downtrodden Jews of Poland and Eastern Europe, and many followed him to become the founders of the religious movement which is still flourishing in Europe and in the large Jewish centers of population in America. Many legends have grown up around the life and character of the Besht investing him with a unique quality and supernatural power.

Under the leadership of some of his disciples the movement developed a considerable theology and philosophy differing in some respects from the main stream of traditional Judaism. One of the most important differences developed in regard to the character and role of the hasidic rabbis, some of whom were believed to possess supernatural powers, able to move the hand of God to perform their will under certain conditions. These men were known as *tsaddikim* (righteous ones), to whom the faithful would come for supernatural help when earthly expedients proved ineffective. This tsaddik cult degenerated some of the Besht's noblest teachings into crude superstitions and brought much of Hasidism into disrepute among the more rationalistic Jews.

However, there was much in Hasidism which influenced all Jewish religious life, especially its emphasis upon spontaneous prayer, humility, joy, and enthusiasm in worship, emotional expression, and an intimately personal relation between man and God.

What Is the Torah?

The word Torah means "teaching or guidance," and in Jewish tradition it is used in two senses.

1. Torah is the parchment scroll placed in the ark in every temple and synagogue in the world. This parchment scroll contains the first five books of the Bible and is ascribed to Moses by Orthodox Judaism. Hence the Torah is sometimes called the law of Moses, for it contains many of the laws and regulations by which the religious, social, and economic life of ancient Israel was governed.

2. Torah in its broader meaning includes the entire Jewish Bible as the embodiment of the word and will of God and all Jewish teaching that has come down to us through the centuries—the teachings of the prophets, psalmists, sages, rabbis, and commentators.

Are There Dogmas in Judaism?

Upon this question there is wide difference of opinion among Jews, even among Orthodox Jews. The reason is that Judaism developed as a way of life with emphasis upon commandments rather than as a theological system with emphasis upon a specific set of beliefs or dogmas, such as those with which Christianity and Mohammedanism began and developed.

Historic Christianity says, "Believe in Christ and ye shall be saved." Mohammedanism says, "There is no God but Allah and Mohammed is his prophet," and if you don't believe that you are an infidel. Judaism says that there is only one God, but it does not require that everybody believe in Him in exactly the same way. It does, however, require that everybody obey His moral Law. Judaism's emphasis has always been on the *right deed rather than on the right creed*. Therefore, creed in Judaism did not assume great importance until comparatively late in Jewish history when Judaism had to defend itself against the creeds of the Persians and later the Greeks, Romans, and Christians.

But even the creeds that developed in Judaism were more in the nature of guides than dogmas upon which a Jew's salvation depended. There was always wide latitude in belief provided the Jew did not deny the existence of God or the divine origin of the Torah and the basic commandments. Through the centuries a number of philosophically minded rabbis did try to formulate Jewish creeds, but none of them were ever accepted as authoritative and binding. The creed most widely accepted by Orthodox Jews is that of Moses Ben Maimon (Maimonides) composed toward the end of the twelfth century c.e. It consists of the following thirteen articles:

1. God is the Creator of the universe.

2. God is one and eternal.

3. God is incorporeal (spiritual being) and cannot be described in any physical terms.

4. God is the First and the Last.

5. Prayer can be addressed only to God. One mustn't pray to any being besides Him.

6. The teachings of the prophets are eternally true.

7. Moses is the greatest of all the prophets and his words are eternally true.

8. The Torah now in our possession was given to Moses by God.

9. This Torah will never change, and there will be no other revelation like unto it.

10. God knows the hearts and deeds of all men; He is all knowing.

11. God rewards the righteous and punishes the wicked.

12. The Messiah will come, and though he delay we shall wait for him.

13. There will be a resurrection of the dead.

Among Conservative and Reform Jews, the only beliefs that might be considered basic are: (1) the belief in one God, Creator and Guide of the universe, Who rules the world by law—physical, psychological, and moral—and love; (2) the belief that the continued existence of the people Israel, the religious Jewish community, is vital to the survival of Judaism and that this community has a special responsibility to help implement the will of God in our world; (3) the fulfillment of God's will on earth through man's cooperation with Him in establishing His kingdom of justice, peace, and human brotherhood; (4) that death is not the end of life but the opening of new and larger opportunities for spiritual fulfillment.

What Do Jews Believe about God?

1. All Jews believe in one God, as they say in the *Sh'mah*, "Hear, O Israel, the Lord our God, the Lord is One" (Deuteronomy 6:4). They believe that God created the world and rules it through law and love. He is the source of all life and all goodness. They believe that God created man in His image as the Bible tells us, by which is meant that man is endowed with a spiritual nature, a soul, which enables him to develop qualities of character that reflect the divinity resident in him.

2. All Jews believe that man's relation to God can best be established by the following fivefold program:

To do the will of God: that is, for man to obey the moral law expressed in the Ten Commandments, the Golden Rule, and the moral and ethical disciplines that flow from them.

To reveal His glory: that is, to explore within ourselves and to develop those qualities of character and soul which show man as made in the image of God.

To hallow His name: that is, to invest life with such dignity, beauty, and goodness that it will be sanctified and reflect the holiness of God Who is the Source and Creator of life.

To imitate Him: that is, so to live that our lives attain godlike qualities in so far as it is possible for a human being to attain them.

To advance God's kingdom on earth: that is, to cooperate with Him in fulfilling the hope of the ages for justice and freedom, peace, and human brotherhood.

3. All Jews believe that man can fulfill that program through:

Learning: that is, through an ever-growing knowledge of

the universe and of himself. Reform and Conservative Jews accept all the verified facts and experiences of the sciences—physical, social, and psychological. These sciences, in addition to personal experiences of God, are the material out of which an adequate faith must be built. Learning also requires a knowledge of Torah, Jewish tradition as it developed through the centuries, the teachings of the lawgivers, the insights of the prophets, the wisdom of the sages, and an understanding and appreciation of the religious institutions developed by Judaism, its customs, rituals, holydays, and festivals.

Orthodox Jews accept the facts and experiences of the sciences only in so far as they do not conflict with or contradict the revealed word of God as contained in the Torah. To the Orthodox Jews the Torah (God's revelation), as contained in the Bible and its extension in the Talmud, is the supreme authority for faith and practice.

Worhsip: that is, through a conscious effort to establish a relationship with God by prayer. Prayer is the language of faith and aspiration. It directs man's heart and mind toward God. It voices the deepest needs, the highest hopes, and the most far-reaching aspirations of man seeking self-realization. Worship is not confined to the temple or synagogue. It may be practiced in the privacy of the home, in the solitude of meditation, in the workshop or the garden. Every reverent thought is a prayer; every impulse to goodness is an act of worship.

Good deeds: that is, by organizing one's life in harmony with the will of God as described in the fivefold program above; so to live that our lives will be a fulfillment of the commandment: "Thou shalt love thy neighbor as thyself"; so to live that each Jew adds to the glory of God in our world and to the sum of human goodness; helping to make the world a little better because he has lived in it.

It is a fundamental concept of Judaism that man is co-partner, co-worker with God in the work of creation, at least on the level of human life and destiny. The rabbis make a very incisive comment on the first chapter of Genesis. They notice that after each act of creation the Bible says, "And God saw that it was good," but when man was created the phrase "and it was good" is omitted. From this omission they deduce that all other creatures were made perfect by God from the beginning. Man alone was left incomplete. However, he was endowed above all other creatures with a creative power for self-improvement which is divine. In that sense the rabbis interpreted the phrase "And God created man in His image."

Since man possesses this divine creative power he can develop his own character and personality in accord with God's will as laid down in the Torah, the moral and spiritual disciplines embodied in God's commandments. Therefore, it is man's duty and responsibility to use the creative power God gave him to perfect himself and his world, working with God to establish His kingdom on earth.

Why Is God Called Jehovah?

In most Christian versions of the Jewish Bible, God is referred to as Jehovah. This name for God arose out of a mispronunciation of the four-letter Hebrew word for God, *Y-h-v-h*, by early Christian translators. The four-letter Hebrew word Yhvh was considered ineffable out of reverence for the Holy Name. It was therefore never pronounced, but a substitute, the word *Adonoy* (Lord, Master), was used. Later, when Hebrew was written with vowel signs, the vowel signs from the word Adonoy were placed under the four letters Y-h-v-h (Yode-hay-vav-hay), which made the word appear as Ye-ho-vah.

Christian translators, not knowing of this vowel interchange, transliterated the four-letter word as Ye-ho-vah which in Latin is Jehovah.

Actually the four-letter word Yhvh is from the Hebrew verb "to be" and signifies "being, existence, eternal." When Moses asked God His name, he was told that the only name he need know is "being." "And God said unto Moses, I Am That I Am. . . . Thou shalt say unto the children of Israel, 'I Am sent me unto you'" (Exodus 3:14).

Note: Hebrew was originally written without vowel signs. These were introduced much later (*see* Hebrew Language and Hebrew Alphabet). To this day the Torah scroll, which is read in the synagogue, is without vowel signs. It is written on parchment by hand. Only printed Bibles have vowel signs—dots and dashes over and under the letters.

What Do Jews Believe about Life after Death?

To Judaism, death is not the end of life. It may be the end of the kind of physical existence to which we are accustomed, but not to life created by God. Life continues in many naturalistic ways, through one's descendants, through one's personal influence upon the world in which he lived, through the memory of those whom one knew or influenced. Life also continues through the immortality of the soul which, being the divine essence in us, is indestructible even as God, the Source whence it came is indestructible.

In biblical times the belief in afterlife was rather vague. It was thought that when a person died he still continued a kind of shadowy, meaningless, and purposeless existence somewhere beneath the earth in a place called *sheol* (the pit). Sheol, unlike the later concepts of hell, was not a place of punishment. The ideas of reward and punishment in heaven and hell were later developments in Judaism, largely influenced by Babylonian and Persian theology.

By the third pre-Christian century belief in life and death was quite well developed, and with it the belief in the resurrection of the body, when the soul of the departed will again unite with the body for the great day of final judgment.

What form life after death takes is vividly described by some of the rabbis in the Talmud, especially in their homiletical discourses in which they allow their fancy-free expression. But most of the rabbis decried the tendency to picture the future life in physical terms, saying that it cannot be described by human imagination or language. The only thing we can say is that the soul of man enters upon a fuller experience of God in the reflection of the *Shekhinah* (Divine Presence). However, folklore would not be denied its imagination of the bliss of the righteous in *Gan Eden* (Garden of Eden, Paradise) and the tortures of the wicked in *Gay Hinnom* (Valley of Hinnom—hell). According to Jewish folklore heaven, Paradise, is a place where the righteous sit and study the Torah all day long without ever getting weary and have all the great Jews of the past there to answer the difficult and knotty problems of interpretation. A special food, the incredibly delicious fish, the mythical leviathan, is enjoyed in abundance at great banquets presided over by the greatest Jewish religious leaders since the world began.

The folkloristic ideas of heaven are much the same among all peoples. They are a projection of the people's highest ideals or their frustrated wishes on earth. Thus among Arabs, living in parched desert lands, heaven is a place of cool waters and abundant food. In Christian folklore heaven is a place for hymn singing and harp playing in cities of gold and precious stones. Among some warring pagan tribes, heaven is a place of heroic combat where death is impossible.

Hell in folklore is a place of torture; the kind of torture depends upon the imagination of the persons describing it.

In Jewish folklore, which Christian tradition has taken over, hell is a place of burning. This tradition is derived from the words *Gay Hinnom* meaning the Valley of Hinnom, a place near Jerusalem which may have been used for human sacrifices in pre-Hebrew times by the pagans and which later was used by the Jews as a refuse dump where rubbish was burned. The word *Gehennah* is taken from the Hebrew *Gay Hinnom*.

Liberal Judaism has abandoned the concepts of heaven and hell as literal geographical areas. It regards them metaphorically as states of being. Hell is estrangement from God which prevents the individual from developing his full potentials as a human being created in God's image. Heaven is complete self-realization and self-fulfillment as a child of God. In this sense Liberal Judaism follows the tradition of the greatest rabbis of the past who said that virtue is its own reward and sin brings its own punishment.

Liberal Judaism does, however, believe in life after death, but it does not attempt to describe what that life is. Liberal Judaism realizes that our human limitations with our finite imaginations cannot possibly describe an existence which is totally beyond human experience. Perhaps some day we shall know more. In the meantime we have faith, as the late Rabbi Milton Steinberg put it, that "though he die, man lives on . . . and the scales of cosmic equity always end up in balance."

What Do Jews Believe about Reward and Punishment?

Closely associated with the belief in life after death is the belief in reward and punishment. Indeed the whole idea of heaven and hell evolved as the result of the need to justify the ways of God to man. If God is ominpotent and just and demands righteousness of His worshippers as the prophets had taught, why do the wicked so often prosper in God's world and the righteous so often suffer?

The author of the Book of Job wrestled with this problem and finally came to the conclusion that there is no answer satisfying to our human understanding—that we must have faith in God believing that what may seem unjust to us with our limited insight may be only a partial experience of a more complete fulfillment which God alone knows and has ordained.

Later, influenced by Babylonian and Persian theology, and in response to the insistent demand for equalizing somewhere, somehow, the inequities of this earthly life, the ideas of heaven as a place of reward for the righteous and hell as a place for the punishment of the wicked became part of the Jewish religious belief about life after death. It is still part of the Orthodox Jewish tradition, as it is of orthodox traditions in Christianity and Mohammedanism, which are derived from Judaism.

There is a story in the Talmud that tries to answer the question of how the divine judgment is executed in life after death—whether judgment is rendered against the soul or the resurrected body. The answer, say the rabbis, is to be found in the parable of the king who owned a beautiful orchard with prize fruit-bearing trees. Fearing that some of the fruit might be stolen by his own watchman he employed two men, one blind, the other lame. One day the lame man said to the blind man, "The fruit in the garden is so beautiful and tempting. Why don't we get some? The king will never miss it." Said the blind man, "But how can we? You can't walk and I can't see." Whereupon they agreed on a stratagem. The lame man climbed on the blind man's back and guided him to the fruit. After a time the king visited his garden and discovered that some of the choicest fruit was missing. When he questioned his watchmen they both denied guilt saying, "How could we have taken the fruit seeing one of us is blind and the other lame?" But the king was wise and guessed what had happened. So he said, "You are right. Neither of you by himself could have stolen the fruit, but both of you together, the seeing lame man using the back and legs of the blind man could have robbed the garden."

So the rabbis say that when the soul and the body come before God on the judgment day, the soul will deny guilt by saying, "How could I, a disembodied spirit, commit any sins? It is the body that is guilty." The body will also deny guilt by saying, "I am but clay and could not sin were it not for the urging of the soul in me." Whereupon God in His wisdom judges both the soul and the body as a unit.

Do Jews Believe in Cremation?

Orthodox and Conservative Jews do not practice cremation, the former because they believe in the resurrection of the body and feel that to burn the body would desecrate it, the latter out of respect to Orthodox tradition. The belief in the resurrection of the body goes back perhaps to the fourth pre-Christian century when Jews were influenced by Babylonian and especially Persian religious concepts. In describing the greatness and power of God, the poet in Isaiah 26:19 (a post-exilic writer whose work was attributed to the great Isaiah) speaks of God's power to raise even the dead from the graves: "Thy dead shall live, their bodies shall rise; O dweller in the dust, awake and sing for joy!"

In the Book of Daniel 12:1-2, the writer carried away by his vision of the future speaks of a time of resurrection: "And many of those who sleep in the dust of the earth shall awake, some to everlasting life and some to shame and everlasting contempt." But the classic passage in the Bible which generations of pious Orthodox believers interpreted as a promise of the resurrection of the body is found in Ezekiel 37, and is known as the vision of the "Valley of Dry Bones." In this vision the prophet, who lived during the Babylonian exile, was trying to comfort his people with the hope of a speedy restoration to their homeland in Palestine. In beautiful imagery he compares the Jews in exile to dry bones in a valley, which God will reanimate with His spirit.

Since Orthodox Jews take the vision of Ezekiel more or less literally, and since cremation reduces the bones to ashes and makes bodily resurrection impossible, Orthodox tradition forbids cremation. Liberal Jews do not believe in the resurrection of the body, and therefore have no religious scruples against cremation.

Do Jews Believe in Asceticism?

Asceticism is the practice of torturing the body to purify the soul. It is self-denial of the physical enjoyment of life for the sake of a richer spiritual fulfillment. Such practices are not considered by Judaism worthy of the wholesome and complete fulfillment of man's obligations either to God or to himself as a child of God. Although ascetic practices were sometimes indulged in by people who aspired to greater holiness than other men, or as penance for sins, the main stream of Judaism never accepted such practices as the way to the good life.

Judaism frowned upon every extremism—upon extremism in sensuality and physical indulgence as well as upon extreme self-denial of the enjoyment of life. It recognized that body and soul had their legitimate needs, and both had to be satisfied if the person were to achieve the fullness of life. Both were given by God; therefore both were intended to fulfill a holy function. In commenting upon the Bible verse, "Thou shalt rejoice before the Lord, thy God," the rabbis said that not only the joys of the spirit were intended, such as study, worship, and good deeds, but also those of the body such as food, drink, raiment, and fellowship.

The Jewish attitude toward life is expressed by the rabbis in this comment: "He who sees a legitimate pleasure and does not avail himself of it is ungrateful to God who made it possible." All of life was given by God for man's enjoyment and use in order that he may fulfill himself. *Every human activity can be spiritual provided it is dedicated to a spiritual purpose.*

That is why Judaism has never looked with favor upon withdrawal from the world. True piety is not achieved in seclusion from the world, but in living in the world according to God's will, helping to make the world a little better because we have lived in it.

Do Jews Still Believe in Animal Sacrifices?

No. It was the belief among the ancient Hebrews, and doubtless among all the ancient peoples, that when a person committed a sin—that is, violated some religious taboo (forbidden act)—he endangered and sometimes forfeited his life to the god whose taboo he violated. To save himself he had to give a life in redemption for his own. In many primitive societies the practice of offering the life of one's child or of some other human being was considered imperative when very important taboos were violated. The story, Genesis 22, describing the interrupted attempt to sacrifice Isaac by his father Abraham, was probably told in its original form as a protest against the practice of child sacrifice, which was not uncommon in those primitive times even among the ancient Hebrews. The prophet Micha refers to the practice of child sacrifice when he says: "Shall I give my first born for my transgressions, the fruit of my body for the sin of my soul?" (Micha 6:7).

But even when human sacrifices were no longer practiced, the belief in the need for the sacrifice of some life in redemption for the sinner's life was retained and became the basis for the animal sacrifice in ancient Israel. Various kinds of animals were used, the value of the animal depending upon the gravity of the sin. Besides the sin offerings there were many other kinds of sacrifices in which animals were used—thanksgiving offerings, peace offerings, and free-will gifts.

The sacrificial cult was the most important feature of the ancient Temple service. The sinner brought to the Temple his sacrifice which the priests offered on his behalf. In addition there were a number of statutory sacrifices which the priests offered daily and on special occasions to atone for the people as a whole. The sprinkling of the blood of the sacrificial animals on the altar was the symbolic giving of the sinner's life in atonement for his sin, for the life principle was believed to reside in the blood.

It was against this mechanical and ritualistic kind of atonement of sins and worship of God that the great Hebrew prophets protested with all the passion of their moral indignation:

> To what purpose is the multitude of your
> Sacrifices unto Me? saith the Lord.
> I am full of the burnt-offerings of rams,
> And the fat of fed beasts;
> And I delight not in the blood of
> Bullocks, of lambs or of he goats . . .
> Wash you, make you clean,
> Put away the evil of your doings
> From before Mine eyes
> Cease to do evil; learn to do good . . .
>
> —Isaiah 1:16

In spite of the prophets' protests, the sacrificial cult continued until the destruction of the first Temple in 586 B.C.E. It was restored when the second Temple was built in the fifth pre-Christian century, and the practice of sacrificing animals for one's sins continued until the destruction of that Temple also in 70 C.E. Since then Jews have abolished animal sacrifices in their worship and turned to the prophetic and rabbinic ideas of worship through prayer, righteous living, and deeds of loving kindness.

Do Jews Practice Baptism?

No. The practice of baptism, that is, ritual immersion in water, was an ancient Jewish practice. It was one of the means by which a sinner purified himself. Every person who committed a sin, or in any way defiled himself, had to offer a sacrifice and also take a ritual bath, that is, be immersed in running water as a symbol of purification. The practice of immersion is still retained to some extent in Orthodox Judaism as a symbol of purification during certain periods of a person's life, especially for women after their monthly periods or after childbirth. The ritual bath is called a *mikveh* (a cistern of water). Liberal Jews have abolished the practice.

The practice came into Christianity through Johanan (John the Baptist). John, to call him by his Greek name, was a Jew who believed in the imminent coming of the Messiah. He believed that in order to hasten the coming of the Messiah the people had to prepare themselves through purification. One means of purification after repentance was immersion in the flowing waters of the Jordan River. He called upon the people to repent and to purify themselves through the ritual bath. The New Testament tells us that Jesus was among those who thus purified himself and that the experience had a profound influence upon his life.

Today the practice of baptism is almost universal among Christians as a symbol of conversion, purification, and acceptance of the Christian faith. In some denominations total immersion is required. In others a symbolic sprinkling of water is regarded as sufficient.

What Is the Jewish Concept of Charity?

There is no word in the Hebrew language for charity, although the practice of charity has been from the beginning one of the basic and most important expressions of Jewish religious life. The reason for this lack of a special word to express the concept of "charity" is that the need for helping the less fortunate was so fundamental a principle in Judaism that it was equated with righteousness. So the word for charity is the same as for righteousness, *tsedakah* from the Hebrew *tsedek* (righteous).

Because Judaism has always been a religion which emphasized the deed, the *mitzvah* (divine commandment), rather than dogma or creed, the stress in Judaism has always been laid upon ethical and moral conduct in one's personal life and in all human relations as the only way to do the will of God. Love of God, the highest commandment of all, can be expressed only in love of one's fellow man. Therefore, charity, the practice of helping one's less fortunate brother man in every way, was a primary duty of anyone who aspired to holiness.

When Jesus said, "Inasmuch as ye did it unto the least of these my brethren, ye did it unto me," he was speaking in the authentic idiom of Judaism and expressing a basic Jewish religious attitude. Whereas the concept of helping the less fortunate was considered a virtue among the more sensitive of the pagans, among the Jews it was the very heart and essence of their religion. The Jewish Bible is vitally concerned with the welfare of the widow, the orphan, the stranger within the gates—the three most underprivileged groups in ancient society; and at every opportunity Moses enjoins his people to care for them, to protect them, to feed and clothe them. The Book of Job has a classic statement of Judaism's attitude toward helping the less fortunate. In trying to justify himself before God, Job reviews his life to prove that he was always very careful in the duty of charity especially:

> If I have withheld aught that the poor desired,
> Or have caused the eyes of the widow to fail;
> Or have eaten my morsel myself alone,
> And the fatherless hath not eaten thereof—
> Nay, from my youth he grew up with me as with
>   a father,
> And I have been her [widow's] guide from my
>   mother's womb.
> If I have seen any wanderer in want of clothing,
> If his loins have not blessed me,
> And if he were not warmed with the fleece of my
>   sheep;
> If I have lifted up my hand against the fatherless,
> Because I saw my help in the gate;
> Then let my shoulder fall from the shoulder-blade,
> And let my arm be broken from the bone.
> For calamity from God was a terror to me,
> And by reason of His majesty I could do nothing
>   [wrong].
>
> —Job 31:16-23

No Jewish community was regarded as complete without its welfare organizations to help the poor, clothe the naked, care for the sick, bury the dead, and its free loan societies for the financially embarrassed. Long before the community chest idea became part of our civilization, Jews had community chests and welfare agencies—as far back indeed as the second Temple more than twenty-three hundred years ago. A literal community chest was placed in the Temple into which pious worshippers deposited their contributions for the welfare of the needy so that neither the giver nor the recipient might know each other. The money was then distributed by proper agencies to those in need. The charity boxes in many synagogues and churches today originated in this ancient Jewish practice.

The great medieval rabbi and philosopher, Moses Ben Maimon (Maimonides), about 1200 C.E. laid down the traditional Jewish concept of charity in the following statement:

There are eight degrees or steps in the duty of charity. The first and lowest degree is to give, but with reluctance or regret. This is the gift of the hand but not of the heart.

The second is to give cheerfully but not proportionately to the distress of the sufferer.

The third is to give cheerfully and proportionately but not until solicited.

The fourth is to give cheerfully, proportionately, and even unsolicited, but to put it into the poor man's hand, thereby exciting in him the painful emotion of shame.

The fifth is to give charity in such a way that the distressed may receive the bounty and know his benefactor without the benefactor knowing him. Such was the conduct of some of our ancestors who used to tie up money in the corners of their cloaks so that the poor might take it unperceived.

The sixth, which rises still higher, is to know the objects of our bounty but to remain unknown to them. Such was the conduct of those of our ancestors who used to convey their charitable gifts into poor people's dwellings, taking care that their own persons and names should remain unknown.

The seventh is still more meritorious, namely, to bestow

charity in such a way that the benefactor may not know the relieved persons nor they the name of their benefactors as was done by our charitable forefathers during the existence of the Temple. For there was in that holy building a place called the Chamber of the Silent wherein the good deposited secretly whatever their generous hearts suggested, and from which the poor were maintained with equal secrecy.

Lastly, the eighth and the most meritorious of all is to anticipate charity by preventing poverty, namely, to assist the reduced fellow man either by a considerable gift or a loan of money or by teaching him a trade or by putting him in the way of business so that he may earn an honest livelihood and not be forced to the dreadful alternative of holding out his hand for charity. To this scripture alludes when it says: "And if thy brother be waxen poor and fallen in decay with thee, then thou shalt relieve him; yea, though he be a stranger or a sojourner, that he may live with thee! This is the highest step and the summit of charity's golden ladder."

—*Union Prayerbook*, Vol. II,
newly revised edition, p. 117

What Is Judaism's Attitude toward Love and Marriage?

The *Zohar*, a mystic commentary on the Bible, says: "When the soul is sent down from heaven it is a combined male and female soul. The male part enters the male child and the female part enters the female. If they are worthy, God causes them to reunite in marriage. This is true mating." Though expressed in the imaginative language of Jewish mysticism it does describe beautifully the Jewish idea of love and marriage. In the first chapter of the Jewish Bible (Genesis 1:24) where the creation of man and woman is described, the writer concludes: "Therefore shall a man leave his father and his mother and cleave unto his wife, and they shall be one flesh."

Although among the ancient Hebrews, as among all Orientals of that day, polygamy was the common practice with those who could afford to support more than one wife, the ideal of love in marriage was extolled by lawgiver, singer, and sage. We are told in Genesis 29:20: "And Jacob served seven years for Rachel; and they seemed unto him but a few days, for the love he had for her." *The Song of Songs* in the Jewish Bible is one of the greatest love poems in literature. Throughout the Bible, and especially in the Talmud, the marriage relation is sanctified and glorified. To this day among all Jews, Orthodox, Conservative, and Reform, the heart of the marriage ceremony is contained in this declaration which the groom makes to the bride: "Be thou consecrated unto me by this ring according to the laws of Moses and Israel." In Reform Jewish ritual the bride makes a similar declaration to her groom. The Hebrew word for marriage is *kiddushin* (sanctification).

Rabbi Milton Steinberg, in his excellent outline *Basic Judaism* (Harcourt, Brace & Co.), describes the Jewish tradition on love and marriage beautifully when he writes:

> Tradition looks upon the love relationship as a high adventure of the human spirit, an opportunity for a man and a woman to make a oneness of their separateness, to confirm each other in strength and support each other in weakness, to be schooled in unselfishness and compassion, and help to hand on from their generation to the next the sacred things of their community.

Marriage in Jewish tradition is indeed a union of souls, an opportunity for two people to produce the spiritual soil and emotional climate which will help both to achieve the highest kind of self-realization and fulfillment. That is why the Jewish home and the Jewish family through the centuries have been almost a byword for the most beautiful relations between husband and wife, and between parents and children.

Do Jews Sanction Divorce?

"He who puts away the wife of his youth, for him God's very altar weeps." This statement of the rabbis in the Talmud expressed the basic Jewish attitude toward divorce. It is a tragedy when a marriage is broken up. But from the very beginning of Jewish history the facts of life were recognized.

Although Jews in their flights of imagination spoke of marriages as made in heaven, they were down to earth enough to realize that marriage, after all, is a human relationship and as such has the fallibility common to all relations between imperfect human beings. In spite of the love that brings young people together, living together brings unforeseen irritations, conflicts, and tensions which are inevitable with normally alert, intelligent, and different personalities. Sometimes the tensions become more than either party can endure or ought to endure. Jewish tradition always recognized such possibilities and therefore provided for divorce where no other solution to marital difficulties was possible.

However, the rabbis hedged the marriage relation with many safeguards, especially to protect the woman, who, in that oriental civilization, had few economic or legal rights. But in spite of the fact that the way was open for the dissolution of an unhappy marriage the divorce rate among Jews has always been very low. Public opinion and the long-established tradition of beautiful Jewish home life served effectively to stabilize and to preserve the integrity of the Jewish home. Only in recent times, with the general breakdown of family life in our modern world, have the foundations of the Jewish family also begun to weaken. For in spite of time-honored traditions and values Jews are a part of the world in which they live and are influenced by their environment.

Jews and Birth Control

There are some differences of opinion on the subject of birth control among the three major denominations—Orthodox, Conservative, and Reform—but the differences are largely in detail, not in basic principle.

The purpose of marriage in Jewish tradition is expressed in the first chapter of Genesis: "And God created man in His own image . . . male and female created He them. And God blessed them, and said unto them 'Be fruitful and multiply and replenish the earth.' "

So the purpose of marriage in Jewish tradition is to beget and rear children and to establish a family, in which and through which all the members may develop and reflect the image of God in which we are created. Therefore, Judaism frowns upon birth suppression, except under certain conditions.

And those conditions go to the heart not only of the Jewish view of marriage and the family, but of Judaism's view of man, the purpose of life, and man's relation to God.

In commenting on the statement in Deuteronomy 8:1, "All the commandments which I command you this day shall you observe to do, that you may live by them," the rabbis added the words "and not die by them." The Torah (God's law and revealed will), say the rabbis, was given to man that he might live more abundantly. Therefore, Jewish tradition rejected dogmatic absolutes as applied to human situations. The rabbis always interpreted the biblical commandments in terms of how they might enhance human welfare and enrich human life. They used these criteria in their interpretation of the commandment to "be fruitful and multiply."

According to Jewish tradition every couple was obliged to bring at least two children into the world in fulfillment of this commandment. But there are exceptions even to this rule, as, for example, where a woman's health is such that to have children might endanger her life.

In all cases where the health of the wife is involved, Jewish tradition permits the use of whatever contraceptives are available to her. In extreme cases she may even submit to permanent sterilization to avoid the danger of accidental conception. In cases where a couple have already brought two children into the world, and although there is no urgent reason for family limitation, their decision to practice birth control is not considered immoral or sinful, provided it is by their mutual consent.

Judaism sees the sanctity of the marriage relation not merely in the process of reproduction (although that is the primary purpose of marriage), but also in the beauty, the harmony, the companionship and love between a husband and wife. So the rabbis will permit a marriage where the woman is past the childbearing age, where the companionship and love can be a source of enrichment to the two people involved.

Modern Judaism, especially in its more liberal interpretations, in its concern for the welfare of the family has extended the principle of birth control wherever in the mature judgment of the people involved limitation and family planning are deemed necessary.

Judaism sees the purpose of life on earth as the building of the kingdom of God in which God and man are co-builders. The family is the institution in which and through which the individual is prepared and equipped for his role as a builder of this kingdom. Therefore, everything that helps the family to help any and all the members toward this end is pleasing to God.

Using this criterion, the question of population limitation in relation to the "population explosion" is from a Jewish view a matter of study into the needs of the human family and its welfare. If such a study were to show that uncontrolled population growth would be harmful to the welfare of mankind, Jewish tradition would sanction birth control as one means of avoiding that danger.

What Is the Jewish Tradition on Manual Labor?

It is a common misconception, fostered by those unfriendly to Jews, that the Jew will not work with his hands or that he looks down upon manual labor. The facts are to the contrary. Most of the Jews in the world today make their living by the work of their hands. It is only because there are many Jews in the professions and in the retail trades with whom the average non-Jew comes into contact that the myth has arisen that Jews do not work with their hands. But these are an insignificant minority of the Jews of the world or even of the Jews in America. How many non-Jews know that there are more than one hundred thousand Jewish farmers in the United States? How many non-Jews know that in New York city one third of the members of the trade unions are Jews?

The fact is that manual labor was always extolled and honored by Jewish tradition. The great rabbis of the Talmud were all engaged in some trade. Their title "rabbi" was merely a term of honor meaning teacher, a title which they earned by their learning and piety. Among the greatest rabbinic names mentioned in the Talmud we find Hillel who was a wood cutter; Joshua Ben Hananiah, a blacksmith; Resh Lakish, a former professional gladiator; Akiba, a shepherd. There were farmers, tanners, fishermen, tailors among them. Indeed they believed implicitly in the injunction given to Adam: "And by the sweat of thy brow shalt thou eat thy bread" (Genesis 3:19).

The famous Rabban Gamaliel, who was the teacher of Saul of Tarsus (Saint Paul), voiced the thinking of the main stream of Jewish tradition when he said: "Excellent is the study of the Torah when combined with a wordly occupation; . . . All study of the Torah which is not supplemented by work must prove futile in the end." It was only during the Middle Ages, when the Jews were forced into segregated ghettoes by the Christian Church and forbidden by the ecclesiastical and secular authorities to engage in economic pursuits other than money lending and occupations considered too ignoble for Christians, that the opportunity for manual labor was denied them except in their own ghettoes among themselves. Moreover, the medieval trade guilds were semireligious organizations to which no Jew could belong and remain a Jew.

To this day discrimination against Jews in employment even in democratic America has forced many Jews to choose trades and professions wherein they can be their own employers. But to say that Jews look down upon manual labor is a travesty of the facts. One has only to see with honest eyes and mind the epic of the building of the modern state of Israel to give the lie to the insinuations which have plagued Jewish life in our own century. The story of the reclamation of Israel from the desert, which centuries of neglect had created, is one of the most heroic and inspiring chapters in the history of human courage, determination, and devotion. Young men and women literally replaced the eroded land with their bare hands and washed the salt out of the desert with buckets. They built great cities out of sand dunes, farms, and gardens where for centuries there was only swamp. Manual labor has always been glorified in Jewish tradition.

THE JEWISH RELIGIOUS YEAR

> Far more than Israel has kept the Sabbath and the holydays, they have kept Israel and enabled him to survive the centuries.
> —An adaptation of Ahad Ha-Am

THE TALMUD tells the story of a heathen who came to Hillel, the leading rabbi of the first pre-Christian century, and asked to have the whole of Judaism explained to him while he stood on one foot. The rabbi replied, "What is displeasing unto thee, do not unto thy neighbor. That is the whole of judaism. All the rest is the commentary. But," he added, "if you really want to understand Judaism you must go and learn the commentary." In this admonition "to go and learn the commentary" Hillel gave a succinct and effective answer to all who ask, "Why are symbols and ceremonies necessary to religion?"

The chief purpose of symbols and ceremonies in religion lies in their function as concrete and dramatic expressions of abstract religious beliefs, ideas, and experiences which are incommunicable through the ordinary means of speech and communication. In an ancient and historic religion like Judaism these aids to a deeper and more satisfying religious life are especially important.

The annual cycle of religious holydays and festivals, the beautiful symbols and ceremonies in the Jew's daily life, are a recurring drama helping to renew and to revitalize for the Jews in every generation their Jewish ideals and traditions, their hopes and dreams for themselves and for mankind. When Jews assemble for worship in the synagogue and take the Torah from the ark they are re-enacting symbolically the great experience of the revelation on Sinai which, according to tradition, set Israel upon its career as the people of God. When they sit at the Seder table (Passover feast) and recite the *Haggadah* (the story of the Passover) and partake of the matzos and the bitter herbs, they are symbolically reliving the bitterness of slavery experienced by their forefathers in Egypt and the story of the redemption which they subsequently achieved. When they light the Hanukah lights year after year, the memory of the heroic struggle and victory of the Maccabees of the second pre-Christian century inspires them to resist tyranny wherever and whenever it may raise its ugly head.

Thus the festivals, symbols, and ceremonies in Judaism enable the Jew to relive the past experiences of his people, to dramatize the beliefs, ideals, and hopes cherished by them, and to revitalize and strengthen the Jewish spirit within himself and his fellow Jews. Incidentally, and quite significantly also, the celebration of these annual festivals and holydays by Jews all over the world at practically the same time and in more or less the same manner is an important experience linking the scattered Jewish communities into a world-wide religious brotherhood. The abstract beliefs and principles of Judaism in themselves would not be sufficient to bind into an effective unity the heterogeneous group of peoples who call themselves Jews. It is the festivals and holydays, the concrete symbols and dramatic presentation of experiences growing out of a common past, that give meaning and power to the sense of kinship between the widely differentiated Jewish communities speaking widely different languages and possessing such widely differing cultures.

There is another reason why we need symbols and ceremonies in religion, especially in organized religion, and it grows out of the fact that the most effective way by which most people are able to obtain impressions of the world is through their senses. We know objects because we can see them, hear them, touch, taste, or smell them. Therefore, the simplest way of imparting knowledge in and appreciation of an object by the human mind is by a direct and concrete stimulation of the senses. We obtain a much better idea of the fragrance of a rose if we actually smell one than if its fragrance is described to us. It is a more thrilling experience to hear a Beethoven symphony than to read about it. And except for those who have been trained to think and to grasp abstract ideas and concepts, most of us still find the concrete and dramatic expression of an idea much easier to understand. The Chinese say, "A picture is worth a thousand words." A picture stimulates our senses and touches us emotionally, which is, after all, the way most of us live and learn. Therefore, the need for symbol and ceremony in all religion, which deals with such profound abstractions as the idea of God, moral values, and man's yearning to establish some kind of relationship between himself and the unseen and often unfelt spiritual world, is even greater than in other realms of human experience. That is why there is not and never has been a great religion without some kind of ritual or ceremonial, however simple it may be.

The great Jewish religious teachers throughout the centuries were fully aware of this psychological need for religious symbolism; and they met that need by developing a rich tradition of custom, symbol, and ceremony touching every aspect of the Jew's religious life.

Judaism is a very ancient religion. Its beginnings are to be found in the first conscious strivings of our distant ancestors to rise above the barbarism which surrounded them. In the course of its development it was molded by contact with nearly every civilization of the ancient world. It learned from Egypt; it was influenced by Assyria and Babylon. It came into contact with the great civilization of the Persians and was enriched by it. The glory that was Greece also left its mark upon Jewish life and thought; nor did the centuries of Roman domination pass Israel without leaving their indelible impress. For four thousand years the Jewish spirit was being molded in the crucible of history. During the course of these centuries it assimilated numberless ideas which it reinterpreted in the light of its own spirit and made its own. These ideas had to be symbolized and dramatized and made meaningful to the mass of Jews. Thus, as the centuries followed each other, Judaism grew richer not only in its ideas and ideals but also in the wealth of its symbolism, customs, and ceremonies which it developed to dramatize those ideals.

But as conditions changed from century to century and from generation to generation many of the ideas and customs and practices that had served well in their own day became in the course of time obstacles in the way of the progressive development of the Jewish spirit. Like the scaffolding erected around a building, which is most useful for its construction but becomes unsightly and a hindrance to the use of the building if it is permitted to remain after the structure is completed, so many of the customs and practices, which had been necessary to Judaism at certain stages of its development, have in the course of time, under changed conditions and under the impact of new ideas, outlived their usefulness and become indeed a meaningless burden.

That is why Reform Judaism and, to a lesser degree Conservative Judaism found it necessary to discard some traditional practices that had become obsolete, to change others more in harmony with changing conditions of Jewish life, and to create new ones growing out of progressively deepening spiritual insights that needed to be dramatized and symbolized. The answers to the questions about Jewish customs, symbols, and ceremonies in the subsequent pages take cognizance of these divergences from tradition and endeavor to explain the reasons why.

> So teach us to number our days that we may get us a heart of wisdom.
>
> —Psalm 90:12

Why Is This Jewish Year 5722?

The year 1961-62 is the year 5722 according to the traditional Jewish calendar. This reckoning is based on the traditional account of the creation of the world as described in the first chapter of Genesis. The year 5722 is arrived at by counting from the first days of creation to Adam, then through the genealogies of the descendants of Adam as told in the Book of Genesis to Abraham; from Abraham to the sojourn in Egypt, the approximately four hundred years of slavery, the deliverance by Moses, the wanderings in the desert, and so on, until the historical period is reached. In a word, according to traditional Jewish reckoning the year 1961-62 is the year 5722 since the creation of the world.

Most Jews realize that the world is older than 5722 calendar years. They accept the findings of science which describe the age even of our planet in terms of hundreds of millions and even billions of years. However, the traditional reckoning is retained in the Jewish calendar even by Liberal Jews for religious and sentimental reasons.

Why Do Jews Use B.C.E. and C.E. instead of the Usual B.C. and A.D. in Their Time Scale?

The letters B.C.E. mean Before the Christian Era, and C.E. means the Christian or present Era. Since Jews do not accept Jesus as the Christ (Messiah) they do not use the designations which have come into our modern calendar through Christianity; that is, B.C. (Before Christ) and A.D., which stands for the Latin, Anno Domini (the year of Our Lord).

Jews do not accept Jesus as "Our Lord"; therefore, they cannot use the term A.D. So they use the terms B.C.E. and C.E. (Before and after the Christian or present Era). Mohammedans also reject the Christian designations, for they count time from before and after the *hegira*, the flight of Mohammed from Mecca to Medina in 622 C.E. This date, 622 C.E., marks the year 1 in the Moslem Era. The Mohammedan year as of 1962 would therefore be 1340 Moslem Era.

Why Do Jewish Holydays Begin in the Evening?

The Jewish religious calendar is based on the cycles of the moon. The ancient Hebrews counted their days from evening to evening. That is why all Jewish holydays begin in the evening. Thus, the Jewish Sabbath begins on Friday evening at sunset or moonrise and ends on Saturday evening at sunset.

Why Do Jewish Holydays Occur on Different Dates Each Year of Our Modern Calendar?

The Jewish religious year is based on the lunar (moon) calendar, whereas our regular calendar is based on the solar (sun) year. The lunar year consists of three hundred and fifty-four days and a fraction, whereas the solar year has three hundred and sixty-five days and a fraction. There is, therefore, a difference of about eleven days between them. Since Jewish holydays are fixed according to the lunar year, they must occur on different days of each solar year.

The Jews of old recognized this problem and found it necessary from time to time to equalize the lunar with the solar year, otherwise the same holydays would come sometimes in the summer and sometimes in the winter. They avoided this difficulty and achieved a balance between the lunar and solar years by arranging for seven lunar leap years in every nineteen-year period. Thus, sometimes at intervals of two years, sometimes of three, a thirteenth month (leap month) was added to the lunar year. This thirteenth month is called *Adar sheni* (second Adar).

What Are the Names of the Months of the Jewish Year?

1. Nisan
2. Iyar
3. Sivan
4. Tammuz
5. Av
6. Ellul
7. Tishri
8. Heshvan
9. Kislev
10. Tebeth
11. Sh'vat
12. Adar

13. Adar sheni (on leap years)

Why Do Some Jews Observe Two Days of the Holydays and Some Only One?

In ancient Palestine the beginning of the month was determined in a rather primitive manner. On the day when the new moon was expected watchers were sent to the shore of the Mediterranean, where the horizon is unobstructed, to watch for the appearance of the new moon. As soon as two reliable witnesses reported having seen it, the Sanhedrin (Jewish Supreme Court) announced the beginning of the month. This news was then relayed by fire signals set up in strategic parts of the country so that during the night the whole country might be apprised of the advent of the new month (moon).

It happened that hostile Samaritans, wanting to embarrass the Jews, sent out false fire signals. To avoid the danger of such further interference, the authorities gave up the fire-signal method and resorted to sending trustworthy messengers to inform outlying communities. This was slow, and often distant communities were left in doubt as to the exact day of the new moon with consequent delays in determining the beginning of the festivals. Therefore, the authorities in Jerusalem ordained that Jews living outside the boundaries of Jewish Palestine should celebrate each of the principal festivals two days instead of one. This usage has persisted among Orthodox and Conservative Jews to the present day, although the calendar is now fixed and it is known with certainty the exact moment of the new moon.

Reform Judaism, seeing no longer the need for the precaution taken by the ancient authorities, has abolished the two days' observance.

Incidentally, the Jews of Palestine never observed more than one day, except on Rosh Hashanah which they observed two days, and still do.

What Is the Sabbath?

The word Sabbath (*Shabbat* or *Shabbos*) comes from the Hebrew word "to rest," and is a day set aside for resting from the ordinary labor of the week in order to devote time to spiritual refreshment through study of sacred literature and to the contemplation and worship of God.

Of all Jewish religious institutions the Sabbath has had the widest appeal and the greatest impact upon the life of mankind. Through the influence of Christianity with its Sunday Sabbath, and Mohammedanism with its Friday Sabbath (both these religions came from Judaism and are based upon the Jewish Bible), the Jewish idea of one day's rest in seven has become a basic institution among most civilized peoples.

The idea behind the Sabbath is essentially ethical and humanitarian. The fourth commandment tells us: "Six days shalt thou labor and do thy work, but the seventh day is a Sabbath unto the Lord thy God; in it thou shalt not do any manner of work, thou, nor thy son, nor thy daughter, nor thy man-servant, nor thy maid-servant, nor thy cattle, nor any stranger that is within thy gates. . . ."

In this commandment is the recognition that "man does not live by bread alone"; that man is a being with a soul as well as a body, and the soul needs refreshment and renewal even as the body needs food and sleep. Although taboo days, days on which certain things could not be done, were observed by many ancient peoples, the Sabbath idea as it developed in Judaism was unique in the ancient world. It was an original Jewish creation born of the spirit of Judaism, which from the beginning emphasized ethical and human values. So the Sabbath became, as it were, a symbol of the Jew's relation to God.

Today the problem of Sabbath observance has become very difficult. The vast majority of Jews live in countries where Saturday is not a day of rest but of work and business, and it has become almost impossible for many Jews, even with the best intentions, to observe the Sabbath in the traditional way. Dr. Claude G. Montefiore has this to say about Sabbath observance in his book, *Outlines of Liberal Judaism:*

> There is no question whatever that by far the most difficult problem in modern Judaism is connected with the keeping of the Sabbath. To shut one's eyes to economic and social facts is the worst possible folly. It is idle to deny that the present conditions of things in the West, in which a vast number of Jews and Jewesses are absolutely unable to "rest upon the Sabbath day" is profoundly unsatisfactory . . . but let me urge and entreat every Jewish parent, man and woman, to remember that because he or she may have to work upon some portion of the Sabbath, that is absolutely no reason for not using the remaining hours sabbathically. On the contrary, it is all the more reason why an attempt should be made to make all the better and finer use of those hours which are left over. It is just here that Liberal Jews should show their fidelity to Judaism and their power of rising above the constraint of circumstances—let not, therefore, those who have to work upon the Sabbath despair. With a good will and with a little trouble, the values and blessings of the Sabbath may still be theirs.

There are many ways in which the Sabbath spirit may be strengthened today. The most effective is by sanctifying Friday evening in the home and the synagogue and making it a unique evening of spiritual experience in which the whole family may participate.

What Is the Significance of the Sabbath Candles?

It is customary to have two candles in silver or brass candlesticks on the Sabbath table. The candles should be white and may be lighted by the mother or one of the children. Among the Orthodox the candles are lit at sunset, but Reform practice has made the lighting ceremony part of the family service at the dinner table just before the meal is served. The reason two candles are used is suggested by the rabbis as symbolic of the two versions of the fourth commandment (Exodus 20 and Deuteronomy 5), one beginning with the word *zokhor* meaning "remember" the Sabbath, and the other beginning with the word *shomor* meaning "keep" the Sabbath.

Light has always been a symbol of religion. The first act of creation was "Let there be Light." When light came into the world the process of creation really began. Light represents truth, enlightenment, and all spiritual values. So it is appropriate for the Sabbath to be ushered in with the lighting ceremony.

Why the Special White Bread on the Sabbath?

Tradition prescribes two loaves of Sabbath bread. They are called *hallos*, which is the plural of the Hebrew word for "loaf." The bread is always white because white bread was regarded as a great luxury only to be indulged in on special occasions. In different communities the *hallos* assumed different shapes. In German Jewish communities the twisted loaf called *barkhes* was adopted and most of the Sabbath loaves we see today are of that shape.

The reason for the two loaves goes back to ancient times when the average family had only one good meal a day during the week but two on the Sabbath, and one loaf was required for each meal. Thus the practice of having two Sabbath loaves became part of tradition. Later, the rabbis explained the custom of the two loaves as symbolic of the double portion of manna, the miracle food described in the Book of Exodus, which was collected on Friday for the Sabbath when the children of Israel were wandering in the wilderness before they entered the Promised Land.

Why Fish on the Sabbath?

The custom of eating fish on the Sabbath is of ancient origin and has no religious significance. Some scholars think that the popularity of fish as the Sabbath food was due to its being regarded as the symbol of fertility.

Later tradition ascribed to the fish a symbolic significance in relation to Jewish survival. Even as the fish persists and multiplies in spite of its numerous enemies, so Israel survives all persecution.

What Is the Significance of the Kiddush?

Kiddush (from the Hebrew word *kodosh* meaning "holy") is the ceremony of sanctification using a cup of wine at the services in the home, and sometimes in the temple and synagogue, to usher in the Sabbath and festivals. It is a symbolic sanctifying of the Sabbaths and holydays as seasons of joy with wine, which is the traditional symbol of joy.

The blessing accompanying the ceremony is: "Praised art Thou, O Lord our God, Ruler of the Universe, Who hast created the fruit of the vine." This is followed by a prayer sanctifying the Sabbath, which reads as follows:

> Let us praise God with this symbol of joy, and thank Him for the blessings of the past week, for life and strength, for home and love and friendship, for the discipline of our trials and temptations, for the happiness that has come to us out of our labors. Thou hast ennobled us, O God, by the blessings of work, and in love hast sanctified us by Sabbath rest and worship as ordained in the Torah: "Six days shalt thou labor and do all thy work, but the seventh day is the Sabbath to be hallowed unto the Lord, thy God."
> —*Union Prayerbook*, Vol. I, newly revised edition, p. 93

In Orthodox Judaism the Kiddush also contains reference to the creation of the world in six days, God's resting on the seventh, and the deliverance from slavery in Egypt.

What Is Havdalah?

Havdalah literally means separation or division. It is a cere-mony observed at the outgoing of the Sabbath on Saturday at sunset, symbolizing the end of the holyday and the beginning of the work week. To the Jews during the past two thousand years, exiled from their homeland in Palestine, mistreated and often persecuted, the one day in the toilsome and difficult week when they felt like human beings sheltered from the animosities of their non-Jewish neighbors was the Sabbath. From sunset on Friday to sunset on Saturday the Jew was king in his own home, honored and respected by his wife, family, and Jewish neighbors. The Sabbath was his day of glory when he could commune with his God in the synagogue, read his sacred scriptures, and become renewed in his faith that all his present misery was merely a transitory phase which would be replaced ultimately by a glorious vindication according to God's promise to Abraham: "And I shall make thee a great people, and all the families of the earth shall be blessed in thee and thy seed" (Genesis 12).

So the Jews looked forward each week to their holy Sab-bath. It was the one bright spot in the week of darkness, and they were loathe to let it go. However, the march of time was inexorable. The hours went by, and as the Saturday sun began to sink in the western sky and the shadows lengthened they realized that their moment of happiness was swiftly running out and the toilsome week lay ahead. Reluctantly they watched the fading sun, and as the first star appeared they began their preparation to usher out the Sabbath Queen with a ceremony worthy of such an honored and precious guest. This ceremony is known as Havdalah, separating the holyday from the rest of the week.

The ceremony includes blessings over a cup of wine— symbol of the joy of the Sabbath—over a box of fragrant spices—symbol of God's great gifts to mankind in his bounty —and over a lighted candle, usually of colored strands of twisted wax—symbolic of the light of the moon and the stars which illumine the night, and of all light which God created to dispel the darkness both physical and spiritual by His creative word and His revealed truth.

What Is Rosh Hodesh (New Moon Observance)?

Rosh Hodesh means the head or beginning of the month. The ancient Hebrews counted time by the phases of the moon. Each new moon beginning a new month was regarded as a holyday. It was observed with the sounding of the *shofar* (ram's horn) and with special sacrifices in the Temple.

The observance of the new moon has continued through the centuries. Among Orthodox and Conservative Jews the new moon (new month) observance is held on the first and often on the first two days of each month with special prayers added to the regular daily services in the synagogue. It is regarded as a semiholyday. Reform Jews observe the advent of the new month by adding a special prayer during the regular Sabbath services at the approach of the new month. It reads as follows:

> Almighty God, grant that the approaching month of ————, which begins on ———— of the coming week, may be a messenger of good tidings to us all. Bestow upon us a life of health and peace, of sustenance and contentment. Help us to spend the month in the love of Thee and in the service of man and so to order our way that it may be pleasing in Thy sight. Amen. (*Union Prayerbook*, Vol. I, newly revised edition, p. 147).

The Penitential Season

A fundamental principle in Judaism is that man is perfectable, that he is endowed by God with the capacity to explore within himself and to develop those qualities of character and spirit which reveal his kinship with God in Whose image he was created. Man can rise from imperfection to ever higher levels of spiritual insight and maturity. This process of spiritual growth is endless, and one of the techniques Judaism provides for such growth is repentance, the consciousness of sin, the recognition of what man is and what in the sight of God he ought to be. To reach for the "ought" is man's purpose on earth. The power to rise to it on ever higher levels is the promise which Judaism gives to every human being who is willing to make the effort and to fulfill the conditions, which are to live by the will of God.

That is why the great holydays in Judaism are called the penitential season ushered in by Rosh Hashanah, the New Year.

What Is Rosh Hashanah?

Literally, Rosh Hashanah means the head or the beginning of the year. This holyday begins ten days of self-examination, self-searching, repentance, and atonement. In Orthodox tradition it was and still is regarded as the Day of Judgment by God of the lives of men. Liberal Jews think of this holyday season as a time for self-judgment in the light of our knowledge of God and His will for mankind.

It is a time for spiritual inventory, when the individual takes annual stock of himself and measures his spiritual achievements against what he knows he ought to be; and if he has fallen short of that goal, he is expected to make greater efforts in the new year. The holyday is spent in worship, in prayer and meditation, and in the outreaching of the spirit for the eternal values in life.

Rosh Hashanah begins on the first day of the seventh month, Tishri. Each new month (new moon) was marked by the sounding of the *shofar* (ram's horn), an instrument used for calling assemblies and announcing important occasions. The seventh month was the most important of all the new moons, probably because of the special significance of the number seven. It was a time for special blasts on the *shofar* and a specially holy day. Probably for that reason the first day of the seventh month was chosen as the beginning of the religious new year. Traditionally Rosh Hashanah is also believed to mark the creation of the world.

The sounding of the *shofar* is still an important part of the Rosh Hashanah service in all synagogues and temples, symbolizing the call to a renewed spiritual life, to make the Jew aware of his responsibilities to God and his fellow men.

It is customary to greet friends on Rosh Hashanah with the Hebrew greeting *L'Shanah Tovah Tikko-Say-Voo* (May you be inscribed for a good year), which refers to the traditional concept of the new year as a time of judgment in which the Heavenly Tribunal goes over the year's life record of each individual to determine whether that person is entitled to reward or punishment in the year to come.

Liberal Jews usually omit the last word because they have abandoned the traditional ideas of the Day of Judgment in favor of the concept of self-judgment in the light of our knowledge of God's will for us. Thus the Liberal Jewish greeting is *L'Shanah Tovah*, a happy or good new year.

It is customary to have something sweet such as apples and honey, or some fruit newly in season, at dinner on the eve of Rosh Hashanah, symbolic of the hope for a sweet and happy new year.

What Is Yom Kippur?

Yom Kippur is the Day of Atonement. It is the most solemn and awe-inspiring of all Jewish holydays and comes as the climax of the penitential season, ten days after Rosh Hashanah. In Orthodox tradition it is regarded as the day upon which the judgment rendered by the Heavenly Tribunal on Rosh Hashanah is finally sealed. Between Rosh Hashanah and Yom Kippur the sinner is given an opportunity for sincere repentance and atonement for any wrongs he may have committed against God or his fellow men. If he repents and atones, then the judgment rendered may be revoked; if not, it is sealed on the Day of Atonement and presumably executed at God's discretion.

The modern interpretation of this entire penitential season has changed the traditional concepts from an external judgment to a self-judgment in the light of what one knows he ought to do and has failed to do. Liberal Jews think of the entire penitential season as a time for self-searching and self-examination, and by prayer, meditation, confession, and fasting to deepen the Jew's spiritual insight so that he may become ever more conscious of his responsibilities to God, to his fellow men, and to himself as a child of God. Yom Kippur, therefore, is really a day of *at-one-ment* when the individual, estranged from God by sin, seeks to become *at-one* with Him through sincere repentance and efforts toward nobler living.

In order to receive God's forgiveness a person must come with clean hands and with sincerity of purpose. Sins committed against one's fellow men, such as lying, cheating, or other wrongs against him, will not be forgiven by God unless the wrongdoer does everything in his power to make amends and seeks forgiveness from the person he has wronged. That person must be ready to forgive if he in turn wishes forgiveness from God.

The Day of Atonement is ushered in with the singing of *Kol Nidre* (all the vows) by the cantor and choir on the eve of Yom Kippur, with a haunting melody which has become famous all over the world. *Kol Nidre* is a prayer asking God to forgive and to annul all vows and oaths made to God and all transgressions committed during the year.

The practice of making vows to God was very common among the ancient Jews as among other religious people. They often made vows and promises to God which it was impossible for them to keep, so that even in biblical times it was necessary to provide for a means of releasing people from rash vows and promises. Sometimes vows made in the heat of excitement or in time of peril were forgotten and never fulfilled. The religious conscience was troubled by the thought of these unfulfilled or perhaps forgotten promises, and also by the feeling that there could be no proper reconciliation with God unless the vows made to Him were either fulfilled or annulled. Out of this sense of guilt grew the need for the remission of vows on the Day of Atonement.

The rabbis frowned upon the whole practice of making rash vows and then seeking to annul them, and some called the *Kol Nidre* a foolish prayer and refused to countenance it. In spite of all opposition, the *Kol Nidre* became part of the liturgy in most Jewish communities. During the religious persecutions in Spain and other countries in the Middle Ages, when Jews were forced to adopt Christianity, the formula became an important part of the ritual for Marrano Jews (forced converts to Christianity) who hoped thus to have the promises, which they made under duress, annulled in the sight of God.

In the nineteenth century the opposition to *Kol Nidre* grew so strong that in some communities the prayer was altogether eliminated and only the melody retained.

From time to time Christians accused Jews on the basis of the *Kol Nidre* prayer that the promise of a Jew was worthless since he could have it annulled on the Day of Atonement. This accusation is based on a misconception of the kind of vows with which the *Kol Nidre* prayer is concerned. Only promises made to God are contemplated. Promises made to one's fellow men, verbal agreements and contracts, *cannot be annulled* on the Day of Atonement. Only the person to whom the promise is made or with whom the agreement is entered into can release the promissor.

The Day of Atonement begins in the evening and lasts until the following evening with the entire period, except for the hours of sleep, devoted to prayer, confession, and soul-searching. Some pious Orthodox Jews remain in the synagogue the entire twenty-four hour period during which they maintain a strict fast, taking neither food nor water.

Why Do Jews Fast on Yom Kippur?

Fasting on Yom Kippur (abstaining from food or drink, from sunset to sunset on the Day of Atonement) is a very ancient practice and is an important part of the observance of the holyday. It is a form of self-denial by which the person shows his repentance. Today the practice of fasting is just another way, together with prayer and confession, of making the Jew aware of his need for sincere repentance and the earnest resolve to live better in the year ahead.

What Is Succos?

Succos or Succoth is the Feast of Tabernacles or Booths. This festival comes on the fifth day after Yom Kippur, on the fifteenth day of Tishri. It is celebrated for eight days, the first and last (for Orthodox and Conservative Jews, the first two and last two) being of special significance. Its name is derived from the little huts or booths (*succos*) which the Hebrew farmers erected on the fields as shelters from the sun during the harvest; for this festival came during the autumn harvest when the farmers gathered their produce from the field and vineyard. The booths are also regarded as a memorial of the shelter used by the ancient Hebrews when they wandered in the desert on their way from Egypt to the Promised Land.

Succos was a time of great rejoicing and was celebrated by a pilgrimage to Jersualem where the farmers brought their gifts to the Temple. The Bible calls it *He-Hag* (*the* festival), for in ancient Palestine it was the most important feast of the year, a thanksgiving celebration.

Symbolic of the booths used in antiquity are the booths erected by pious Orthodox Jews in their own yards, in which they eat their meals throughout the festival. In Reform congregations *succos* (booths) are erected in the temple or in the garden of the temple, and the pulpit is decorated with autumn fruits and flowers symbolic of the time when our ancestors were farmers in Palestine, and in gratitude for God's goodness in providing nature's bounty (*see* Exodus 23 and Leviticus 23).

In many congregations the children are encouraged to bring fruit, vegetables, and canned goods which they place upon the pulpit as a thanksgiving offering. After the festival the gifts are taken to the various children's institutions of the city.

Symbols of the Feast of Tabernacles include the lulav (Palm leaves bound together), the esrog (Palestinian citron), myrtle, and willow of the brook. All these are ordained in Leviticus 23.

The rabbis have drawn spiritual lessons from these four symbols. The lulav is beautiful but has no fragrance, like some people who are all outward show with no inner piety or virtue. The myrtle is fragrant but not beautiful, like some people who are humble but virtuous. The willow of the brook is neither beautiful nor fragrant, like some people who are neither learned nor virtuous. The esrog is both beautiful and fragrant, like people who are learned, pious, and good. The combining of all these symbols represents the brotherhood of mankind composed of all kinds of people.

Our American Thanksgiving festival was modeled on the Feast of Tabernacles. The Pilgrim Fathers were pious students

of the Jewish Bible (Old Testament) and used it as their guide
to life. When their first harvest was successful they thanked
God in the manner of the ancient Hebrews by a thanksgiving
feast.

What Is Simkhas Torah?

Simkhas Torah (rejoicing for the Torah) is a festival that
comes on the last day of Succos. Even as the Feast of Tabernacles is a thanksgiving for the bounty of nature, so Simkhas
Torah is a thanksgiving for the gift of the Torah, the Jewish
faith and the discipline of the commandments, the spiritual
gift of God. The festival is celebrated with a procession of the
synagogue leaders, each carrying a Torah scroll in a circuit of
the synagogue. This is called *hakofos* (circuit). Special hymns
are sung during this ceremony, which takes place on the eve
of the festival.

On the following morning, as part of the ritual of reading
from the Torah, the last chapter of Deuteronomy is read and
the first chapter of Genesis to symbolize that the study of the
Torah never ends. In many temples the festival is celebrated
by a special service consecrating children who are about to
begin their religious education.

Among Orthodox and Conservative Jews, the day before
Simkhas Torah is Sh'mini Atzeres, Eighth Day of Conclusion,
with Simkhas torah being a special extra holyday. Among
Reform Jews, Sh'mini Atzeres and Simkhas Torah are usually
combined.

What Is Hanukah?

Hanukah means dedication, and refers to the rededication
of the Temple in Jerusalem when, under the leadership of
Judas Maccabeus and his brothers, the Jews fought a successful war for religious freedom against their Syrian-Greek overlords who tried to destroy Judaism and to force all Jews to
worship the heathen gods. The war was fought for three years
from 168-165 B.C.E. Against tremendous odds the Jews won
an almost miraculous victory, drove the Syrian-Greeks from
Jerusalem, cleansed the Temple which had been polluted by

heathen rites, and rededicated it to the worship of God; hence the name of the festival.

The festival begins on the twenty-fifth day of the month of Kislev, the ninth month of the Jewish calendar, and is celebrated for eight days by the lighting of candles in the menorah, an eight-branched candelabrum. One candle is lit the first night, two on the second, three on the third, and so on, until eight lights are burning on the eighth night, symbolic of the ever-increasing light and power of the Jewish faith.

Another explanation for the eight lights is a legend which tells that when the Jews came to rededicate the Temple there was no holy oil for the altar lamps. After an intensive search a small cruse of oil was discovered which still bore the unbroken seal of the High Priest of a former day. Miraculously this small cruse of oil lasted for eight days until fresh holy oil could be prepared.

In Jewish religion schools the festival is celebrated by pageants and dramatic presentations of the Hanukah story, by the exchange of gifts, and by remembering the less fortunate. In the home children's parties are held, and every night of the festival candles are lit with appropriate blessings and with the singing of the hymn *Mo-Oz-Tsur* (*Rock of Ages*).

Although Hanukah is a Jewish festival it can have significance for Christians also. Had not the Jews been victorious in their war for religious freedom and survival, Judaism would have disappeared more than a hundred years before Jesus was born, and the entire history of the world might have been different; for Jesus was born into Judaism and his disciples were all Jews.

What Is Purim?

Purim (Festival of Lots) comes on the fourteenth day of Adar, one month before Passover, and derives its name from the word *pur* (lot, or drawing lots). It is based on the Book of Esther in the Bible and commemorates the deliverance of the Jews of Persia from their archenemy, Haman, prime minister of Persia, the arhcetype of all anti-Semites. Haman wanted to destroy the Jews of Persia and plotted their extermination on a certain day which he chose by casting lots, hence the name Purim. Happily, his evil designs were frustrated by Esther, a Jewess, chosen in a nation-wide beauty search to be Queen of Persia. She pleaded with the king to spare her people, pointing out that Haman had only selfish motives for his evil plan. Haman was punished by being hanged on the very gallows he had prepared for Mordecai, the leader of the Jews.

The festival is symbolic of divine retribution and of God's watchfulness over Israel. It is celebrated in a joyous spirit by the exchanging of gifts and remembering of the needy. In the synagogue, the story of Esther is read from a special scroll, *Megillah*.

Since Haman's argument against the Jews is contained in the allegation that they were different from the other Persians in their religious beliefs and customs, the festival has become symbolic of the Jew's eternal struggle for the right of differences to exist and against all forms of totalitarianism.

A special kind of triangular cake filled with poppy seed or fruit is eaten on Purim. It is called *Haman Taschen* from the German (Haman's Pockets) to commemorate the frustration of his evil designs.

What Is the Passover?

Passover (*Pesakh*) is one of the oldest religious festivals in the world. It probably began as a festival of the ancient Hebrew shepherds rejoicing for the increase of their flocks during the spring lambing season. Later, when the Hebrews became farmers in Canaan, it assumed the additional role of a spring harvest festival. It was not until much later that its present historical character, commemorating the deliverance of the Hebrews from Egyptian bondage, assumed its significance for Jews.

According to biblical tradition the name *pesakh* is derived from the paschal lamb which was sacrificed during the festival, and perhaps also from the legend describing how the angel of death "passed over" the homes of the Hebrews on the night when the firstborn of the Egyptians were slain (*see* Exodus 12).

Passover begins on the fourteenth day of the month of

Nisan, the first month of the Hebrew calendar, corresponding to March-April, and continues for seven days. Orthodox and Conservative Jews observe the festival for eight days. The eve of the Passover is celebrated with a special feast called Seder during which the *Haggadah*, the narrative describing the deliverance, is read. Orthodox and Conservative and many Reform Jews celebrate the Seder for two nights. No leavened bread may be eaten during the entire period of the festival.

Today the festival has become for Jews an annual reminder of the precious heritage of freedom and a call to maintain it in every generation by eternal vigilance and self-discipline.

Passover is a family celebration, an opportunity for the scattered members of the family to come together in family reunion. Heinrich Heine, the German-Jewish poet of the nineteenth century, expressing his own fond memories of that happy festival, offers this tribute to the Passover: "It thrills the heart as though one heard the lilt of some sweet lullaby. Even those Jews who have fallen away from the faith of their fathers in the mad pursuit of other joys and other glories are moved to the very depths of their being when, by chance, they hear again the old Passover melodies once so dear to them."

The Passover festival is rich in symbolism especially in the Seder observance. Among the symbols used at the Seder feast are the following:

Matzah, unleavened bread, also called the bread of afflic-tion. It is a flat cake made of white flour and water without salt or leavening. It is symbolic of the bread which the Hebrews made in haste when they left Egypt, not having time to permit their dough to leaven. Matzah is the most important symbol of the Passover and is the only kind of bread permitted during the festival.

Moror, bitter herbs (horseradish), symbolic of the bitter-ness and hardships the Israelites endured as slaves in Egypt.

Haroses, a kind of paste made of apples, nuts, raisins, and wine, symbolic of the mortar used by the Israelites in the con-struction, as Egyptian slaves, of Pithom and Raamses.

Shank bone, a roasted bone, symbolic of the paschal lamb that was sacrificed on the eve of the Passover and eaten roasted.

Roasted egg, symbolic of the free-will burnt offering

brought every day of the festival while the Temple was still in existence. The egg is also a symbol of life and springtime when life is renewed in nature.

Four cups of wine are drunk during the Seder, the Passover meal. They commemorate the four promises of redemption which God made to Moses (*see* Exodus 6:6-7).

Cup of Elijah, symbolic of a fifth promise, "and I shall bring you" into the land of Canaan. Some of the rabbis suggested that because of this fifth promise there ought to be a fifth cup of wine at the Seder; others disagreed. Popular belief left all disputed questions of ritual and law to the decision of the prophet Elijah, the great hero of Jewish legend; hence the cup of Elijah.

Jewish tradition also regarded Elijah as the forerunner of the Messiah who would usher in the kingdom of God. Since Passover was the time of Israel's redemption it was also believed to be the time for the world's redemption with the coming of the Messiah which Elijah would announce. Therefore, the cup of Elijah is a gesture of welcome to the messenger of the glad tidings (*see also* Passover and Easter).

What Is Shovuos?

Shovuos or Shabuot is the Feast of Weeks, sometimes called Pentecost, Feast of the Fiftieth Day. It is so called because it comes seven weeks after Passover, counting from the second day of Passover. Originally it was an agricultural festival, the time when Jews from all over Palestine made a pilgrimage to Jerusalem to offer gifts of their first ripe fruits to the Temple. It was known as *Haag Habikkurim*, the festival of the first ripe fruits. Later it was associated with the giving of the Ten Commandments on Mount Sinai and came to be known as *Zman Mattan Torosenu*, the season of the giving of the Torah.

Today the latter aspect of the festival has become most important and it is celebrated by holding confirmation services, at which time Jewish children are confirmed in the faith which their ancestors accepted thirty-five centuries ago. It is observed one day by Reform and two days by Orthodox and Conservative Jews. It is the birthday of the Jewish religion celebrated as a time for rededication to Judaism and its spiritual values (*see* Leviticus 23 for the biblical account).

What Is Tisha B'Av?

Tish B'Av, ninth day of Av, the fifth month in the Jewish calendar, is a day of mourning and a fast day for Orthodox and Conservative Jews. According to tradition it was on the ninth day of Av in the year 586 B.C.E. that King Solomon's Temple was destroyed by the Babylonians, and on the same day, 656 years later in 70 C.E., the second Temple was destroyed by the Romans. Because these two tragedies in Jewish history occurred on this day it has become a day of mourning in Jewish life.

Orthodox and Conservative Jews observe the three-week period prior to the ninth day of Av as a period of semi-mourning during which no marriages or other joyous occasions are permitted. The last nine days are a period of more severe mourning, reaching a climax on the ninth of Av when Orthodox and Conservative Jews hold a special service during which the Book of Lamentations is read.

Most Liberal Jews have dropped the ninth of Av from their religious calendar on the theory that the destruction of the Temple, while an undoubted tragedy at the time, was part of God's design to further His purpose among the nations. By the destruction of the Temple and the dispersion of the Jews throughout the world they were enabled to carry the message of Judaism, refined, deepened, and purified throughout the world. However, out of respect for the feelings of the Orthodox, many Reform congregations observe the ninth day of Av as a time when entertainment and other joyous occasions are discouraged.

What Is Lag B'Omer?

Lag B'Omer, the thirty-third day of the Omer, is a semi-holyday in Jewish tradition. It goes back to the ancient practice of bringing a measure (omer) of barley every day as an offering to the Temple, beginning on the second day of Passover, and continuing for forty-nine days until Shovuos (see Leviticus 23:10-11). In Orthodox and Conservative synagogues this forty-nine day period is observed by reciting a special prayer each day during which mention is made of the number of days which had already elapsed. This counting is called S'firah.

In Orthodox and Conservative tradition this forty-nine day period of S'firah is regarded as a period of semi-mourning to commemorate the tragically unsuccessful revolt of the Jews against their Roman oppressors under the leadership of Bar Kokhba, 125-135 C.E. It seems that during the war with Rome a period between Passover and Shovuos was the occasion for a terrible massacre of Jews which ceased on the thirty-third day of the S'firah. The people saw in what they regarded as a miracle the symbol of divine forgiveness for the sins which they believed occasioned the massacre. So the rabbis relaxed their prohibitions against joyous occasions during the S'firah and made this thirty-third day a semiholyday. Today Lag B'Omer is the only day during the forty-nine-day period between Passover and Shovuos when marriages and other joyous occasions are permitted among Orthodox and Conservative Jews.

What Is Hamisha Asar Be Shvat?

Hamisha Asar Be Shvat (fifteenth day of Shvat) is generally known as Jewish Arbor Day. It is a semiholyday commemorating the tree-planting season in ancient Palestine. The rabbis recognized three new years—the first day of Nisan (the first month in the Jewish calendar) which they regarded as the secular new year, the first day of Tishri (seventh month of the calendar) which is the religious new year (Rosh Hashanah), and the fifteenth day of the eleventh month (Shvat), the new year for trees.

The month of Shvat corresponds to our month of February and was evidently the season for tree planting in ancient Palestine. Today this occasion is still observed by many Jews out of sentimental attachment to the ancient homeland. Since the reestablishment of the state of Israel the festival has assumed increasing importance in that country and, out of traditional sentiment, also in other lands where Jews dwell, especially among the Orthodox and Conservative Jews. In this country it is observed in many Jewish religion schools by planting trees in the school grounds.

HOW DO JEWS WORSHIP?

The synagogue is the sanctuary of Israel. It was born out of Israel's longing for the living God. It has been to Israel throughout his endless wanderings a visible token of the presence of God in the midst of the people. It has shed a beauty that is the beauty of holiness and has ever stood on the high places of the earth. It is Israel's sublime gift to the world. Its truths are true for all men; its love is a love for all men; its God is the God of all men, even as was prophesied of old: "My house shall be called a house of prayer for all peoples" —*Union Prayerbook,* Vol. I, newly revised edition, p. 327

PRAYER IS Israel's only weapon, a weapon tried in a thousand battles.

—Talmud

How Did the Synagogue Begin?

Until the destruction of Jerusalem by the Babylonian Nebuchadnezzar in 586 B.C.E. the Temple was the center of Jewish religious life. Three times a year pilgrims flocked to Jerusalem from all parts of Palestine and other places of Jewish habitation to bring their gifts and to offer their sacrifices in the Temple. The priests and Levites (members of the tribe of Levi) ministered to the sanctuary, offering the daily sacrifices and carrying on the worship services.

With the destruction of the Temple and the exile of part of the people to Babylonia it seemed that an end had come to the Jewish religion. What saved Judaism during this critical period were the teachings of the Hebrew prophets, many of whom had lived and delivered their message before the great catastrophe. They had all taught that God could be worshipped anywhere in the world, for He was the Creator of the world

103

and Father of all men. Wherever people's hearts turned to Him in sincerity and in righteousness, there He would come and help them.

In their despair and loneliness the exiled Jews began to turn to the comforting teachings of the prophets. They would meet in private homes and perhaps later in public quarters to study the words of the prophets and to comfort each other in the land of their conquerors. Perhaps the meetings would begin with a word of prayer expressing the hope for forgiveness by God and for a speedy restoration to their homeland. At any rate these meetings became the basis of the synagogue. The word *synagogue* is Greek for "meeting place."

When Cyrus, the conqueror of Babylonia, permitted the exiled Jews to return to their homeland in 538 B.C.E. and to reestablish themselves in Palestine under Persian rule, they took with them the institution of the synagogue. It became the meeting house of the village and also of the city dwellers, especially outside of Jerusalem, and even there. It was called *Bes Haknesses* (house of assembly). In the course of time it also became the community school *(Bes Hamidrash)*.

When the second Temple was destroyed by the Romans in 70 C.E., these meeting houses were already well established and recognized as part of Jewish religious life, and were ready to take over the functions of the Temple, thus ensuring the survival and continuity of Judaism. The people were aided in this readjustment by the teachings of the rabbis who were the leaders of the synagogues. The rabbis taught, in harmony with what the great Hebrew prophets had taught centuries before, that God could be worshipped anywhere. "In every place where I cause My name to be mentioned, there I will come and bless thee," says the prayerbook. Prayer and righteousness were more acceptable to Him than the Temple sacrifices, the rabbis said.

Thus, although the destruction of the Temple was a crushing blow, it was not fatal because the synagogue, serving as the religious, educational, and social center of Jewish life, enabled the people to survive and to flourish in the dispersion, and helped to unite the scattered communities into a strong religious brotherhood.

What Is the Difference between a Temple and a Synagogue?

Temple and *synagogue* are two names for the same institution. They both mean a Jewish place of worship. The word synagogue comes from the Greek meaning a "meeting house." The word temple is from the Latin *(templum)* meaning a place of worship. Reform places of worship are often called temples. Orthodox and Conservative places of worship are called synagogues.

Is There a Titular Head of the Jewish Faith?

There is no one head of the Jewish faith. Unlike the Pope among Catholics, Jews have no one spiritual head nor any hierarchy of religious leadership. In the United States every congregation is an independent and sovereign unit bound together with other congregations in very loose federations for mutual aid. There are several such federations of synagogues —the Union of Orthodox Congregations, the United Synagogues of the Conservatives, the Union of American Hebrew Congregations of the Reform Movement, and the Union of Sephardic Congregations (Orthodox).

There are also several rabbinical organizations—the Union of Orthodox Rabbis, the Rabbinical Council, Rabbinical Alliance, and Agudas Ho-Rabonim, all Orthodox; the Rabbinical Assembly of the Conservatives; and the Central Conference of American Rabbis of the Reform Group. These rabbinical organizations are also loose federations whose function is to guide and to some extent to discipline their members, but they cannot control them.

In the state of Israel there are now two Chief Rabbis among the Orthodox, representing the Sephardic and Ashkenazi communities who are recognized as more or less the heads of the Jewish religious community in that country; but in no sense do their powers or prerogatives correspond to that of the Pope among Catholics. They are the presidents of the rabbinical organizations in that country. There is also a Chief Rabbi in Britain, who is the titular head of Orthodox Judaism in the British Empire.

What Is the Function of a Rabbi? Is He a Priest?

The word rabbi comes from the Hebrew *rav*, master or teacher. The rabbi has no authority other than that which his Jewish learning gives him. He is not a priest, and in no way is he an intermediary between the individual and God. The rabbi does not pray for his people; he often leads them in prayer. He cannot absolve them from sin; only God can do that when the sinner repents.

Among Orthodox Jews the rabbi often acts as judge interpreting Jewish law and questions of ritual. Today most rabbis are ordained by some recognized rabbinical college.

What Is a Minyan?

No Jewish public worship service, according to Orthodox and Conservative usage, can be held without a minimum of ten adult males. This is called a *minyan*, from the Hebrew word "to count." The adult males must have attained their thirteenth birthday (thirteen years being the age of bar mitzvah when a Jewish boy is considered to have reached the age of religious responsibility and to be eligible for the minyan).

The origin of the practice of the minyan is believed to come from the biblical *edah* (a congregation of ten), the smallest administrative unit. To insure that a quorum (minyan) would always be available, every community was expected to have ten adult males whose work, if any, was such as to permit them to be called at all times to make up the necessary minyan for public services.

Reform Judaism has dispensed with the need for a minyan, and Reform Jews are able to hold public worship with less than the ten adult males. Moreover, women are regarded equal to men for all religious purposes.

Why Are Men and Women Separated in the Synagogue?

Among Orthodox Jews there is a more or less rigid separation of the sexes in public worship, whether the service is held in the synagogue or in a private home. In the development of Judaism the motive for separating the sexes in worship was to prevent the sexual orgies which often took place in the worship of the heathen peoples on the borders of Palestine. Thus, in the Temple at Jerusalem, there was a special section exclusively for women worshippers known as *Ezras Nashim,* the women's court.

Another reason for separating the sexes in the synagogue may be no more than the survival of the oriental custom which separated the sexes socially.

Liberal Judaism has abolished the practice of separating the sexes in the synagogue because it desires to emphasize family worship, which it regards as of supreme importance in the development of wholesome family life.

Is Instrumental Music Forbidden in Synagogues?

Among Orthodox and some Conservative Jews the use of instrumental music such as the organ is forbidden in synagogue worship. This prohibition is a token of mourning for the destruction of the Temple in 70 C.E.

The Temple in Jerusalem used to have instrumental music and a famous choir of Levites, which sang the psalms at the great pilgrim festival services. Tradition tells us that an organ of a thousand notes enriched the Temple services, and the psalms were usually rendered with orchestral accompaniment. The destruction of the Temple caused all these instrumental musical accompaniments to be abolished in token of grief for the loss of the sanctuary, and the ban is still mantained in Orthodox and some Conservative synagogues.

Liberal synagogues, however, reintroduced instrumental music early in the nineteenth century with the beginnings of Reform Judaism in Germany. The founders of the Reform movement felt that instrumental music was necessary for the enrichment and beauty of the worship services. Since Reform Judaism never held the same attitude toward the destruction of the Temple as Orthodox Jews do, the leaders of Reform had no scruples about reintroducing instrumental music into the synagogue.

Why Do Some Jews Cover the Head in Worship?

As with so many Jewish practices derived from antiquity we do not know for certain how the custom of covering the head began. In Exodus 28:36-38, we are informed that the priest had to wear a special head dress (mitre) while officiating in the Temple, but there is no indication that the ordinary worshippers had to have their heads covered. It is very likely they did, following the oriental manner, which showed respect by covering the head and removing the shoes. In the story of the burning bush, Moses is told to remove his shoes for he is standing on holy ground (*see* Exodus 3:5).

At the beginning of the Christian Era the custom of covering the head in worship was generally recognized among Jews, and the more scrupulous would not walk four cubits (about six feet) with their heads uncovered. However, it was not a legal ordinance; it was not a sin to go with uncovered heads, though it was regarded as bad manners.

Among the Babylonian Jews, who assumed the religious leadership of world Jewry about the fourth century c.e., the custom of covering the head as a sign of respect was more rigidly followed. To cover the head as a mark of respect was the custom of the country and Jews found that custom congenial; thus, from a matter of personal piety, it became a general rule for all Jews who were influenced by the Babylonian traditions.

In the Middle Ages, especially in Spain under the influence of the Moors, an oriental people, the custom was further strengthened, but not in France and Germany where the oriental influence had not reached. As late as the twelfth century it seems that covering the head was not obligatory among the Jews of France.

It was only when persecution compelled Jews to fight for their very existence that they became very scrupulous about the observance of customs and manners which served to accentuate their distinctiveness from the Gentiles. It was probably then that the custom of wearing the hat in worship and even at home and at work became a universal practice among Jews to avoid the danger of following "the custom of the Gentiles" (*Hukas Ha-Goim*).

Reform Jews have largely abolished the practice of wearing the hat in worship. Since Reform Judaism looks to the meaning and purpose behind a ceremony rather than to its traditional usage, it has reinterpreted the practice of covering the head in the light of our Western custom and manner of showing respect. We show respect in our Western world by removing the hat. We do so in the presence of a lady, when we enter a home, in the presence of the flag of our country. It is our way of showing respect and doing homage. So in the synagogue, when we stand in the presence of God, we show our reverence in our customary manner by sitting or standing bareheaded.

Do Jews Kneel in Prayer?

No; except on the Day of Atonement during the adoration when pious Orthodox Jews will prostrate themselves on the floor in token of reverence.

Prostration, bending the knee and touching the forehead to the ground, was a common form of worship among the ancient Hebrews. This practice has generally been abolished, perhaps because kneeling has become a Christian form of worship and prostration a Mohammedan practice, and the rabbis tried to keep the Jews from following the customs of non-Jews for fear of assimilation.

However, prostration has been retained by Orthodox Jews for one special occasion, during the adoration prayer on the Day of Atonement, a recollection of the ancient Hebrew practice.

What Is the Significance of Reading from the Torah?

The reading from the Torah (the first five books of the Jewish Bible), which is today an integral part of every Sabbath morning and festival service among Reform as well as among Orthodox and Conservative Jews, probably began with the reforms introduced by Ezra, about 438 B.C.E. Ezra helped to establish the Torah (the five books attributed to Moses) as God's revealed law and constitution for Jewish life. Since books were not available and the parchment scrolls were few and expensive, only some method of public instruction could achieve Ezra's purpose of making the people familiar with the divinely revealed law by which their lives were to be governed. So we are told in the Book of Nehemiah that Ezra ordered the people to come to Jerusalem and to assemble in the street by the water gate to listen to the reading of the Torah. "So they read in the book of the law of God distinctly and gave the meaning and caused them [the people] to understand the reading" (Nehemiah 8:8). This was probably the beginning of the custom of reading from the Torah.

In the course of time the practice of reading from the Torah became a regular feature of public worship, for the gatherings at such times were large and the opportunity for instruction favorable. Market days were especially opportune, for then the Jewish peasants would came to town to sell their produce and to buy for their needs. Monday and Thursday were the usual market days. Thus the practice developed of reading from the Torah on these days in addition to the Sabbaths and festivals, a practice which is still retained in Orthodox congregations.

Why Are People Called Up to Read the Torah?

The custom of calling men up to the reading of the Torah (*aliyah*—going up) is very old. Originally Ezra himself seems to have read the Torah to the people. It was always considered a great honor to be chosen to read the Torah, an honor which was given only to those who were sufficiently learned in the text.

We don't know exactly when the practice of calling seven persons to read the Torah began, but we do know that those who were thus honored had to read their portion by themselves. The number seven was always considered sacred by the Jews.

The seven were divided into a Cohane (a member of the priestly caste), a Levi (a member of the Levite group), and five ordinary Israelites. The Cohane (from which the name Cohen and all its derivatives came) was honored by being the first to be called up; the Levi (from which the name Levy and all its derivatives came) was given the second place of honor; and the others were more or less of equal importance except number three and number seven and the *maftir* (the reader of the Haftarah, a portion other than from the first five books of the Bible), which were next to the Levi in rank.

The men chosen for these honors, other than the Cohane and Levi, were selected on the basis of their scholarship, piety, and general merit. Each person called up had to read his own portion, and this practice continued until about the twelfth century C.E.

The first concession to ignorance, of which we have some record, occurred about the ninth century. An uneducated Cohane had to be called up, no other one being available. Since by that time the calling up of seven had become an established practice, and the necessity of having a Cohane first was generally recognized, the uneducated Cohane was given the honor but had to be prompted by the reader who stood by. That was the first step.

The next step came with the reader prompting some who were called up in the intonation of the reading, for the Torah was not read but chanted according to a definite musical form, and still is in Orthodox synagogues. Later, the desire not to shame men who were not proficient either in the reading or the chanting gave rise to the practice of having the reader chant every portion himself for the scholar as well as for the less learned person whom the community wished to honor.

By the fourteenth century the whole weekly portion was chanted by the reader; the seven persons called up merely recited the benedictions before and after the reader chanted his portion. Only the Haftarah, the additional reading, was chanted by the person called up. This portion was much easier to read than the Torah because, unlike the Torah, it is vocalized, punctuated, and is printed together with the cantillation marks (the musical notes) to help in chanting. The Torah is without vowel signs, punctuation, or cantillation marks.

The practice of reading from the Torah was, however, retained for the boy who celebrated his bar mitzvah (his coming of age religiously at the age of thirteen). He was expected to have studied enough to be able at least to read from the Torah scroll.

The Weekly Portion

In almost all synagogues and temples the Torah is divided into fifty-two portions, one of which is read each Sabbath. They are called *Sidras* (orders or arrangements) and are arranged so that the entire first five books of the Bible (Pentateuch) are completed every year from Simkhas Torah to Simkhas Torah. This custom is designed to fulfill the commandment that the study of Torah should never cease from our lips.

Each Sidra is divided into seven portions called *perasah* (*perashot*, plural). In all Orthodox and Conservative synagogues all seven portions are chanted during the service. In most Reform synagogues, perhaps in all, only one of the seven portions is read. It is often chosen by the rabbi with reference to his sermon subject or the idea which he wishes to convey as the theme of the Sabbath service. This practice has the disadvantage that certain portions of the Torah are seldom if ever read in the synagogue. It has the advantage of selecting portions of the Torah which have the greatest pedagogical and spiritual value and using them as the Torah was originally intended to be used, for religious instruction and inspiration.

In one respect the Reform practice of Torah reading is much nearer to the original practice instituted by Ezra twenty-four hundred years ago than is the Orthodox or Conservative. When Ezra began the custom of reading the Torah in public he introduced a system of interpretation and translation for the benefit of the uneducated, and for many years the Torah portion was chanted in Hebrew and translated into Aramaic, the vernacular. In modern Orthodox synagogues there is no attempt to translate the Torah. It is assumed erroneously that the people understand the Hebrew. Therefore the Torah reading has lost its original purpose and has become just another ritual. In most Reform temples the Torah portion is both translated and explained.

What Is the Haftarah?

It is not certain when the custom of reading the Haftarah (the additional portion) originated. Undoubtedly the writings of the Bible other than the first five books were known and studied even before the destruction of the first Temple, and interest in them was greatly stimulated by the Babylonian exile. But they did not become part of the synagogue liturgy until much later, perhaps during the persecutions under Antiochus IV, the tyrant of the Hanukah story (*see* Hanukah).

Antiochus attempted to unify his empire by compelling all his subject peoples to adopt his religion, the religion of the Greeks. Judea was then one of his provinces and the only one where he met with stubborn resistance. To break that resistance he endeavored to destroy Judaism root and branch, and forbade, among other things, the reading of the Pentateuch (first five books of the Bible) on pain of death.

Since the Pentateuch was not allowed, the people began to study the other biblical books more seriously and to substitute them for the Pentateuch. With the defeat of Antiochus by Judah Maccabee and his followers, the practice of reading from the prophetic books and other writings was retained and was added to the regular reading of the Torah. Incidentally, the Christian practice of reading two scripture lessons is probably taken from the synagogue practice of reading from the Torah and the Haftarah.

What Is the Tallis?

The *tallis* (prayer shawl) is a shawl-like garment made of silk or wool, but not mixed, with black or blue stripes at the end and with fringes at each of the four corners. The fringes are the most important part of it from a ceremonial point of view, and the blue in the fringes was their principal feature. The reason for the blue we do not know, but the Talmud (rabbinic commentary on the Bible) explains it on the ground that "blue resembles the sea; the sea resembles the sky; the sky resembles the throne of Glory." Thus, looking at the blue in the fringe is a reminder of God, fulfilling the commandment in Numbers 15:37.

The blue color was obtained from a kind of snail according to a secret formula known only to the people of Acre in Palestine. After the destruction of Jerusalem by the Romans and the subsequent dispersion of the Jews, either the secret was lost or the snail could no longer be obtained, and the use of the blue thread in the fringes had to be discontinued. So today the fringes are white or ivory color.

By the first century B.C.E., the tallis with *tzitzis* (fringes) was the recognized Jewish garb, a kind of uniform by which a person could be readily recognized as a Jew; it was the Jewish national as well as religious costume. After the destruction of the Jewish State, however, Jews found themselves scattered among people where the tallis was an outlandish garb, marking the Jews as foreigners and subject to all the inconveniences which being a foreigner involved.

Some Jews gloried in this distinctiveness, but the majority in the course of time adopted the dress of the countries where they lived and discarded the tallis as their ordinary garb; but they retained it as a symbol of their former Palestinian life. Like many other former Palestinian customs transplanted into the European environment, the tallis became a religious symbol worn during the daily morning, the Sabbath, and festival services in the synagogue or at home.

There was, however, the specific commandment in Numbers 15 that the tzitzis (fringes) should be worn all the time as a reminder of God, and without the tallis there could be no tzitzis. A compromise solution was reached by the use of the tallis *koton* (the small tallis), a silk or woolen cloth with a hole in the center to fit over the head and with fringes at its four corners, which could be worn under one's ordinary clothes. Thus the commandment to wear the tzitzis continually was fulfilled and the wearer did not have to appear outlandish. This small tallis is also known as *arba kanfos* (four corners) or simply as tzitzis (fringes). It is still worn by Orthodox Jews.

Reform Jews have abolished the wearing of the tallis and tzitzis. In some Reform congregations the rabbi wears a stole that resembles the tallis but without the traditional fringe.

What Are T'fillin (Phylacteries)?

One of the privileges which the bar mitzvah (the ceremony inducting the Jewish boy into the community as a religiously responsible adult at the age of thirteen) carries with it is wearing *t'fillin* in morning prayer. According to Orthodox tradition it is the duty of every adult Jew to put on t'fillin every morning except Sabbaths and festivals.

The word t'fillin comes from the word t'fillah (prayer). The t'fillin consist of two small black boxes to which are attached long leather straps. One box is placed on the forehead and the other on the arm near to the heart. The box on the forehead contains four compartments in which are four strips of parchment each inscribed with one of the following four passages from the Bible: Exodus 13:1-10, Exodus 13:11-16, Deuteronomy 6:4-9, and Deuteronomy 11:13-21.

The box on the arm has only one compartment containing one parchment on which all four of the above passages are inscribed. The reason why these passages have been chosen is that they contain a reference to the most important event in Jewish history, the deliverance from Egypt, and the most significant passage in the Bible, the *Sh'mah* (Deuteronomy 6:4-9), and each passage contains the words referring to "a sign on thine hand and frontlets between thine eyes."

Today the wearing of t'fillin in daily morning worship is considered of primary importance by Orthodox Jews, and great significance is attached to teaching a boy approaching his bar mitzvah the proper way to put them on. Indeed, a special technique has been evolved and is carefully observed. It may be of interest to describe it. The box for the arm is put on first. It must be put on the left arm above the elbow turned toward the heart—symbolic that the words of God are close to the heart.

The strap attached to it is then wound about the arm seven times (the mystic number seven) and three times about the hand to form the shape of the Hebrew letter *shin*, the first letter in the word *Shaddai*, meaning Almighty God. Then the box for the forehead is placed in position by means of a circular strap attached to it. The box must be in the center of the forehead ("frontlets between thine eyes"). To the circular strap two long straps are attached which are thrown over both shoulders and allowed to hang down in front. As the t'fillin are put on special benedictions are recited.

The practice of wearing the t'fillin has been generally abolished by Reform Jews, although there are individuals who still observe it. There is, of course, nothing in Reform Judaism condemning the wearing of t'fillin if the person wearing them appreciates their symbolism and is helped thereby to worship more sincerely and to live more in harmony with Jewish ideals and values. The danger which Reform Judaism tries to guard against in the use of the t'fillin is exactly the same against which the rabbis warned, that they should not be used as magical charms or amulets, or that they should not become a merely mechanical performance.

Why Do Some Jews Hold Three Daily Services?

Among Orthodox Jews, and to some extent among Conservative Jews, three daily public services are obligatory—in the morning, after midday, and after sunset. These three daily services are a recollection of the three daily sacrifices which Jewish ritual prescribed for the ancient Temple in Jerusalem. At each of these services at least ten male adults are required for a quorum. In Hebrew the three services are designated *Sha-haris* (morning), *Minha* (afternoon), and *Maariv* (evening). Of course any Jew may read the services in the privacy of his home.

What Is the Significance of the Ark in the Synagogue?

The most important ceremonial object in the synagogue is the ark in which the Torah scrolls are kept. It occupies a central place in the architecture of the synagogue and much of the artistry in the synagogue's interior is lavished upon it. It is the most sacred part of the building, and is never approached except with reverence. It is called *A-rone Ha Kodesh,* the holy ark. The ark is described in the Book of Exodus as the symbol of God. It is called "the Ark of the Covenant."

When King Solomon built the Temple in Jerusalem, the ark was its most important feature and stood in the Holy of Holies, and in the course of time became venerated as the most important religious symbol in Judaism. When the Temple was destroyed the synagogue took over many of its functions. Prayer and righteous conduct became the substitutes for animal sacrifices. The priesthood was replaced by rabbis, men learned in the Torah.

Insofar as possible the Temple symbols and ceremonial objects of the Temple were retained in the synagogue which became known as the "small sanctuary." So the ark, so central in the Temple worship, also became central in the synagogue, the symbolic dwelling place of God. That is why in the most solemn moments of worship Jews turn to the open ark.

Synagogues are usually built (among Orthodox Jews always) so that the ark is in that part of the synagogue which is in the direction of Jerusalem, the holy city. In countries west of Jerusalem, the synagogue faces east; in countries east of Jerusalem, the synagogue and ark face west. So when worshippers turn toward the ark in the synagogue they are always facing toward Jerusalem.

What Is the Significance of the Perpetual Light?

In all synagogues in front of the ark there is a perpetual light, *Ner-Tamid*—eternal light. This is a recollection of the fire that was kept burning day and night before the altar in the Temple at Jerusalem. Today it is symbolic of the presence of God in the sanctuary.

What Is the Significance of the Seven-branched Candelabrum?

In describing the sanctuary which Moses was to erect during the Israelites' wandering in the desert, the Bible provides for a candelabrum of seven branches as the lighting fixture at the altar. The number seven, corresponding to the seven days of the week, was always considered a sacred number by the ancient Hebrews. That is probably why the candelabrum, *menorah*, is seven-branched.

In the synagogue, which replaced the Temple after its destruction by the Romans in 70 C.E., the rabbis tried to maintain as much of the Temple furniture and ceremonial objects as possible. The menorah is one of these ceremonial objects. There is also an eight-branched menorah, which is used dur-

ing the celebration of the Hanukah festival (*see* Hanukah).
The word menorah means candelabrum, from the Hebrew
word *nor*.

What Is the Significance of the Six-pointed Star?

The six-pointed star, actually two interlaced equilateral triangles, is known as *Mogen David* (Shield of David). It is a
symbol of great antiquity and was known among the ancient
Egyptians, Hindus, Chinese, and other peoples as well as
among Jews. The first record of it in Jewish history goes back
to the seventh century B.C.E. when it was found on a Hebrew
seal. It was also found on a Jewish tombstone in the third
century of the Christian Era. Arabs used it, too. It was known
as the "Seal of Solomon" by the non-Jews.

It was not until about 1150 C.E. that we find a record of its
being called the "Shield of David" in Jewish literature, and
after that time it begins to appear frequently as a Jewish
symbol in synagogues and on seals and art objects.

Under the influence of Cabalistic teaching, the teachings of
Jewish mysticism, the six-pointed star was invested with spiritual meaning. The Cabalists related it to their conception of
two worlds, the upper and lower. The two triangles, one pointing upward, the other downward, symbolize the inner linking
of the visible and the invisible worlds, the material and the
spiritual.

The two triangles were also related to the days of the week.
The hexagon in the center, a perfect six-sided figure, symbolized the perfection of the Sabbath. The six triangles on the
outer side symbolize the six days of the week.

In modern times the two interlaced triangles making a
six-pointed star have become a specifically Jewish symbol,
sometimes called the "Jewish Star." The Nazis used it as an
emblem which Jews were compelled to wear on their garments
to distinguish them from their non-Jewish neighbors. Today,
the six-pointed star is used in all synagogues, on art objects,
and the like, as a decorative motif. It is also used in the flag
of the state of Israel.

What Is a Mezuzah?

The word *Mezuzah* literally means "door post." The Mezuzah is so called because it is fastened to the door post of the house. It is a small wooden or metal container in which a piece of parchment inscribed with passages from Deuteronomy 6:4-9 and 11:13-21, which contain the *Sh'mah* ("Hear, O Israel, the Lord our God, the Lord is One") and injunctions to live by God's law if the people wish to be prosperous and happy, and to place the words of God on the door posts of the houses and upon the city gates.

On the outer side of the parchment is written the Hebrew word *Shaddai*, meaning Almighty God. The word *Shaddai* appears through an opening in the container. The Mezuzah must be fastened in a slanting position to the upper part of the door post on one's right as one enters the house, with the upper end pointing inward. It is customary for the pious to touch the Mezuzah with their fingers, then to put their fingers to their lips when they enter or leave the dwelling, reciting at the same time the words: "May God keep my going out and my coming in from this time forth and forever."

FROM THE CRADLE
TO THE GRAVE

Ye shall be holy, for I the Lord, your God, am
Holy.

—Leviticus 19:1

MITZVOS (COMMANDMENTS) were given that we may live
by them.

—Tosefta (addition to the Talmud)

What Is the Significance of the Bris Millah (Circumcision)?

The custom of circumcising Jewish male babies at the age
of eight days goes back to the tradition in the Bible which
describes Abraham as establishing the rite of circumcision as
a covenant, *Bris,* between him and his descendants and God
(Genesis 17:9-14).

Circumcision is often called *Os Bris* (sign of the covenant).

Among Orthodox and Conservative Jews, the rite is performed by a *Mohel* (man trained to perform the rite) and is
accompanied by an elaborate ritual and festivity. Among
Liberal Jews the rite is sometimes performed by a doctor with
a rabbi present to read the prayers.

What Is the Significance of the Pidyon Ha-Ben (Redemption of the Firstborn)?

On the thirtieth day after the birth of a male child, if he is
his mother's first-born child, there is a ceremony known as
Pidyon Ha-Ben, the redemption of the firstborn. In this ceremony the father symbolically redeems his son from the priest,
a person who traces his descent from the ancient priestly caste,
by giving him five silver coins, which the priest usually returns
to the father if he is a poor man, or else gives to charity.

This custom goes back to very ancient times when the first-

121

born child of the mother, if it was male, was dedicated to the Temple, and could be redeemed by payment of a certain sum, later computed at five *shekalim*, a shekel being the equivalent of our silver dollar (*see* Exodus 13:11).

The ceremony of Pidyon Ha-Ben has been largely discarded by Liberal Jews because they believe that the whole basis of the ancient Temple cult and of the priesthood has lost its validity since the destruction of the Temple in 70 C.E.

What Is Bar Mitzvah?

Bar Mitzvah is a Hebrew phrase meaning "son of the commandment." It refers to the ceremony in which a Jewish boy, having attained his thirteenth birthday, assumes personally his religious responsibilities as an adult, that is, obedience to the commandments of God. Until then his parents are responsible for his conduct. Among the privileges which the Bar Mitzvah ceremony gives the Jewish boy is to be counted as an adult among the ten men (minyan), the quorum, which is required for all public religious services among the Orthodox and Conservative Jews.

The Bar Mitzvah ceremony is a kind of confirmation in Judaism for Jewish boys. It consists of the boy being called up to read a portion of the Torah and also the Haftarah, the weekly portion read from one of the other books of the Bible. This calling up (*Aliyah*) is restricted to male adults. In Conservative and in some Reform congregations girls also participate in a *Bas* (daughter) *Mitzvah* service.

What Is Confirmation?

Confirmation of both girls and boys at ages from thirteen to sixteen, depending upon local custom, was introduced into Judaism by the Reform movement which began in Germany about 1811. It was intended to mark the religious maturity of girls as well as boys. In America, where Reform Judaism made its greatest advances, the ceremony of confirmation in many congregations has been substituted for the Bar Mitzvah ceremony, and both boys and girls attaining the age prescribed by the congregation are confirmed as a class in a beautiful service, which is designed to strengthen the religious consciousness of the young people.

Today in most Reform congregations the ceremony of Bar Mitzvah is still retained for boys, but they are expected to continue their religious education until they are fourteen, fifteen, or sixteen, when they are confirmed with girls of their age in the confirmation service which usually takes place during the festival of Shóvuos in the summer. The festival commemorates the giving of the Ten Commandments to Moses on Mount Sinai. It is, therefore, a most appropriate occasion for the induction of Jewish children into the faith of their fathers.

Why Is a Canopy Used at Jewish Weddings?

The wedding canopy, *huppah*, is the covering, usually of velvet, held up by four posts under which the bride and groom take their marriage vows in Orthodox and Conservative marriage ceremonies. Reform Judaism does not require a huppah, though Reform rabbis have used it at the request of the couple.

The huppah is a relic of the Bedouin type of life of the ancient Israelites when they lived in tents, and a special tent was set aside for the young couple.

When the Jews, no longer nomads, lived in substantial dwellings the custom of having a tent for the bridal couple was retained in the marriage ceremony. The huppah is a continuation of that ancient custom.

The rabbis interpreted the huppah as a symbol of the harmony of the couple's future life. Even as they take their vows under the same covering, so hope is expressed that the future may always be a mutual sharing of life in full and equal partnership. In Reform temples the huppah is often made of flowers.

What Is the Kesubah?

No marriage ceremony among Orthodox and most Conservative Jews is valid without the Kesubah (Kethubah). The word *Kesubah* means literally "that which is written," and refers to the document which the bridegroom gives to the bride in which he declares his obligation to her during their marriage and in the event of their divorce or his death. The Kesubah was instituted by the rabbis of the Talmud in the second pre-Christian century for the protection of the wife.

In the oriental civilization in which Judaism developed women had few legal and economic rights. Before marriage they belonged to their fathers or male relatives. After marriage they were the chattels of their husbands. Very early in the development of the Jewish religion the Jewish lawmakers and sages tried to improve the position of women; the Kesubah became the instrument through which they achieved their purpose.

The Kesubah states in detail the obligations which the husband assumes to care for his wife during their marriage and the settlement he must give her in case of divorce or his death. This settlement becomes the first lien on all his property both real and personal. It takes precedence over all other obligations.

The Kesubah is written in Aramaic, the vernacular used by the Jews during the Talmudic period, and is read by the officiating rabbi in that language as part of the wedding ceremony. It is often also translated into English. The Kesubah must be signed by two witnesses and must be given to the wife before the marriage can be consummated.

Reform Jews have abolished the Kesubah, relying upon the civil laws to protect the wife against divorce or in case of the husband's prior death. However, where the couple wishes, Reform rabbis will use the Kesubah.

Why Is a Glass Broken at Jewish Weddings?

The custom of breaking a glass at the conclusion of Orthodox and Conservative wedding ceremonies is of ancient origin and was perhaps founded on various superstitious beliefs about driving away evil spirits with noise at a time of joy when they were particularly bent on doing mischief. After the destruction of the Temple in Jerusalem the custom was interpreted by the rabbis as a reminder to the young couple and all the congregation that in the midst of their joy they should remember that the Temple was destroyed and that the people were in exile. Often a valuable vase or dish was shattered on such occasions. Today a small wine glass is used. The groom steps on it and crushes it.

Later generations tried to spiritualize this custom by interpretations such as that even in the time of greatest joy one should be mindful of the fact that life is a mingling of joy and sorrow, and that even while the young couple may be full of joy, elsewhere in the world there is sorrow and suffering.

Reform Judaism has abolished the glass breaking, although many Reform rabbis will permit it if requested by the couple.

Why Are Marriages Forbidden during Certain Periods?

There are certain times of the year when in Orthodox tradition no marriages are permitted. One of these is the forty-nine days between Passover and Shovuos (Feast of Weeks). It is called the period of S'firah (counting).

No marriages or other joyous celebrations are permitted during this period except on Lag B'Omer, the thirty-third day of this S'firah period (see Lag B'Omer, for further explanation).

Another period when marriages are forbidden is the three weeks before the ninth day of Av (usually the end of July and the first half of August). It was during this period that the first Temple in Jerusalem was besieged and destroyed by the Babylonians in 586 B.C.E., and later the second Temple was destroyed by the Romans in 70 C.E. during this same period. It is therefore regarded as a time of mourning (see Tisha B'Av).

Marriages are also discouraged during the ten days between Rosh Hashanah and Yom Kippur (the ten days of penitence) out of the mistaken notion that these are days of gloom. However, there is no actual prohibition against marriages during this period.

Among Liberal Jews the forbidden periods are generally disregarded.

What Is the Meaning of Shivah?

In Orthodox Judaism a person who loses a parent or near relative by death observes a strict period of mourning for seven days (*Shivah*—seven). During this period he remains at home, sits on the floor or on a low stool, does not cut his hair or do any business. The mourner is usually visited by friends who bring him food during the week and participate with him in the daily services at his home during which he recites the Kaddish prayer, a prayer in which he expresses submission to the will of God who is Lord of life and death.

After the Shivah period, the traditional Jew usually observes another twenty-three days of semimourning during which he attends the synagogue daily, carries on his business, but abstains from all forms of entertainment.

After the thirty-day period the mourner continues his daily attendance at the synagogue to recite the Kaddish for another ten months. During this period he abstains from most forms of entertainment.

Liberal Jews have softened the rigors of the mourning period emphasizing the inward rather than the outward show of grief.

What Is the Yahrzeit?

On the first anniversary of a near relative's death and every year thereafter, the bereaved observes the *Yahrzeit* (German for anniversary) of his loved one. On this day he attends services in the synagogue and recites the Kaddish. In most cases a Yahrzeit candle is lit that burns for about twenty-four hours, symbolic of the saying in Proverbs: "The soul of man is the lamp of the Lord."

In most Reform synagogues the names of those whose Yahrzeits occurred during the week are mentioned during the memorial part of the Sabbath service.

During the religious year there are several general memorial services, *Yizkor* (remembrance), for all departed. These occur on the last day of Passover, on Shovuos, Shmini Atzeres, and on the Day of Atonement. In some Reform synagogues a memorial service is held only on the Day of Atonement.

Why Are Garments Torn at a Funeral?

Cutting part of one's wearing apparel at a funeral is a sign of mourning going back to biblical times when it was the custom to tear one's garments and pour ashes on one's head as a sign of grief. Reform Jews have abolished the practice.

Why Are Mirrors Covered in a House of Mourning?

In the house where a death occurs it is customary among Orthodox and Conservative Jews to cover mirrors during the seven-day period of mourning. The reasons for it are lost in the mists of ancient superstition. The rabbis, however, gave the practice a spiritual interpretation as they have done for many customs and practices of antiquity. The mirror is the symbol of vanity, and in time of bereavement one is made conscious of the vanity of earthly things and of the reality of the spiritual values of life.

What Is the Kaddish?

Kaddish comes from the same root as *Kiddush*; hence they are often confused. Both mean sanctification, but whereas the Kiddush is a joyous ceremony sanctifying the Sabbath and festivals, Kaddish is a prayer glorifying God which is recited at funerals and at all memorial services.

Originally the Kaddish had nothing to do with the dead or memorial services. It began as a brief response to the reader in public worship calling upon the worshippers to praise God. Later it was used as a liturgical formula praising God at the end of a sermon or lecture in the synagogue expressing the hope for the coming of the Messiah when death would be abolished forever.

In the course of time it came to be recited by orphans at the death of parents and later at all memorial services. It is a prayer extolling God for His greatness and goodness and expressing man's submission to His will in life and death.

Why Is the Pig Forbidden as Food?

Refusal to eat pork or the products of the pig has become almost a symbol of Jewishness. In the eyes of many non-Jews the refusal to eat pork or ham is synonymous with being a Jew. Actually, the pig is only one of many animals forbidden by the dietary regulations of the Bible.

In Leviticus 11 and in Deuteronomy 14, it is clearly stated that of the animals only those that both chew the cud and have cloven hooves may be eaten. The pig has cloven hooves but does not chew the cud, hence is forbidden. Other animals forbidden are the camel, the hare, and the badger. But of all the forbidden animals the pig has assumed a special importance, not merely because of health reasons as is usually assumed, but because historically the pig was used by the pork eaters, Romans and Greeks, as an anti-Jewish symbol with which to taunt the Jews; and during the Middle Ages it was used in the same way by the Christians.

Why Don't Some Jews Eat Meat and Milk Together?

The prohibition against eating meat and milk together, or the products of meat and milk, is an outgrowth of the teachings of the rabbis in the Talmud. The Bible says: "Thou shalt not seethe a kid in its mother's milk" (Exodus 23:19). On the basic rabbinic principle that they must build a fence around the Torah, the rabbis extended the prohibition to exclude any mixing of milk and meat products. Thus, if a Jew is scrupulous about not mixing meat and milk products, he will certainly not violate the law against "seething a kid in its mother's milk."

Why this prohibition was instituted we do not know. It is thought that it goes back to the time when the Hebrews were practicing many Canaanite heathen rites. As part of their worship the rite of boiling a newborn kid in its mother's milk may have been an important ritual. In order to wean the people away from such heathen rites and worship, the ancient lawgivers forbade the practice altogether.

Another explanation is that a kid boiled in its mother's

milk was a great delicacy, and the prohibition of the practice was instituted for economic reasons to prevent the people from destroying their flocks by overindulgence in this practice.

Another explanation is grounded in Jewish humanitarian sensibilities. It seemed unnecessarily cruel to boil a kid in its mother's milk.

Why Do Orthodox Jews Have Two Sets of Dishes, for Milk and Meat?

This practice grew out of the prohibition against eating meat and milk together. It is an extension of the principle of "making a fence around the Torah." If separate dishes are used there is even less danger of Jews violating the prohibitions against eating meat and milk, and therefore of boiling a kid in its mother's milk.

How Did the Kosher Laws Develop and Why?

The word *kosher* means "ritually proper or clean." It has come to refer to the elaborate dietary system which traditional Judaism developed. The dietary regulations in the Bible are quite simple, referring only to the kinds of animals, birds, and fish that may or may not be eaten. These are found in the Bible in Leviticus 11 and Deuteronomy 14.

The reason for these dietary regulations are not really known, but scholars have suggested a number of them. One is health, on the theory that the animals, birds, and fish forbidden are disease-bearing, or for one reason or another less healthy than other living things for human consumption.

Another reason is that the forbidden animals were often used as sacrificial animals to the heathen gods, or were worshipped as gods themselves. Hence, to wean the people from idolatry and heathen rites the animals, birds, and fish were made taboo, unclean for Jewish use.

The most valid reason seems to stem from the fundamental objective of the Bible writers. Their chief aim was to make the ancient Israelites "a kingdom of priests and a holy people" as is described in Exodus 19. It was a common practice for the priests and holy men of Egypt, Babylon, and other nations to abstain from eating certain animals, especially carnivorous animals, and certain fish and birds. This dietary discipline was a symbol of their holiness. The ancient lawgivers and writers of the Bible, in their effort to make the entire people holy to God, compelled them all to adhere to a certain dietary discipline. What only the priests of other people were forbidden to do the entire Israelite nation was forbidden, for they were to be a "kingdom of priests."

Later, under the influence of the rabbis in the Talmud, the dietary laws developed into an elaborate system of *kasherut* (ritual cleanliness) for two reasons: (1) to build a fence around the Torah; (2) to build a fence around the Jew. By fencing him in with an elaborate system of dietary regulations, it became almost impossible for the pious Jew to have any social contact with his non-Jewish neighbors. Since he couldn't eat their food, he could have no real social intercourse with them, which minimized the chances for intermarriage and assimilation.

Today Orthodox Jews still adhere strictly to the whole dietary system on the theory that it is part of the divine commandments of the Torah tradition. Conservative Jews also adhere more or less strictly to the dietary laws on the ground that they are a vital factor in the survival of the Jew. Liberal Judaism leaves the observance of the dietary rules to the discretion of the individual. If it helps him in self-discipline and increases his consciousness of the Jewish ideals and values, he is encouraged to observe them.

What Is the Origin of the Practice of Ritual Slaughtering of Animals?

Among Orthodox and Conservative Jews no meat may be eaten unless the animal has been slaughtered according to traditional Jewish rites called *Shekhita* (slaughtering). The official who slaughters the animal is called a *Shokhet*.

The origin of the practice of slaughtering animals and fowl by cutting through the air tube in the throat (fish are not subject to slaughter) is uncertain, though it was probably derived from the method of slaughtering sacrificial animals in the ancient Temple. In early times no meat could be eaten by the

Hebrew unless it was first offered on the altar as a sacrifice and parts of it were either burned or given to the priests.

With the great religious reformation of Josiah about 621 B.C.E., sacrifices were forbidden except at the Jerusalem Temple. This made eating meat very difficult for people living far from Jerusalem, so a special provision was made at that time permitting the eating of meat without sacrifice (Deuteronomy 12:2); but the animal had to be slaughtered. Jews were not allowed to cut limbs from living animals, a common practice among the heathen. Thus, no Jew could eat meat which was not first slaughtered, and doubtless the method of slaughter was copied from the Temple usage.

At first every Jew was allowed to slaughter his own animals, but in the course of time a special group of *Shokhetim* (ritual slaughterers) developed who had to study the art and were awarded a certificate of competence by the ecclesiastical authorities. Under rabbinic influence the slaughter ritual was surrounded with numerous regulations and safeguards. A special knife with a perfect edge had to be used. A minute nick in the knife's blade is enough to make the slaughtered animal *t'refah* (literally, torn or unfit for food). The Shokhet must also examine the slaughtered animals for any signs of disease which would make them unfit for use. In modern times special slaughtering pens have been invented which enable the Shokhet to perform his task very quickly and efficiently, causing the animal the minimum amount of pain.

SACRED LITERATURE
OF THE JEWS

In the poorest cottage are books, is one Book,
wherein for several thousands of years the spirit
of man has found light, nourishment, and an interesting response to whatever is deepest in him.
—Thomas Carlyle, *Essay*

And God said: "Let there be light."
—Genesis 1:3

To THE ORTHODOX Jew and Christian the Bible is in a literal
sense the word of God revealed to mankind through the
verbally inspired minds of the lawgivers, prophets, and poets
named therein. As the word of God, the Bible is sacred, altogether beyond human criticism, analysis, or comparative
study. That is why the critical study of the Bible is of comparatively recent origin. It began only within the past century
when the growth of liberalism weakened the power of orthodoxy to stem the tide of scientific progress. Since then much
has been achieved in the study and understanding of the Bible,
of its nature, origin, and development.

Liberal thinkers, both Jewish and Christian, have been profoundly influenced by this new approach to the Bible and
have contributed much to our knowledge about it. Out of
this critical study has grown a deeper insight into the nature
of religious inspiration and a more realistic understanding of
man's relation to God and of his spiritual potentials.

The Bible, no longer considered to be a book handed down
by God at one time in the past and for all time as Orthodox
Judaism teaches, has, through reverent research and the examination of devoted scholarship, become an incomparable
spiritual literature, revealing man's quest for an ever-growing knowledge and an ever-deepening awareness of God and
of his relation to Him. As such literature, the Bible is for us
Jews our most treasured possession, not only for the truths
and inspirations it contains, but because it is the expression

of our people's growth from spiritual infancy to maturity in their quest for and understanding of God and the good life. It holds an equally significant position in Christianity.

The word Bible comes from the Greek word for books. The Bible is not one book, but many books bound together in one volume. These books contain historical narratives, laws, legends, songs, poems, sermons, prayers, and the science of the time when they were written. They cover a long period of the history of the Jewish people. Some parts of the Bible go back to perhaps 1200 B.C.E., based on much earlier legends and traditions. Others were written more than a thousand years later. All these different writings were collected and edited and finally put together in the form in which we know the Bible today.

The Jewish Bible, the "Old Testament," as we have it today contains thirty-nine books. They are divided into three groups. The first is called Torah, often translated as law, which also means instruction. Another name for the Torah is the Greek word "Pentateuch," five (in Hebrew *Humosh*), and refers to the first five books, known as the Books of Moses.

The five books of the Torah are:

Genesis (Greek, meaning the "beginning"). The Hebrew name for the book is *B'reshis*, "in the beginning." This book contains an account of the creation of the world and of man and the beginnings of the Hebrew people. Highlights of the book include stories of Noah, Abraham and his covenant with God, Isaac, Jacob and Joseph, and how the Hebrew settled in Egypt.

Exodus (Greek, meaning "going out"). The Hebrew name is *Shmose*, "names," because it begins with the words, "These are the names." The book tells the story of the Hebrew slaves in Egypt, their deliverance from Egypt by Moses, and the origin of the Passover. It tells of the wanderings in the desert, the revelation of God on Mount Sinai, and the giving of the Ten Commandments. It also describes some of the early laws and customs of the Hebrews and gives an account of the building of the sanctuary and its furnishings.

Leviticus (Latin, meaning "priestly"). The Hebrew name

is *Va-Yikro*, "And He called," from the first words in the book. This book describes the sacrificial cult in great detail, the kinds of sacrifices that must be offered to atone for the different kinds of sins, the service in the Temple, the duties and the prerogatives of the priests, laws of health and cleanliness, and some of the dietary laws.

It also describes the holydays and festivals and how they are to be observed. Chapter 19 of the book ("Holiness Code") contains some of the loftiest ethical ideals in the Bible including the famous commandment, "Thou shalt love thy neighbor as thyself" (Leviticus 19:18).

Numbers, so called because it contains a census of the Hebrews. The Hebrew is *Bamidbor*, "in the wilderness," because it also tells of the wanderings in the wilderness on the way to the Promised Land, Canaan. It describes the difficulties which Moses encountered from complaining and even rebellious groups who were discouraged by the hardships they encountered, and were forever reminding him of the fleshpots of Egypt.

The book also contains the beautiful priestly benediction so often used in churches and synagogues: "On this wise thou shalt bless the children of Israel; you shall say unto them: The Lord bless thee and keep thee; The Lord make His face to shine upon thee, and be gracious unto thee; The Lord lift up His countenance upon thee, and give thee peace" (Numbers 6:24-26).

Deuteronomy (Greek, meaning "the second law"). This book is so called because it was thought to be a restatement of the laws and experiences contained in the first four books. It is regarded traditionally as Moses' farewell address before he turned his leadership over to Joshua, his successor. The Hebrew is *D'vorim*, "words," because it begins, "These are words."

This book shows the influence of prophetic teachings in the ethical ideals it contains and in the lofty concepts of the nature of God and Israel's relation to Him. The *Sh'mah*, "Hear, O Israel, the Lord our God, the Lord is One, and thou shalt love the Lord thy God with all thy heart, with all thy soul and with all thy might," recited at every religious service, is contained in this book (Deuteronomy 6:4); so also is another version of the Ten Commandments (Deuteronomy 5).

The Historical Prophetic Books

The second division of the Bible is called *N'viim*, "Prophets." This section contains the historical books of Joshua, Judges, Samuel, Kings, and the prophetic books: Isaiah, Jeremiah, Ezekiel, Hosea, Joel, Amos, Obadiah, Jonah, Micha, Nahum, Habakkuk, Zephanaiah, Haggai, Zechariah, and Malachi.

Joshua: This book derives its name from the central hero of the story, Joshua, the successor to Moses, who according to tradition led the conquest of Canaan and won the Promised Land for the Israelites. The book tells of a speedy and miraculous conquest of the land and the settlement of the twelve tribes of Israel in Canaan (Palestine).

Judges: This book is a collection of stories which give a more accurately historical account of the conquest of Canaan. Far from one sweeping advance as described in the Book of Joshua, the Book of Judges tells of a difficult and costly penetration covering a long period of time, about three hundred years. During this period there was no unity among the Israelites. The tribes warred against the inhabitants singly and only rarely as a coalition, and often fought among themselves. The stories of Samson, Gideon, Jeptha, and Deborah are among the highlights of this book.

Samuel I and II: These two books tell of the welding of the twelve tribes into a nation under the leadership of Samuel, a religious leader, who inspired Saul to become the first king of the infant nation, and David to become his successor. The book tells of the wars with the Philistines for mastery over Palestine, the exploits of David, and the final achievement of unity with the capture of Jerusalem and its establishment by David as the national and religious capital.

Kings I and II: These two books describe the history of the united kingdom under Solomon and that of the two kingdoms after the secession of the ten northern tribes following Solomon's death, when Palestine was divided into the kingdom of Israel in the north and the kingdom of Judah in the south.

The Books of Kings are not strictly historical books. History is used by the writers as illustrative material to teach their basic religious philosophy, that undivided loyalty to God brings prosperity and happiness and deviation from that singleness of purpose leads to disaster. The books tell the story of the northern kingdom culminating in the destruction of the state by Assyria in 722 B.C.E., and that of the southern kingdom until its destruction by the Babylonians in 586 B.C.E. The influence of the great Hebrew prophets is seen throughout these books.

The Prophets of Israel

> O Lord, Thou hast enthralled me, and I was enthralled,
> Thou hast overcome me, and thou hast prevailed;
> I am become a laughing stock all the day;
> Everyone mocketh me.
> For whenever I speak, I cry out;
> I cry, "Violence and destruction!"
> For the word of the Lord has become
> A reproach and derision all day long,
> And if I say, "I will not mention Him,
> Nor speak any more in His name,"
> There is in my heart as it were a burning fire
> Shut up in my bones,
> And I weary myself to hold it in,
> But I cannot.
>
> —Jeremiah 20:7-9

The contribution of the Hebrew prophets to religion is immense. Their influence upon Judaism was so profound that one cannot think of it without them. Without Judaism, Christianity would have been impossible, and also the religion of Islam. From the appearance of Amos about 740 B.C.E. across the centuries we have been immeasurably enriched by the legacy which these religious geniuses left us. Most of what is permanent in Judaism derives from them. Our ideas of God and man's relation to Him, our pursuit of righteousness, our future hope were all inspired by their insights. It is true that they built upon the religious tradition of ancient Israel, but so revolutionary was their teaching and so deep the impress of their personalities upon Jewish life and thought that it is not an exaggeration to say that they created the Judaism which has inspired the religious life of mankind.

How they came and why we do not know. No study of their background or the history of their people can altogether explain them. We must accept their own simple account of their life and work. "God took me from following the flock," Amos tells us in his impressively simple manner, "and said unto me, 'Go prophesy unto My people Israel.'" God simply called them and they answered. We say they were inspired. If to be consumed with a passion for righteousness so that all one's being cries out against evil in any form is to be inspired, they were divinely inspired. If to be overwhelmed by an irresistible compulsion to proclaim truth regardless of consequences to themselves is God revealing Himself to men, they were indeed the vehicles of divine revelation. They were not philosophers speculating about the nature of God nor theologians interested in founding and maintaining a religious system. They were men who felt God in their innermost being, and out of their own deepest experience of Him emerged the convictions they proclaimed with such commanding authority, saying, "Thus saith the Lord. . . ."

And the convictions which possessed them were that God was absolutely righteous, demanding of His worshippers uncompromising obedience to His moral law. In the light of this conception of God we can understand the vehemence with which the prophets condemned the religion of their time. Their unmeasured denunciation of the sacrificial cult and the scrupulous observance of the prescribed feasts and fasts was their protest against the religious smugness and complacency which characterized both priests and people. The people believed that so long as they provided sufficiently rich sacrifices and were unstinting in their oblations of wine and oil, God was satisfied with them. Good fortune was accepted as proof of such favor, disaster as evidence that the sacrifices had not been lavish enough or the manner of their offering had been at fault. The attitude toward God was formal, ritualistic, mechanical. It was this attitude which the prophets lashed with the fury of their tongues.

I hate and despise your feasts, saith the Lord,
And I take no delight in your festivals . . .
But let justice roll on as a flood,
And righteousness as an unfailing stream

—Amos 5:21-24

I desire love and not sacrifices,
The knowledge of God rather than burnt offerings. . . .

—Hosea 6:6

Micah summed up the whole of prophetic teaching in his magnificently simple appeal:

It has been told thee, O man, what is good and
What the Lord requires of thee, only to do justly,
To love mercy and to walk humbly with God.

—Micah 6:8

All this flowed from their inspired vision of God as absolute goodness, demanding goodness of those who would be His worshippers. Apart from living as God would have men live, worship had no value, religion no meaning for them. Only as men were radiant with the light of God so that its rays shone upon everything they thought, felt, and did were they true believers in Him. There were no half measures in prophetic religion. God demanded complete and undivided loyalty, the whole dedicated personality, without reservation, without compromise.

Out of this wholehearted devotion to God emerged all the moral ideas and values which constitute prophetic religion, and also their unique and revolutionary conception of God as the one and only Ruler of the universe. Until Amos appeared, the belief was universal that every tribe and nation had its own tribal and national gods who possessed power only over their own people and over the territory occupied by that people. The Jews were no exception. They believed that the one God they worshipped was their special Lord and Protector, that He was only one among many in the world.

The prophets were the first to challenge that belief, and they based their challenge not on any logical inference from creation to a creator, or from the unity of nature to a one first cause, but as Dr. Leo Baeck writes: "The divine unity became unshakably certain to them in the inward experience that there is only one justice, one holiness." God is the one God of the world because He is a God of justice, holiness, and love, and these are universal moral values, absolute, the same for all people, everywhere. Their sensitive, inspired conscience could not accept moral compromises or different kinds or degrees of moral behavior. There could not be one moral law for Jews and other moral laws for other nations. So out of their own deepest experience and intuitions emerged their world-changing view of a universal God Who demands righteousness. That is what is known as "ethical monotheism."

And out of this conception of ethical monotheism arose the glorious visions of the future which the prophets foresaw for the Jews and for humanity. If their own deepest experiences were true, and how could they doubt it, then God's law was the foundation of the universe and goodness was at the heart of it. All creation moved under His guidance toward one perfect goal. To the prophets this was crystal clear, beyond all argument. That is why they interpreted the world-shaking events of their time, the rise and fall of nations and empires, as the handiwork of God. Assyria, Babylon, Persia were all instruments of God's will, though they themselves were not aware that they were being used to carry out His purpose. All history was an unfolding of that purpose. And its fulfillment was inevitable. There may be much suffering because of spiritual blindness, great travail because of human stupidity, and deep searching before mankind discovers its soul, but "in the end of days it shall come to pass." To the prophets this was as certain as the movements of the seasons in their cycle and the stars in their courses. And out of that unshakable faith was born the messianic hope of a world brotherhood founded on a knowledge and love of God and established in righteousness.

> They shall not hurt nor destroy in all My holy mountain,
> For the earth shall be full of the knowledge of God
> As the waters cover the sea.
>
> —Isaiah 11:9

So what began as an intuitive awareness of their own highest nature ended as a wondrous vision of a divinely ordained human destiny. That is the great legacy which the prophets gave to the world. It consists not only in what they taught but in the spirit of the men themselves. For they were the very embodiment of the ideals they proclaimed, and their lives were the fulfillment. That is why Dr. Baeck so rightly says that the prophets, as personalities, count for so much more than their speeches. It is no exaggeration to say that they were the spirit of Judaism incarnate, the point at which the religious genius of the Jew found its fullest expression. Even as the essence of beauty can be appreciated only through beautiful things, so the essence of religion must be revealed in religious personalities. In the great Hebrew prophets the spirit of Judaism was supremely revealed.

The Prophetic Books

The prophetic books bear the names of the men who wrote them, or to whom they were ascribed by the editors who compiled the biblical literature. They contain the utterances of the great religious teachers who flourished from about the middle of the eighth century B.C.E. down to about the third century B.C.E. These moral and spiritual giants introduced not merely a new type of religious literature, but also a new movement in the spiritual history of mankind which still profoundly influences religious thought and aspiration.

The prophetic books are here listed as they appeared in history (the order in the Bible is not chronological).

AMOS (about 750 B.C.E.)

The Book of Amos is a collection of sermons (some scholars think it is one sermon) delivered by Amos, a shepherd from the village of Tekoa, who preached in the streets of Beth El, the religious center of the northern Kingdom of Israel.

Amos was the first to proclaim that God was Lord of the universe and Father of all mankind. He challenged the accepted beliefs that God was only the national deity of the Jews and delighted in animal sacrifices and in the meticulous performance of the rites and rituals of the Temple cult. God rules the world in righteousness according to a moral law, said Amos, and only those who worshipped Him in justice and in righteousness were acceptable to Him. Unless the people changed their thinking and their living God would destroy them and their land.

This was a revolutionary and heretical doctrine. It brought upon Amos the wrath of the people as well as of the priests so that he was driven from the city. However, the seed of his idea took root in the hearts and minds of a few who became his disciples. They preserved his message for posterity, a part of which we now cherish in the book bearing his name in our Bible.

HOSEA (about 745-735 B.C.E.)

Hosea's message parallels that of Amos except that the different temperaments of the two men influenced their ultimate conclusions. Amos was a rugged, uncompromising moralist to whom the inexorable working of the moral law spelled inevitable doom for wayward Israel. Hosea was of gentler nature and couldn't accept the doom of his people as irrevocable. His own domestic experience convinced him that somehow God's love of Israel could effect the people's redemption.

It seems that Hosea married a woman named Gomer whom he dearly loved. But Gomer proved a faithless wife, and after a time ran away with a lover leaving Hosea with three small children. In spite of her faithlessness Hosea never ceased to love Gomer. One day, several years later, he saw her being auctioned as a slave in the marketplace. She had been abandoned by her lover. Hosea bought her and took her back to his home. We are not told the details of what happened but we are left to assume that under Hosea's tender care and love, Gomer repented of her folly and became a changed woman. This experience Hosea interpreted as a sign that God wished him to become a prophet to His people to urge them to repentance with the promise of God's forgiveness if only they would return to Him in truth and righteousness.

Hosea's contribution to the religious insights of Judaism lies in his profound understanding of the redemptive power of God's love.

ISAIAH (about 738-700 B.C.E.)

The Book of Isaiah as we have it in the Bible contains sixty-six chapters. Modern scholars suggest that this book contains the work of at least three men, which is roughly divided in Chapters 1-39, the writings of the real Isaiah; Chapters 40-56, the work of an unknown author who lived and preached during the Babylonian exile, 586-538 B.C.E., and who is called Deutero-Isaiah, the second Isaiah; Chapters 56-66, the work of an unknown author who lived during the period of the restoration and is called Trito-Isaiah, the third Isaiah.

The real Isaiah was a son of the nobility and a friend of the royal family. He was not only a man of deep spiritual insight but a farseeing statesman who tried to keep his country out of entangling alliances with the great empires warring for mastery of the ancient world.

Isaiah believed that the strength of his country and of his people lay in their singlehearted devotion to God and not in alliances or in armaments. "In quietness and in confidence is your strength," he pleaded. So long as the king and the people were faithful to God and lived by the ethical principles and the moral code He taught them, they had nothing to fear. God would protect them, for He was ruler of the world and the Arbiter of the fate of all nations, using them as instruments of His will.

In matchless poetry Isaiah pleaded with his people, condemning them for their folly and their blindness, berating them for their wickedness and ingratitude, threatening them with utter destruction, but also expressing the conviction that they would some day see the truth and thus help to usher in a world of justice, harmony, and peace.

MICAH (about 730-722 B.C.E.)

Micah was a contemporary of Isaiah and is somewhat overshadowed by the latter's greatness. However, though the remains of his work are contained in but a few chapters and though we know little of his life, what we have of his teaching places him among the great prophets. Micah belonged to the common people and championed the cause of the plain folk against the oppression both of princes and priests.

In Micah 6:8, we find the classic expression of prophetic religion ending in one of the most movingly beautiful passages in the whole Bible:

> It hath been told Thee, O man, what is good,
> And what the Lord doth require of thee,
> Only to do justly, to love mercy
> And to walk humbly with thy God.

ZEPHANIAH, NAHUM, HABAKKUK
(about 626-600 B.C.E.)

These three small books contain the preaching of three men who lived at about the same time. They differed from each other in temperament and somewhat in their thinking. All of them were profoundly influenced by the teaching of the great prophets before them, Amos, Hosea, Isaiah, and Micah.

About 626 B.C.E. the Scythians were threatening to engulf Palestine in their march of conquest. Zephaniah saw in this Scythian invasion the visitation of God upon all the wicked nations, but especially upon Judea because of its social and religious corruption. So he called upon his people to repent of their sins that God might forgive them, and that they might escape the terrible judgment. His hope that they might repent and be saved is expressed in Chapter 3:11-13:

> The remnant of Israel shall not do iniquity, nor speak lies;
> Neither shall be found in their mouth a deceitful tongue;
> For they shall feed and lie down,
> And none shall make them afraid.

A younger contemporary of Zephaniah was Nahum, who was probably inspired to preach by the approaching destruction of Assyria. Nahum was an ardent nationalist and full of vengeance and hatred for Israel's enemies. He saw in the doom that was confronting Assyria the vengeance of God, and he exulted in it. Though a good poet, and probably very popular in his day, in the history of the progressive development of Judaism he holds an insignificant place.

Habakkuk's great problem was to resolve the seeming inconsistency between God's undoubted righteousness and the evil that existed in the world. How could a righteous God tolerate so much wickedness in both Israel and the other nations?

> O Lord, how long shall I cry,
> And thou wilt not save.
> I cry out unto thee, "Violence!"
> And thou wilt not save.
> Why dost Thou show me iniquity
> And look upon perverseness?
> For destruction and violence are before me . . .
> For the wicked compasses about the righteous;
> Therefore justice goes forth perverted.
> —Habakkuk 1:2-4

An answer seemed to come when Babylonia conquered the arrogant Assyrians. Babylonia was God's instrument of punishment, thought Habakkuk. But Babylonia also showed herself arrogant, cruel, and wicked, and yet she seemed impregnable and unconquerable. Again his problem tormented him. Only after much soul-searching did he find an answer that satisfied him: God is the Ruler of the universe. Of that there is no doubt. He will also visit punishment on the wicked. Of that there can be no doubt. Only man must wait and have faith, for the solution is God's and will be revealed in God's appointed time.

> Though it tarry, wait for it,
> Because it will surely come, it will not delay.
> —Habakkuk 2:3

JEREMIAH (about 625-586 B.C.E.)

Jeremiah was born about 650 B.C.E., the son of a priestly family in a small town near Jerusalem. It was during the invasion of the all-conquering Scythians, which threatened also to engulf Palestine about 626 B.C.E., that Jeremiah felt himself called to become a prophet to his people.

Like his predecessors he saw the great historical movements of the past and of his own time as the unfolding of a divine purpose. The rise and fall of nations and empires was God's way of righting the moral balance in the world. So it was inevitable that he should interpret the threatened danger to his people as a warning and visitation from God because of their sins. How could he stand by and see the threatened destruction of his people without at least trying to warn them of their danger? It was this conviction that impelled him against his better judgment and natural inclinations as a rather shy and retiring person to become a prophet unto his people.

Jeremiah's preaching brought him into conflict not only with the religious and lay authorities, but also with the people whose cherished religious beliefs and prejudices he challenged. Wherever he went he encountered abuse, ridicule, and even violence until it became impossible for him to enter Jerusalem without risk of bodily harm, even death.

Many times he felt like giving up the struggle. People didn't want to hear his message. They didn't understand him, nor did they want to. He felt that he was wasting his life and accomplishing nothing. In some of the most poignant confessions in all literature, Jeremiah described his inner conflicts, cursing the day he was born to be a man of strife, the day he accepted the mission of prophet, and wishing he could escape it all. But he could not escape his destiny.

> And if I say, I will not make mention of Him,
> Nor speak any more in His name;
> Then there is in my heart as it were a burning fire
> Shut up in my bones,
> And I weary myself to hold it in,
> But I cannot.
>
> —Jeremiah 20:9

Here Jeremiah describes eloquently the character of the true prophet, who is driven by an irresistible compulsion to speak truth regardles of consequences to himself.

When Jeremiah found that he could no longer deliver his message in person since the authorities wouldn't allow him to enter the city, he commissioned one of his disciples, Baruch, to write down his messages and to read them whever he could and to whomever would listen. Thus some of the greatest spiritual utterances in all literature have been preserved to inspire all the generations since then with a deeper understanding of God.

EZEKIEL (about 597-580 B.C.E.)

In the first conquest of Judah by the Babylonians in 597 B.C.E. there was a young priest among the leaders of the people whom the Babylonians took into captivity. This priest was destined to exert a profound influence upon the religious life of his people. His name was Ezekiel. Until the final destruction of Jerusalem in 586 B.C.E. Ezekiel, like his predecessors by whom he was greatly influenced, preached inevitable doom because of the people's sinfulness. But after the destruction and the second deportation he became a prophet of hope.

In order to give the individual Jew hope that he was not irrevocably lost, he rejected the generally accepted belief of his day that children were tainted with the sins of their parents and nothing they might do would alter the divine punishment. "The fathers have eaten sour grapes and the children's teeth are set on edge" (Ezekiel 18:12) was the common proverb. Ezekiel challenged this proverb by proclaiming that "God is righteous and will judge every one after His own ways."

There is no hereditary guilt and there will be no hereditary punishment. Every man stands or falls by his own deeds. Thus Ezekiel gave hope to the exiles that God might give them another chance and restore them to their homeland. In the famous Chapter 37 Ezekiel sees the Jews in exile as dry bones in a valley which will come to life because God will restore flesh and spirit to them. In this vision of the "Valley of Dry Bones" Ezekiel tried to bring hope to his despairing and hopeless people.

Ezekiel's influence in his own time was very great, especially for his emphasis upon ritual holiness and the importance of the Temple and its service. The Book of Leviticus owes much to Ezekiel's teaching. In the history of prophetic religion and in the progressive development of Jewish idealism, however, his emphasis upon the Temple cult is regarded as a retrogression.

DEUTRO-ISAIAH (about 550-538 B.C.E.)

The work of this prophet of the Babylonian exile whose real name is unknown is contained in Chapters 40-56 of the Book of Isaiah. It reaches a high point in prophetic religion. The most important people of Judah had been taken captive to Babylonia in 586 B.C.E. The Temple had been destroyed and the holy city, Jerusalem, which the people believed inviolate, lay in ruins. The people's faith in God was severely strained. It was in such a time and to a people despairing of the future that this prophet came with a message of hope.

He had watched eagerly the victorious progress of Cyrus the Mede, ruler of Persia, and in harmony with his prophetic conviction that God was ruler of the world and director of all movements in history, he saw Cyrus as a divine instrument sent by God to humble the arrogant Babylonians and to restore the Jews to their homeland. "Comfort ye, Comfort ye, my people, says your God," he called to them; and throughout the sixteen chapters of his book, he encourages the people to deepen their faith in God.

Their suffering was part of God's plan, he told them. It was to test their faith and to deepen their spiritual insight so that they might more effectively fulfill their divine mission as God's servant and become witness to His unity and His truth before all the world.

. This conviction came to the prophet with all the power of an original discovery. It made all the contradictory events fit into a wonderful, purposeful pattern for him. In a series of poems, great both in their beauty of expression and in their lofty conception, he proclaimed his interpretation of Israel's destiny in the spiritual life of mankind.

> Listen, O Isles, unto me, and hearken ye people from far;
> The Lord hath called me from the womb . . .
> And said unto me, Thou art My servant, O Israel,
> In whom I will be glorified. . . .
>
> —Isaiah 49:1-4

> I, the Lord, have called thee in righteousness,
> And will hold thine hand, and will keep thee,
> And give thee for a covenant to the people,
> For a light unto the nations. . . .
>
> —Isaiah 42:6

Israel is the servant of God chosen from the beginning for a special mission. Nor let the people be disturbed by their present helplessness, wondering how they, a despised and exiled minority, can possibly influence the mighty nations who are their conquerors. God has His own ways of doing things, ways beyond human comprehension:

> For My thoughts are not your thoughts,
> Neither are your ways My ways, saith the Lord.
> For as the heavens are higher than the earth,
> So are My ways higher than your ways,
> And My thoughts than your thoughts.
>
> —Isaiah 55:8-9

> Fear not, thou worm, Jacob,
> And ye men of Israel.
> I will help thee, saith the Lord.
>
> —Isaiah 41:14

Deutero-Isaiah reaches the heights of prophetic insight in his development of ethical monotheism, the belief in one God Who rules the world in righteousness. In sublime poetry he describes Israel as the servant of God destined to bring all mankind ultimately to a true knowledge and worship of the one living God. He thereby gave a meaning and purpose to Jewish suffering and survival, which is still a challenge and inspiration.

The fifty-third chapter of Isaiah is interpreted by Christians as describing the suffering of Jesus. Jews, however, interpret that chapter as relating to the people of Israel who are the suffering servants of God through whom the world will ultimately learn God's truth and, knowing it, will fulfill its destiny.

OBADIAH (after 586 B.C.E.)

This is the shortest book in the Bible, containing only twenty-one verses, mostly concerned with the punishment of Edom, Israel's hereditary enemy.

HAGGAI and ZECHARIAH (about 520 B.C.E.)

Shortly afer the fall of Babylonia, permission was given by Cyrus the Great for the exiled Jews to return to Palestine and to rebuild their homeland under the protection of Persia. Many took advantage of the opportunity and eagerly set out for their homeland. But their return was full of disappointment. The journey back was difficult, not at all as glorious as the promise made by Deutero-Isaiah during the exile. Drought and famine added to their misery and hostile tribes had overrun the country. The people were disillusioned and in danger of losing faith in God altogether.

In 520 B.C.E. Haggai and Zechariah began to preach to the people, calling upon them not to lose faith, but rather to go to work to make the land acceptable to God. Here they were building homes and palaces while the Temple was in ruins. How could God remain among them if His sanctuary was neglected?

The prophets' call met with an enthusiastic response and the work began on the restoration of the Temple. When the people were discouraged because the restored Temple was far inferior to the splendid Temple which Solomon had built, Haggai and Zechariah encouraged them by saying that God

Himself would provide the splendor and beauty for the Temple. At least He had a dwelling place among them.

TRITO-ISAIAH (about 500 B.C.E.)

The work of this prophet whose real name is unknown is contained in Isaiah 56-66. He lived during the restoration and was not in sympathy with the insistence upon the rebuilding of the Temple and the emphasis upon the sacrificial cult. He objected to the return of ritual religion and urged a spiritual revival:

> Thus saith the Lord,
> The heaven is My throne,
> And the earth is My footstool;
> Where is the house that you may build for Me?
> And where is the place that may be My resting place?
> For all these things hath My hand made,
> And so all these things come to be, saith the Lord.
> But on this man will I look,
> Even on him that is poor and of a contrite spirit.
> And trembleth at My word. . . .
>
> —Isaiah 66:1-2

God did not need temples because the whole earth belonged to Him; nor did He desire animal sacrifices. A contrite spirit was more acceptable to Him and the human heart was His real sanctuary. Here we see a re-emphasis of the tradition of the great pre-exilic prophets.

MALACHI (about 440 B.C.E.)

The real name of this prophet we do not know. *Malachi* is merely the Hebrew word for "my messenger". Malachi lived after the Temple was restored and the sacrificial cult was re-established, but religious conditions had deteriorated after the first enthusiasm had worn off. The cost of maintaining the Temple was high. Heavy taxes and bad harvests made it even more difficult.

Many people resorted to sorcery, magic, and witchcarft to

better their fortunes. Faced with this problem Malachi tried to restore confidence in God and in His worship. To the challenge that the wicked seem to go unpunished, Malachi said that God was taking note of their evil doings and would punish them in time and the righteous would be rewarded.

One of the great statements in the Book of Malachi proclaiming the fatherhood of God and the brotherhood of man is in Chapter 2:10:

> Have we not all one Father?
> Hath not one God created us?
> Why do we deal treacherously every man against his
> brother? . . .

JOEL (about 450 B.C.E.)

The Book of Joel shows the influence of the priestly tradition after the Babylonian exile. To Joel the most important thing in religion was the maintenance of the sacrificial cult, for he believed that it was through the daily sacrifices in the Temple that the relationship between God and Israel was maintained.

JONAH (about 400 B.C.E.)

The Book of Jonah is an alegory and was probably written as a protest against the narrow nationalism which had developed in Judea after the Babylonian exile. Jonah represents that narrow religious nationalism. He is commanded by God to preach to Nineveh, a Gentile city, and to call it to repentance so that it may be saved from destruction. Jonah does not like Gentiles and refuses to go. He tries to escape his mission by putting out to sea, but a storm rises for which Jonah is blamed. The sailors throw him into the sea and he is swallowed by a fish where he remains for three days. While in the belly of the fish Jonah realizes that he cannot escape the arm of God that reaches everywhere, so he decides to accept the mission.

The fish then spews him up and Jonah goes to Nineveh where his call to repentance meets with a ready response. The people promise to reform their ways. This response does not please Jonah who would rather see the Gentile city destroyed. In the meantime the heat of the day causes him much suffering, so he prays for shelter. In answer God causes a gourd to spring up which shelters Jonah from the heat, but in one day it withers. Jonah is much distressed that his shelter has disappeared and complains to God about it. This gives the author a chance to proclaim his great universal message.

And God said unto Jonah: "Art thou greatly distressed for the gourd?" And he said: "I am greatly distressed even unto death!" And the Lord said: "Thou hast pity on the gourd for which thou hast not labored neither madest it grow, which came up in a night and perished in a night. Should I not have pity on Nineveh, that great city, wherein are more than six score thousand persons that cannot discern between their right hand and their left hand, and also much cattle?"

This thought that God is Father of all mankind, a God who has regard for Gentiles no less than for Jews, is an echo of the universalism of the great pre-exilic prophets which later generations forgot in their reversion to narrow nationalism. It is a protest against the religious chauvinism which followed in the wake of Ezra's reform about the middle of the fifth pre-Christian century, and a call to that universalism which gave to prophetic Judaism its pre-eminence in world religious thought.

The Book of Jonah also teaches the omnipresence and omnipotence of God from Whom it is impossible to escape; for His power reaches everywhere, even into the depths of the sea. That is the meaning of the allegory of the fish swallowing Jonah, an allegory which, because it was taken literally by the Orthodox, has caused so much difficulty and has given ammunition to the scoffer and the skeptic.

Did the Hebrew Prophets Foretell the Future?

One of the chief differences between Orthodox and Liberal Jews, and perhaps also between Orthodox and Liberal Christians, is their attitude toward the prophets of the Jewish Bible. To the Orthodox Jews and Christians the Hebrew prophets were regarded as mouthpieces of God. They were believed to have the power to repeat God's revelation of what was to happen in the near and distant future. These revelations were believed to come to the prophets in dreams and visions, in signs and portents. Therefore, the Orthodox interpreters of the writings of the prophets, believing that the prophets' visions were revelations from God, found in those writings allusions to events of their own times, and today are continuing to find allusions to things that happen in our modern world.

To read into the scriptures our own experiences and events is not difficult when sentences are taken out of their context and words are interpreted differently from their original meaning. The ancient writers were human beings faced with moral, spiritual, social, and political problems not unlike our own. The milieu may have been different, but the human nature that lived in it and reacted or responded to it was not too much different from our own. There were greed and selfishness, hate and prejudice, anxiety and aggression, lust for power and international jealousies, even as there are today. People were subject to fears, insecurities, and frustrations just as we are, and they probably reacted or responded in much the same way as we do. That is why it is not difficult to find allusions to our own experiences in the writings of these ancient religious teachers.

The Liberal Jewish attitude toward the great Hebrew prophets, whose literary work is contained in the Bible in books bearing their names, is quite different from the Orthodox. To the Liberal Jew the prophets were not foretellers. They were moral teachers and preachers. They were men who felt deeply a moral compulsion to speak in the name of a moral God ruling the universe according to a moral law. They knew intuitively, through divine inspiration we say, that a moral God could not tolerate an immoral world; that the moral law was as inexorable as any physical law, and its violations must bring punishment even as violation of physical laws result in disaster. That is why they spoke of doom and destruction when the people persisted in their evil ways. That is why they pleaded for a return to God in truth and righteousness. Only a wholehearted return to God and obedience to His moral law could save mankind.

This conviction, that any violation of the moral law would result in certain punishment, was so strong in these God-inspired men that they felt a compulsive urge to bring their message to the people as a direct command from God Himself, as though they were voicing the very words of God. So they spoke in God's name and with the authority of a command from God, saying, "Thus saith the Lord. . . ."

Occasionally some of these great prophets went into detail in describing future events, but in no case did they speak of events in the limitless future. Even when they said, "And in the end of days it shall come to pass," they spoke in general terms, as any preacher today might speak of the golden age of the future when men shall have learned to live by the will of God, or as one might say that we must live together in peace or we shall die together in atomic war. It is taking the words of these ancient preachers out of context, and changing their meaning out of all relation to what the writers really intended to make their prophecies seem to foretell events that were to take place hundreds and even thousands of years after their death.

It is a pity that the word prophet is applied to them, and that the word "prophet" and to "prophesy" have come to mean in our language foretelling the future. Actually, the Hebrew word for these men was n'viim, which does not mean to foretell. It simply refers to "speakers," people who move their lips. There were several kinds of n'viim (speakers, lip-movers) in biblical times. Some of them were professional foretellers, who would reveal for a fee what the gods had in mind. They were not unlike our modern fortune tellers, crystal-ball gazers, palm readers, and mediums. These men would, for a fee, tell a person whether a certain day was auspicious for a journey or for the launching of a new business or where to find a lost article. The foretellers were also called n'viim.

Unfortunately, generations of pious believers applied to

these foretellers the term "prophet," in the same manner as they applied it to the great moral teachers like Amos, Hosea, Isaiah, Jeremiah, and many others whose lives and teachings have so significantly shaped and influenced Jewish and world religious thought. By translating the word n'viim as "prophets," we have put the foretellers and seers in the same category as the great spiritual geniuses of ancient Israel, thus creating and continuing misunderstanding of the true character, purpose, and message of the great Hebrew prophets.

The Holy Writings

The Lord is my shepherd, I shall not want.
He maketh me to lie down in green pastures;
He leadeth me beside the still waters;
He restoreth my soul;
He guideth me in straight paths for His name's sake.
Yea, though I walk through the valley of the
Shadow of death, I will fear no evil,
For Thou art with me;
Thy rod and Thy staff, they comfort me.
Thou preparest a table before me in the presence
Of mine enemies; Thou hast anointed my head
With oil; my cup runneth over.
Surely goodness and mercy shall follow me
All the days of my life, and I shall dwell
In the house of the Lord forever.

—Psalms 23

The third section of the Bible is known as K'suvim, holy writings, and includes the Psalms, Proverbs, Job, Song of Songs, Ruth, Lamentations, Ecclesiastes, Esther, Daniel, Ezra, Nehemiah, and Chronicles I and II.

THE PSALMS

The Book of Psalms contains one hundred and fifty religious poems. These poems are traditionally ascribed to King David, known as the "sweet singer in Israel." The authorship of most of them is unknown, but it is quite certain that they were composed by different poets over a long period of time, men who poured out their hearts in these magnificent utterances.

The psalms express almost every human emotion. The consciousness of sin; awe in the presence of nature's wonders; the bitterness of frustration; the cry of pain; the hope for a happier future; the aspiration for justice, righteousness, truth, holiness, human brotherhood; the yearning for communion with God—all these find noble expression in the psalms. No wonder the psalms have become the greatest devotional literature in the world. Not only among Jews, but among Christians, too, men have found comfort in sorrow, strength in need, and every kind of spiritual satisfaction and inspiration in the winged words of the psalter.

In the days of the Temple the choir of Levites put many of the psalms to music and sang them during the various pilgrim festivals and holydays. Today many of the hymns sung both in synagogue and church are translations or adaptations of the psalms.

THE PROVERBS

The Book of Proverbs is part of the wisdom literature. It is a collection of aphorisms, wise pithy sayings, expressing the everyday wisdom and philosophy of the Jews, compiled in thirty-one chapters. The proverbs are traditionally ascribed to King Solomon, known as the wisest of men. Their real authorship is unknown. Most of them are anonymous sayings that grew out of the experience and daily living of the people, homely sayings that passed from generation to generation. Many of the proverbs reveal the influence of the great Hebrew prophets in their emphasis on personal and social righteousness.

Selections from the Book of Proverbs

FAITH IN GOD

Fear (Reverence) for the Lord is the beginning of wisdom.

(1:7)

Trust in the Lord with all thy heart, and lean not on thine
own understanding. (3:5)

The confidence of fools shall destroy them. (1:32)

Be not wise in thine own eyes. (3:7)

The spirit of man is the lamp of the Lord. (20:27)

WISDOM AND FOLLY

Reprove a wise man, and he will love thee. (9:8)

Where there is no wise direction, a people falleth;
But in the multitude of counselors there is safety. (11:14)

In the multitude of words there wanteth not trangressions;
But he that refraineth his lips is wise. (10:19)

Every wise woman buildeth her house;
But the foolish plucketh it down with her own hands.

(14:1)

A scorner seeketh wisdom and findeth it not. (14:6)

He that is slow to anger is of great understanding. (14:29)

A good name is rather to be chosen than great riches.

(22:1)

He that soweth iniquity shall reap vanity. (22:8)

The wicked flee when no man pursueth;
But the righteous are secure like a young lion. (28:1)

HUMAN RELATIONS

Hatred stirreth up strife;
But love covereth all transgressions. (10:12)

He that despiseth his neighbor lacketh understanding.

(11:12)

The hearth knoweth its own bitterness;
And with its joy no stranger can intermeddle.   (14:10)

He that oppresseth the poor blasphemes his Maker;
But he that is gracious unto the needy honoreth Him.

(14:31)

A soft answer turneth away wrath;
But a grievous word stirreth up anger.   (15:1)

It is an honor to man to keep aloof from strife;
But every fool will be snarling.   (20:3)

Rejoice not when thine enemy falleth,
And let not thy heart be glad when he stumbleth.   (24:17)

Whoso diggeth a pit shall fall therein;
And he that rolleth a stone, it shall return upon him.

(26:27)

A rebuke entereth deeper into a man of understanding
Than a hundred stripes into a fool.   (17:10)

Even a fool when he holdeth his peace is counted wise.

(17:28)

A word fitly spoken
Is like apples of gold in settings of silver.   (25:11)

Answer not a fool according to his folly,
Lest thou also be like unto him.   (26:4)

Seest thou a man wise in his own eyes?
There is more hope for a fool than for him.   (26:12)

Go to the ant, thou sluggard.   (6:6)

THE GOOD LIFE

Treasures of wickedness profit not,
But righteousness delivereth from death.   (10:2)

The memory of the righteous is for a blessing.   (10:7)

In the way of righteousness is life;
In the pathway thereof there is not death.   (12:28)

Righteousness exalteth a nation;
But sin is a reproach to any people. (14:34)

To do righteousness and justice
Is more acceptable to the Lord than sacrifice. (21:3)

He that spareth the rod hateth his son;
Be he that loveth him chasteth him betimes. (13:24)

Train up a child in the way he should go;
And even when he is old he will not depart from it. (22:6)

He that trusteth in riches shall fall. (11:28)

A tranquil heart is the life of the flesh,
But envy is the rottenness of the bones. (14:30)

Better is a dinner of herbs, where love is,
Than a slaughtered ox and hatred therewith. (15:17)

Better a dry morsel and quietness therewith,
Than a house full of feasting with strife. (17:1)

He that is slow to anger is better than the mighty;
And he that ruleth his spirit than he that taketh a city.
(16:32)

Pleasant words are as honeycomb
Sweet to the soul, and health to the bones. (16:24)

A merry heart is a good medicine,
And a broken spirit drieth the bones. (17:22)

Pride goeth before destruction;
And a haughty spirit before a fall. (16:18)

A man's pride shall bring him low;
But he that is humble in spirit shall attain honor. (29:23)

Boast not thyself of tomorrow;
For thou knowest not what a day may bring forth. (27:1)

Faithful are the wounds of a friend;
But the kisses of an enemy are importunate. (27:6)

THE BOOK OF JOB

One of the greatest books in the Bible and perhaps in all literature is the Book of Job. In form it is a drama; in content it deals with the most difficult problem in religion, the problem of evil in a world ruled by a just God. The author of Job was not satisfied with the conventional doctrine of his day that human suffering is a punishment for sin, whereas happiness, prosperity, and success are the rewards for virtue. That was not life as he saw it. The wicked often flourished, whereas the righteous often suffered. His challenge to the conventional beliefs is the burden of the book.

The author takes the well-known story of Job as his theme. Job, a truly righteous man, is visited with great misfortune. He loses his wealth; his children die; and he himself is smitten with a loathsome disease—all this for no apparent reason. When Job's three friends come to comfort him, and by their silence imply that all this suffering is a visitation from God for some sin that Job had committed, Job can no longer contain himself. He curses the day of his birth and gives way to utter despair. This opens a debate between Job and his friends giving the author an opportunity to discuss the whole subject of human suffering and evil.

Job's friends represent the conventional ideas that sin and suffering are correlative. Job challenges them to show wherein he had sinned either openly or in secret, either knowingly or unwittingly; and in justifying himself the author makes Job express some of the finest ethical ideas in the Bible:

> If I have withheld aught that the poor desired,
> Or have cause the eyes of the widow to fail;
> Or have eaten my morsel myself alone,
> And the fatherless hath not eaten thereof—
> Nay, from my youth he grew up with me as with a
>   father,
> And I have been her guide from my mother's womb . . .
> If I rejoiced at the destruction of him that hated me,
> Or exulted when evil found him;
> Yea, I suffered not my mouth to sin

By asking his life with a curse.
The stranger did not lodge in the street;
My doors I opened to the roadside.

—Job 31:16-18, 29-32

Job's self-justification is a challenge to God's justice, which God answers by a counterchallenge to Job. How dare he question the justice of God when he, Job, cannot understand even the simplest revelation of God's power and majesty? How dare an insignificant mortal question the ways of the Creator of the universe Whose mysterious power is evident in every living thing. Job, overwhelmed by this challenge and recognizing his ignorance and his insignificance in the presence of Almighty God, admits his error in presuming to doubt even for a moment the moral order of the universe.

Then Job answered the Lord and said:
I know that Thou canst do everything,
And that no purpose can be withholden from Thee . . .
Therefore have I uttered that which I understand not,
Things too wonderful for me which I knew not.

—Job 42:1-3

The problem of evil is still unanswered. It is still a mystery why the righteous often suffer and the wicked prosper; but the reason is not that God is not just, or that there is no moral law in the universe. The reason, concludes the author, why the problem troubles us is that we do not understand the whole pattern of life. We must have faith that God is righteous; that He governs the world in justice, even though we mortals cannot see or understand the complete pattern of the divine plan.

THE SONG OF SONGS

The Song of Songs is a collection of love poems sung perhaps at wedding feasts telling of passionate love between a man and a woman, a love that is as "strong as death." Though these poems are attributed to King Solomon, who is mentioned several times, they are really anonymous songs that were sung by many generations of Jews. These love songs got into the Bible because they were interpreted allegorically by the rabbis who established the Bible Canon, the lover being God, and the beloved, Israel.

EZRA and NEHEMIAH

About the middle of the fifth century B.C.E. Nehemiah, a Persian Jew, was sent to Palestine as governor-general to supervise the country, which at that time was a Persian province. Nehemiah describes in his book the disorder that he found there and the reforms that he instituted.

Some years later, about 438 B.C.E., Ezra, a priestly scribe, came to the country to help rebuild its religious life. His experiences are recorded in the book bearing his name. Both Nehemiah and Ezra, espeically the latter, exerted a far-reaching influence upon shaping the course of Judaism. Ezra is sometimes called the "Father of Judaism," because of the great influence of his reforms upon the development of Talmudic Judaism from which present-day Orthodoxy derives so much of its inspiration and content.

RUTH

When Ezra and Nehemiah came to Judea from Persia to straighten out the tangled political, social, and religious affairs of the restored commonwealth, they introduced a number of reforms, among which was the prohibition of intermarriage. They ordered all Jews to divorce their non-Jewish wives. There was much protest against this decree. One of the most beautiful expressions of these protests is contained in the Book of Ruth.

The story tells of the loyalty and devotion of Ruth, a non-Jewess married to a Jew who had died. Although she is urged by her mother-in-law, Naomi, to go back to her own people, Ruth refuses to leave and pleads to be allowed to share with her mother-in-law whatever fortune or misfortune may lie in store for them. Her plea has become the great classic of loyalty and devotion:

Entreat me not to leave thee
And to return from following after thee;
For whither thou goest I will go,
And where thou lodgest I shall lodge.
Thy people shall be my people, and thy God my God.
Where thou diest I will die,
And there will I be buried.
The Lord do so unto me, and more also,
If aught but death part thee from me.

—Ruth 1:16-17

ESTHER

The Book of Esther is an historical novelette. The setting is laid in Persia during the reign of Artaxerxes. Esther is a Jewess who is chosen in a nation-wide beauty contest to become the favorite Queen of the Persian King. Her exalted position gives her the opportunity to save her people from threatened destruction.

It seems that Haman, the prime minister, wishing to revenge himself upon Mordecai, the leader of the Persian Jews, for some fancied slight, decides to destroy all the Jews of Persia. To that end he complains to the king that the Jews are different from all the other peoples in the empire, having a different religion and different customs, and therefore they ought not to be tolerated—an argument which has been used against Jews ever since by anti-Semites.

The king agrees to Haman's plan and gives him a free hand. Haman decides to exterminate the Jews on a certain day which he chooses by casting lots. Mordecai, hearing of Haman's wicked plan, pleads with Esther to intercede with the king. Esther agrees to risk her life for her people, for the king is unaware that she is a Jewess.

Her intercession is successful. The king revokes Haman's decree and permits the Jews to defend themselves. Haman is condemned by the king and executed upon the very gallows he had prepared for Mordecai, while the latter is elevated to Haman's position as prime minister. All turns out well for the Jews, and the festival of Purim is ordained to commemorate the great deliverance (see Purim).

LAMENTATIONS

The Book of Lamentations is a collection of poems written during the destruction of Jerusalem by the Babylonians in 586 B.C.E. and the captivity that followed. It describes with terrible vividness the tragedy of that period. Different writers are responsible for these poems, but all are weighed down by the sense of the people's tragedy. Though they realize that the destruction of the commonwealth was a punishment for the sins of Zion, they still hope that God may forgive them and restore them to their homeland.

The Book of Lamentations is still chanted in Orthodox synagogues on the ninth day of Av, the anniversary of the destruction of the Temple.

ECCLESIASTES

About the third century B.C.E. a writer reflecting on the meaning of life wrote a little book which is now part of the Bible under the name Ecclesiastes (Hebrew, *Koheles*). He approaches the problem of life with a gentle cynicism growing out of many years of living and wide experience.

In order to make his message more effective the author ascribes the book to King Solomon who had every opportunity to drain the cup of life, to indulge all his whims and fancies. After indulging them all he comes to the conclusion that "all is vanity and a chasing after wind." Life really has no meaning, he concluded. It is merely a round of activities without purpose or goal.

However, Koheles is no sour pessimist. Life may have no ultimate meaning, but it is sweet nevertheless. Work is good; wisdom is desirable; much enjoyment can be derived from living if one is sensible and takes advantage of one's opportunities. Koheles advocates the golden mean in everything. Wise, moderate, and sensible living is his ideal.

Frankly cynical in its philosophy of life, the book would not have found its way into the Bible had not pious editors changed some of its more offensive passages and added the following postscript which took the sting out of the book's cynicism:

This is the end of the matter, all has been heard. Fear God and keep His commandments, for this is the duty of every man. For God will bring every work unto judgment, with every hidden thing, whether it be good or evil.

—Ecclesiastes 12:12

DANIEL

The Book of Daniel was probably written during the Maccabean period, about 168 B.C.E., when Judaism was struggling for its existence against attempts to destroy it by the Syrian-Greek overlords of Palestine. Antiochus Epiphanes, the Syrian King, tried to unify his empire politically and religiously by compelling all his subject peoples to adopt his religion. The Jews opposed his plan and rebelled under the leadership of a village priest, Mattathias and his sons, among whom was Judas Maccabeus. It seemed hopeless for the band of Jewish rebels, untrained and poorly armed, to fight against one of the world's greatest powers.

It was during this crisis that the Book of Daniel appeared to encourage the people in their struggle for religious freedom. The book describes the experience of Daniel and his friends during the Babylonian captivity; how God saved Daniel from a den of lions and his friends from a fiery furnace because they were loyal to Him and refused to waiver in their faith. The moral pointed up by the story is that God will always protect the faithful and preserve them from all harm, if only they remain steadfast and loyal to Him.

CHRONICLES I and II

The two Books of Chronicles, written about the third century B.C.E., are a kind of summary of Jewish history from Adam to the restoration of the commonwealth after the Babylonian exile. The books are not strictly history, though the chronicler, like the writers of the Books of Samuel and Kings, uses historical material to illustrate his thesis that God is sovereign and rewards loyalty and punishes faithlessness. He was greatly influenced by the priestly tradition and emphasizes the importance of the Temple and the priestly code.

The Bible Canon

The Bible as we have it today is known as the Canon, or official Bible, and contains only the books which the canonizers believed were divinely inspired and were therefore regarded as sacred and authoritative. Partly as the result of a religious controversy with the Samaritans about the fourth pre-Christian century, and later because of the conflict with the new Christian movement, the rabbis fixed the end limit of divine inspiration as of the time of Ezra and Nehemiah (about 438 B.C.E.). Anything written before that period was considered divinely inspired; anything after that period was not, hence not worthy to be included in the Canon or official Bible.

The Book of Daniel, actually written about 168 B.C.E., was included because it purported to be the work of a prophet who lived during the Babylonian exile, before the time of Ezra and Nehemiah. *The Song of Songs* was included because it was believed to have been written by King Solomon and was interpreted allegorically.

The Bible Canon was finally established and fixed as we have it today at a convention of the rabbis at Jabneh about 100 C.E. From that time on, that compilation became the official version and text; all others were destroyed.

There were, however, a number of books which were known to have been written after the end limit of divine inspiration as decided by the rabbis. Some of them were very popular and were read by the people with enthusiasm. These were placed in a collection known as the Apocrypha (Greek for "hidden things"), but were excluded from the official Jewish Bible. The most important of the apocryphal books are:

The Wisdom of Solomon.

The Wisdom of Joshua, the Son of Sirach (ben Sirach).

The Book of Tobit, the story of a good man.

Judith, the story of a brave Jewess who saved her people in time of grave danger.

The Book of the Maccabees, two books telling of the Maccabean War for religious freedom in the days of Antiochus. Our Hanukah story is based on the account in the two books of the Maccabees.

Bible Translations

The Jewish Bible was originally written in Hebrew; but several centuries before the books of the Jewish Bible were canonized, Hebrew ceased to be a spoken language among Jews and was replaced by the vernacular Aramaic. So it became necessary to translate and explain the Hebrew text to the people in Aramaic. This was done orally by way of explanation and interpretation, beginning perhaps in the fourth century B.C.E. The first written translation in Aramaic was that of Onkelos, a convert to Judaism, and was completed some time in the first century B.C.E.

The most important translation of the Hebrew Bible was in Greek, popularly known as the Septuagint, and was completed about the third century B.C.E. for the Greek-speaking Jews, especially for the large Jewish community of Alexandria in Egypt. Legend has it that the King of Egypt commissioned seventy Hebrew scholars to do the translation. To insure accuracy he placed each of them in a separate chamber so that they might not consult one another. When the work was completed the seventy translations were compared and it was found that they were almost identical in every detail. That is why the first Greek translation is called Septuagint, "the translation of the seventy."

Since then there have been many translations in every language of the world. The official Catholic version is largely the work of Father Jerome was translated the Bible from the original Hebrew into Latin in the fourth century C.E. It is known as the Vulgate.

The classic English Protestant translation was made under orders of King James I in 1611. It was an attempt to reconcile the various English versions produced since the fourteenth century. The King James Version was accepted as the official English Protestant version used in most American Protestant churches. It was revised in 1885 and was again revised in 1952 in an edition called the Holy Bible, revised standard version (Old and New Testaments). This new revision is the work of the Standard Bible Committee, appointed in 1929 by the International Council of Religious Education on behalf of forty Protestant denominations associated in that body. The new version attempts to translate the King James English into the English idiom of our twentieth century, and does an excellent job.

The great difficulty with all Bible translations has been that there is no universally accepted text from which a translation can be made. There is no originl Hebrew text in existence. Moreover, what Hebrew versions there were lost some of their original meaning when translated into Greek or other languages. The translators were often so careful to preserve the accuracy of the Hebrew original that their translations were stilted and pedantic, thus missing the flavor of the original Hebrew idiom and sometimes even missing the meaning entirely.

In the *Universal Jewish Encyclopedia,* published about 1940, Dr. Simon Cohen, author of the article on the Bible, says:

Among the more noteworthy cases where the Bible translations have failed to give the best rendering of the Hebrew are the following:

Ordinary Translation	*More Exact Translation*
Isaiah 11:5 "A little child shall lead them . . ."	Any little child will be able to lead them.
Habakkuk 2:2 "That he who runs may read . . ."	That one may quickly read it.
Job 13:15 "Though He slays me, yet will I trust in him."	Lo! He slayeth me, I have no further hope.

In the last example the translation changes the entire meaning of the author's thought.

What Are the Dead Sea Scrolls?

The Dead Sea Scrolls are part of the library of an ancient Jewish community that lived in the desert near the Dead Sea in Israel. The community may have been part of a Jewish sect known as the Essenes who lived a kind of communitarian monastic life, withdrawn from the world and devoted to the study of the Torah and governed by special disciplines in their pursuit of holiness.

When the Romans destroyed the Jewish commonwealth in 70 C.E. the Essenes disappeared from history, but the community that lived by the Dead Sea had hidden their library of sacred scrolls in stone jars in caves nearby, some of which were accidentally discovered in 1947 by Arab shepherds. That is why they are called the "Dead Sea Scrolls." Some of the scrolls were in very good condition, others in fragments of various sizes.

The Dead Sea Scrolls are ancient manuscripts of the Jewish Bible (Old Testament), the oldest manuscripts by at least one thousand years discovered up to now. The scrolls also contain writings not found in the Old Testament—certain thanksgiving hymns written perhaps by the members of the sect, a manual of discipline governing the community and its members, and commentaries on some of the Old Testament prophets, especially on Habakkuk. Since the scrolls belonged to a Jewish sect living perhaps from the second century before Jesus until thirty-seven years after his death, they are the most valuable source for an understanding of the period between the Old and New Testaments that have yet been discovered. They throw a new light upon many problems that have baffled scholars for centuries. And what is equally important, being the oldest manuscripts of the Old Testament ever discovered, they help us to compare and to correct the texts we have been using up to now.

One of the scrolls, the "Manual of Discipline," gives us a detailed description of the community and its organization. It seems that membership in the community was attained by a process of election after a long period of training and preparation. An applicant for membership had to pass an examination as to his intellectual and moral fitness. Having passed the test, he was subjected to a year's probation, during which time he had no share in the community's resources nor was he permitted to eat at the common table. At the end of his probation year the applicant come up for another examination. Having passed the second test, the candidate went through another year's probation, but this time within the community, yet not part of it. He still was not permitted to participate in the common meal or to enjoy the resources of the group, although his own property had to be placed in trust with an overseer of the community. Only after successfully completing his second year's probation was he admitted to full membership into the community by a general vote of the members and by swearing an oath of allegiance to the community and to its principles.

The supreme authority of the community was vested in priests assisted by Levites, in an elaborate system of ranks and precedence in office and in all community activities. All the material resources of the community were owned in common. The members ate in a common dining room, and were assigned their tasks by an overseer or superintendent.

Prayer and study was a most important part of the daily activity and one third of the nights of every year had to be spent in extra study of the Torah. Breaches of the rules of the community were punished by temporary ostracism from the community life and exclusion from the normal food rations. Repeated infraction of the rules was punished by irrevocable excommunication.

What influence the Dead Sea Scrolls and the community that lived by its rules and teachings exerted on the origins of Christianity is a much discussed question. Theodor Gaster, in his excellent book *The Dead Sea Scrolls* (Doubleday Anchor Books, New York, 1957), in discussing the question "Do the Dead Sea Scrolls restore to us a long-lost forerunner of Christianity?" says:

The answer is Yes and No. Yes, in the sense that they furnish a picture of the religious and cultural climate in which John the Baptist conducted his mission and in which Jesus was initially reared. They portray for us, in vivid but authentic colors, the environment whose spiritual idiom John and Jesus spoke, whose concepts they developed and transmuted and whose religious ideas served largely as the seedbed of the New Testament. They also mirror a form of religious organization many elements of which were adopted by the primitive Church.

No, in the sense that what we have in these documents is, as it were, but the rude clay as yet unmolded by Christian hands. There is in them no trace of any of the cardinal theological concepts [of Christianity]—the incarnate Godhead, Original Sin, redemption through the Cross, and the like—which make Christianity a distinctive faith.

Professor Millar Burrows in his fine work *The Dead Sea Scrolls* (Viking Press, New York, 1957) sums up their value in these words:

> The doctrines and practices of the convenanters (the community by the Dead Sea) substantially enrich our knowledge of Judaism at the time just before and during the origin and early growth of Christianity. . . . The enlarged understanding of Judaism contributes in turn to our understanding of the New Testament in relation to its background and derivation, and all the more so because the beliefs, ideals, organization and rites of the convenanters, as compared with those of the early Church, exhibit both impressive similarities and even more significant contrasts.

The Talmud

> In the darkness of exile hath God refreshed us.
> He gave us the Talmud.
>
> —Talmud

The word *Talmud* is from the Hebrew *lomed* "to teach." It refers to a vast body of literature created by the sages and rabbis in their endeavor to interpret the Torah (the Jewish Bible) as a discipline for daily Jewish living. Their monumental activities began perhaps in the fourth pre-Christian century and continued to the sixth century of the Christian (present) Era, a period of about one thousand years.

The Talmud is composed of two sections.

The *Mishnah* (repetition, or teaching) is the Bible commentary of the sages and rabbis covering a period from about 350 B.C.E. to about 200 C.E. It is their explanation of the Bible, explaining and amplifying its laws, its regulation of the festivals and holydays, and its ethical and moral ideals and spiritual values. The Mishnah was finally compiled and edited about 200 C.E. by the great patriarch and leader of the Jewish communities of the Roman Empire, Judah Hanasi

(Judah the Prince), and in its modern printed edition contains several large volumes.

The *Gemara* (completion) is the rabbinic commentary and explanation of the Mishnah. It is an even vaster body of literature covering a period from about 200 C.E. to about 500 C.E. In its present printed edition it contains many large tomes which cover every aspect of Jewish belief, custom, ceremony, tradition, and all the laws regulating man's relation to God and to his fellow men. The Mishnah and the Gemara together make up the Talmud.

The Talmud is sometimes called the "oral law" as distinguished from the Torah, the "written law." Tradition viewed with disfavor the writing down of the rabbis' commentaries on the Torah for fear that the Torah might be displaced. It was not until the teachings and commentaries of the rabbis became so voluminous, and there was danger of their being lost in the troubled world conditions, that it became necessary to edit them and write them down in a permanent form. Thus, although the Talmud actually is a written literature much greater in volume than the Bible, it is still referred to as the oral law.

There are two editions of the Talmud, one compiled in Palestine, called the Jerusalem Talmud, and one developed in Babylonia, known as the Babylonian Talmud. The latter is the most complete and the most authoritative for traditional Judaism.

The Talmud is a veritable encyclopedia of Jewish literature touching all phases of life and thought. It contains legal arguments and decisions of the rabbis on all civil, criminal, and ritual law. In contains also parables and homilies, sermonettes and legends, wise sayings of the rabbis, proverbs, and moral discourses. And all of these are so commingled that the Talmud is an exceedingly difficult literature to read. Only a proficient scholar can navigate safely in the "sea of the Talmud." It is not a literature to read but to study, and for centuries after the Talmud was completed it was the chief subject of scholarship in Jewish life. Among Orthodox Jews it still is the most important subject of study for those who would aspire to Jewish learning.

Through the centuries various scholars have tried to organize the literature of the Talmud according to its subject matter and to codify its legal decisions. These efforts have been very valuable in making the Talmud available for the ordinary student. However, even with all these aids, and even with the modern translations of the Talmud from its original Hebrew and Aramaic into English, it is still a difficult literature to negotiate without guidance.

SAYINGS FROM THE TALMUD

The rabbis, whose discussions, interpretations of the Bible, and decisions on Jewish law, custom, and practice comprise the bulk of Talmudic literature, lived and worked during a period of about a thousand years, from about 350 B.C.E. to 600 C.E. They were not paid functionaries of the synagogue as ministers are today. They were laymen learned in the Torah and recognized as leaders by virtue of their scholarship and piety. Most of them were men in very ordinary economic circumstances. Some were even very poor. Among them were farmers, artisans, blacksmiths, and shopkeepers. But all of them were men of deep understanding and insight into the meaning and purpose of life, and all of them had a profound and unyielding faith in God and in the destiny of Israel. Their wise and pithy comments, cherished and preserved through the generations, became household guides to wise and wholesome living. The following are only a few of these comments taken from various anthologies of rabbinic wisdom.

HUMAN RELATIONS

The world rests upon three things: truth, justice, and peace.

Be of the disciples of Aaron, loving peace and pursuing it, and loving all creatures.

Say little and do much, and receive all men cheerfully.

God sends a messenger to punish for every sin committed except the sin of abusing or insulting another without cause. That sin God Himself punishes.

An aged man, whom Abraham hospitably invited to his tent, refused to join him in prayer to the one living God. Learning that the stranger was a fire worshipper Abraham drove him from his tent. That night God appeared unto Abraham in a vision and said: "I have borne with that ignorant man for seventy years; could you not have patiently suffered him one night?"

The heathen is thy neighbor, thy brother; to wrong him is a sin.

To cheat a Gentile is even worse than cheating a Jew, for besides being a violation of the moral law it bring Judaism into disrepute and desecrates the name of God.

The just among the Gentiles are priests of God.

Deeds of mercy are the Gentiles' offering, reconciling them with God.

When God created Adam He took earth from the site of the sanctuary, and from the four corners of the world, and breathed into his nostrils the breath of life. Hence all men are equal in God's sight.

"Thou shalt love thy neighbor as thyself." Who is my neighbor? Every man, for he is created in the image of God.

Look not at the pitcher but at what it contains.

There are three crowns: the crown of the Torah, the crown of the priesthood, the crown of royalty; but the crown of a good name excels them all.

The righteous among all the nations shall have a share in the world to come.

What is hateful unto thee do not unto thy neighbor. That is the whole of Judaism. All the rest is commentary.

If I am not for myself, who will be for me? But if I am for myself only, what am I? And if not now, when?

Which is the right course that a man should choose for himself? That which honors him in his own eyes and in the eyes of his fellow men.

Separate not thyself from the community. Pass no judgment upon thy neighbor until thou are come into his place.

In a place where there are no men, strive thou to be a man.

Open not thy mouth to speak evil.

Hospitality is an expression of divine worship.

Thy friend has a friend, and thy friend's friend has a friend. Be discreet.

Mention not a blemish which is thine own in detraction of thy neighbor.

Man sees the mote in his neighbor's eye, but knows not of the beam in his own.

When love is great both find room enough upon one board of the bench; afterwards they may find themselves cramped in a space of sixty cubits.

When a liar speaks the truth he finds his punishment in the general disbelief.

Without law civilization perishes.

He who is loved my man is loved by God.

He who gives charity in secret is greater than Moses.

The Bible was given us to establish peace in the world.

Let the honor of thy neighbor be as dear to thee as thine own.

The sword comes into the world because of justice being perverted.

He who has acquired a good name has enriched his manhood.

When the Egyptian hosts were drowning in the Red Sea, the angels in heaven were about to break forth in songs of jubilation. But the Holy One, blessed be He, silenced them with the words: "My creatures are perishing and ye are ready to sing!"

THE GOOD LIFE

Who is wise? He who learns from everybody.

Set a fixed time for the study of the Torah.

The chief thing is not knowledge but the use to which it is put.

He alone possesses knowledge who is aware of how little he knows.

Only the ignorant is really poor.

Much have I learned from my teachers, more from my companions, most from my pupils.

If thou hast learned much, do not pride thyself on it; for that thou wast created.

Knowledge is compared to water. As water flows off from high places, so knowledge can flourish only among modest men.

The horse fed too liberally with oats becomes unruly.

First learn then teach.

A single light answers as well for a hundred men as for one.

A myrtle even in the desert remains a myrtle.

Teach thy tongue to say, "I do not know."

Rather skin a carcass for pay in the public streets than lie idle dependent upon charity.

He who mixes with unclean things becomes unclean himself; he whose associations are pure becomes more holy with each day.

If a word spoken in its time is worth one piece of money, silence in its time is worth two.

The place honors not the man; 'tis the man who gives honor to the place.

Two pieces of coin in one bag make more noise than a hundred.

The rivalry of scholars advances knowledge.

The camel desired horns and his ears were taken from him.

There is no occasion to light thy lamp at noontide.

Silence is the fence around wisdom.

Into the well which supplies thee with water cast no stones.

A small coin in a large jar makes a great noise.

Use thy noble vase today; tomorrow it may break.

Commit a sin twice and it will not seem to thee a crime.

The world is saved by the breath of school children.

Even to rebuild the Temple the schools must not be closed.

There is a great difference between one who can feel ashamed before his soul and one who is only ashamed before his fellow men.

Who gains wisdom? He who is willing to receive instruction from all sources. Who is the mighty man? He who subdues his temper. Who is rich? He who is content with his portion. Who is deserving of honor? He who honoreth mankind.

What Is the Cabala?

The Cabala (Kabbalah) is a body of literature developed by Jewish mystics speculating about the nature of God and the universe. The name is derived from the Hebrew verb *Kobel* (to receive), hence Cabala means literally "tradition, transmitted teaching."

When these mystic activities began is unkown. It may have been under the influence of Greek philosophy in the first century C.E. They attained their greatest influence, however, during the Middle Ages. The mystical ideas of the Cabala are supposed to have been handed down by certain initiates, men specially gifted to understand the hidden mysteries of God and the universe, to others who also possessed such gifts. Therefore the knowledge thus transmitted was esoteric, hidden from ordinary people, and incapable of transmission to them through the ordinary rational channels of communication.

In the thirteenth century C.E. a book appeared in Cordova which has since become the Bible of Jewish mysticism. It is called the *Zohar* (illumination). It is acribed to a great rabbi, Simon Ben Yohai, who lived in the second century C.E., and who was supposed to have written it while hidden in a cave for fourteen years to escape Roman persecution. Most scholars believe that the *Zohar* was compiled by Moses de Leon, a famous Jewish mystic of the thirteenth century. It is a veritable encyclopedia of Jewish and non-Jewish mysticism up to that time. It is believed by cabalists to be an esoteric interpretation of the Hebrew Bible, containing secret interpretation which enables the initiated to understand mysteries of God's revelation incomprehensible to ordinary men.

Stimulated by the *Zohar*, Cabalism achieved its greatest power both in its mystical speculations and its parctical application. In its speculative aspects it tried to explain the mysterious nature of God's essence and man's relation to God.

God is *En Sof*, the endless, the infinite, beyond human comprehension. In order to become intelligible to man God had to become active and creative, but since He is purest spirit He can operate in the material universe only through a series of emanations *(sefiroth)*—ten of them—each lesser in its spiritual nature, the lowest being the substance out of which the material universe was created.

Man represents the highest product of creation. He is the harmony between the material and the spiritual world because he possesses a soul. The destiny of the soul is to return to the source whence it came—God—but before it can do so it must be thoroughly purified, since in its origin it is composed of three parts—*nefesh*, the lowest part, representing man's animal nature; *ruach*, the moral nature of man; *neshamah*, the most pure, hence the divine, part of man. Since the soul cannot return to its source, God, unless perfect, the doctrine of reincarnation came into Cabalism; that is, the soul continues to inhabit one body after another until the last person it inhabits is himself a perfect individual worthy of having a perfect soul. Then on the death of this perfectly righteous person the soul ceases to travel and rests in the source whence it came—the *En Sof*, the infinite God.

In its interpretation of the Bible, Cabalism taught that the words of the Bible are not ordinary human words. Every letter, every syllable, every arrangement of the letters has a hidden meaning. So the cabalists developed a system of interpretation known as *Gematria*, the art of discovering the hidden meaning of a word by the numerical equivalent of its letters. Other forms of interpretation were *Notarikon*, by which every letter of a word was taken as an initial or an abbreviation of some other word, and *Temurah* (transformation), by which one letter is substituted for another preceding or following it in the alphabet.

With these kinds of interpretation the cabalist could make the words of scripture mean anything his vivid imagination desired.

In its doctrine of evil Cabalism anticipated Christian Science by its denial that evil has an independent existence; it is only a negation of good, representing the other side of divinity, the left side of God. Man fell into evil when he strayed from God rather than seeking union with Him. Creation is continually disturbed by the influence of evil powers, but ultimately evil will be eliminated and Satan (the devil) himself will be converted to goodness when the Messiah will come and God's kingdom will be established on earth as in heaven. Through such speculations, the Cabala developed interesting philosophical ideas. Some of its ideas influenced modern theosophy and many of the other mystical movements of modern times, including Hasidism, a Jewish mystical movement which began in Poland in the seventeenth century (see Hasidism).

In its practical application, claiming the power to influence the course of human life and even nature itself by the use of its esoteric knowledge, Cabalism dabbled in all kinds of magic and superstition. It produced amulets to help women in childbirth, to ward off evil spirits and control them, and developed incantations capable of producing supernatural results. One of the most important objectives of practical Cabala was to hasten the advent of the Messiah who is to usher in the kingdom of God on earth, perfecting the whole universe so that even Satan will renounce his wickedness.

The Shulchan Arukh

The *Shulchan Arukh* (Prepared Table) is the official code of religious life, custom, and practice according to which Orthodox Jews and to a lesser extent Conservative Jews are guided and governed. Reform Jews do not recognize the religious authority of the *Shulchan Arukh,* although where possible they follow its tradition.

The *Shulchan Arukh* was composed by Joseph Caro, and was published in Venice in 1565. It is a condensation by Joseph Caro of a much greater attempt to codify and arrange the vast body of rabbinic law as contained in the Talmud, which was known as *Bet Yoseph,* the "House of Joseph."

The *Shulchan Arukh* is a simplified, systematic, pithy presentation of Jewish law and ritual as it developed across the centuries through the rabbinic interpretations of the Bible in the Talmud and its commentaries.

By the time Caro lived (sixteenth century) the Talmud and its commentaries had become so vast and so complex a literature that only the most erudite scholars could navigate what was known as the "sea of the Talmud." Ordinary people had to rely altogether upon rabbinic scholars to make known to them what Judaism expected of them. Many attempts were made before Joseph Caro's *Shulchan Arukh* to arrange, systematize, and simplify this complex literature. Joseph Caro built upon the work of his many predecessors and perfected the process in his monumental *Shulchan Arukh.*

Joseph Caro was a Sephardic Jew, a descendent of a Spanish-Portuguese Jewish family, and his interpretations were influenced by his Sephardic tradition. As such it was unacceptable to the Ashkenazi Jews of the Rhineland and Poland. Through the critical comments made on the *Shulchan Arukh* by a famous Polish rabbi, Moses Isserles, the *Shulchan Arukh* in time became acceptable and authoritative for all Orthodox Jews.

TWO PATHS TO ONE GOD

THE SON of David (the Messiah) will come when no one expects him.

—Talmud

Jesus in His Jewish Setting

Ever since the destruction of the first Judean State by the Babylonians in 586 B.C.E., the Jews, exiled from their homeland, hoped and prayed for their return to Judea and for the restoration of their independence and the glory of their commonwealth under a king of the Davidic dynasty. This king was to be their *Moshi-akh*, their Messiah, the anointed one promised by the Hebrew prophets.

The restoration to their homeland was accomplished about 538 B.C.E., but not quite as the Jews expected. It was not a Jewish Messiah, but the Persian conqueror, Cyrus the Great, who made their return possible; and it was to Judea as a Persian province, not as an independent state, that they returned. However, though the returned exiles were disappointed, they found comfort in the fact that the first part of the prophetic promise had been fulfilled. They had returned to their homeland; the rest of the promise would be accomplished in God's good time, they hoped.

The years lengthened into decades, the decades into centuries, and the Messiah, son of David, did not come. Persian domination was succeeded by Greek; Greek by Roman. Little Judea writhed under the heel of one conqueror after another. However, there was one turbulent interlude when they thought that perhaps their hopes had at last been realized. It was during the short period of the Hasmoneans, the dynasty established by the descendants of the Maccabees who had won a glorious struggle for Jewish religious freedom from the Syrian-Greeks in 165 B.C.E. But that period of independence was short-lived. The Romans soon took over, and the heavy yoke of imperial Rome was now being felt.

The country was seething with discontent. Burdened by oppressive taxes, torn by internal political and religious strife, angered by the insult to their God because of the presence of the Roman Eagle in their holy city where no graven images were permitted, the Jews felt that conditions could get no worse. These were indeed the *Hev-lay Ha-moshi-akh*, the tribulations preceding the messianic age which the apocalyptic writers had foretold. Surely, they thought, this must be the darkness before the promised dawn. So they looked for the imminent advent of the Messiah who would deliver them from their oppressors and restore them to their former greatness and glory.

It was to a people hoping, praying, and waiting for the imminent coming of the Messiah that John, known as the Baptist, appeared upon the Jewish scene, calling upon them to repent of their sins and to purify themselves by immersion in the sacred waters of the Jordan in preparation for the longed-for messianic fulfillment.

Not all the Jews, however, believed in the coming of the Messiah, nor even desired it. There were those who actually feared any such eventuality because of what it might do to the status quo which suited them perfectly. Among these were the Sadducees, a religious political group composed largely of the priests, the aristocracy, and the wealthy who were well satisfied with the power and stability which Roman rule had brought to the country and were loathe to see it end.

Opposed to the Sadducees were the Zealots, fiery patriots who carried on a ceaseless guerilla war against the Roman invaders. They organized themselves into terrorist bands which roamed the country, robbing and killing all collaborators with the Roman authorities.

A third group or party in Judea in the time of Jesus was the Essenes, a comparatively small group who turned their backs on all worldly conflicts and devoted themselves to a strict religious discipline far from the turbulent political strife which surrounded them. They were organized into small religious brotherhoods and lived a kind of monastic life, sharing the fruits of their labor with complete equality in their communal settlements. Some scholars think that Jesus either belonged to this sect or was profoundly influenced by it (*see* the Dead Sea Scrolls).

The largest and most powerful group in Judea in the time of Jesus was the Pharisees. They were the leaders of the masses of the Jews. Among them were the rabbis and sages who interpreted the Torah as a guide to daily living. They were the great stabilizing force in the country, avoiding the worldliness of the Sadducees, the political extremism of the Zealots, and the other worldliness of the Essenes. Their chief interest was in the study of the Torah and obedience to its commandments —moral and ritualistic. They might be compared to the great stable religious middle class of our own country.

While the Pharisees hated Roman domination no less than the Zealots, they were willing to accept the stability which Roman power had established and maintained, provided the Romans did not interfere with their religious autonomy. It was Johanan Ben Zakkai, a leader of the Pharisees and probably an older contemporary of Jesus, who helped to salvage Judaism from the wreck of the Judean State after the Romans destroyed Jerusalem in 70 C.E.

These were the four major groups in Judea when Jesus appeared upon the Jewish scene. He came at a time of grave religious, social, and political tension. It was a time when emotions were easily aroused and when feelings ran very deep. It was a time of unparalleled religious excitement, of wild speculations and equally wild hopes.

It is only in the light of such conditions that one can understand the role which Jesus played among the Jews of his time. It is only against the social, political, economic, and religious background of his time that one can understand his life, activities, and crucifixion. The New Testament becomes much more meaningful as we know the milieu in which the events it describes occurred. The very words of Jesus, so often misunderstood, take on a new and deeper significance when seen in the light of the circumstances in which he uttered them. His greatness as a man and as a Jewish religious teacher stands out in bold relief against the background of the religious conflicts of his time—the conflicts between those who emphasized the forms of religion and those who, like the great Hebrew prophets of old, stressed the religion of the heart, the soul, and the deed. Certainly his acceptance as the Messiah by some of the Jews and his rejection by others cannot be understood except in the light of the conditions of those days.

Why Didn't All the Jews Accept Jesus as the Messiah?

The reason that the vast majority of Jews didn't accept Jesus as their Messiah is that he did not fit their concept of what the Messiah was to be, nor did he fulfill their expectations of what the Messiah was to achieve. They looked for a Messiah who would deliver them from the Roman yoke, and Jesus told them to "give unto Caesar that which was Caesar's," as though he was not at all concerned with the Jewish aspirations for political freedom. They looked for someone who would miraculously usher in the golden age of justice, peace, and brotherhood promised by the Hebrew prophets, and, as far as they could see, Jesus did not fulfill that hope. Moreover, the fact that Jesus, who was to save the Jews, could not even save himself from death at the hand of Roman executioners seemed to the Jews of his day conclusive evidence that he was not their Messiah. Let us not forget that to the Jews of Jesus' day he was not what he became to later Christians and is to-day, the third person of the Christian Trinity. For these reasons Jesus was not accepted as the Messiah by the vast majority of his Jewish contemporaries.

Who Were the Pharisees?

Today in almost every dictionary the word *pharisee* is explained as synonymous with hypocrite. The unfortunate association is due to the hatred on the part of the writers of the New Testament for a group of Jewish leaders who refused to recognize Jesus as the Messiah. Through New Testament stories and teaching, the word pharisee has come into our language as a term of contempt.

Actually the word pharisee means "separatist" and refers to a group or party in ancient Judea who were distinguished from other Jews by their adherence to a stricter religious discipline. There may have been among them some who were scrupulous about outward piety and less careful about their inner integrity, even as today among all religious groups there are those who make a great show of outward piety and church allegiance but whose ethical conduct and human relations leave much to be desired.

However, among the Pharisees were also the greatest rabbis, scholars, and saints in ancient Judea. The Pharisees were the religious teachers of the Jews. They were the leaders in the synagogues and the judges who interpreted Jewish law according to the Bible tradition. Hillel, one of the great saints in Jewish history and the gentlest and most tolerant of men, was a leader of the Pharisees. It was he who told the heathen that the essence of Judaism lay in the Golden Rule: "What is displeasing unto thee, do not unto another."

Because the Pharisees emphasized the importance of the Torah and its ritual as well as its moral commandments, Jesus who placed his primary emphasis on the moral and spiritual values in Judaism, and upon the inwardness of religious piety, rather than on the ritualistic and ceremonial forms, turned upon them and in anger called them "hypocrites." Thus, through the New Testament the word pharisee has come into our vocabulary as a term of abuse and contempt.

What Is behind the Story of Jesus Chasing the Money-changers from the Temple?

Much has been made of the New Testament story of Jesus chasing the money-changers out of the Temple in Jerusalem, giving the impression that the Temple was a place of cheating and corruption which Jesus tried to clean up. The account in the Gospel according to Matthew says: "And Jesus went into the Temple of God, and cast out all that sold and bought in the Temple, and overthrew the tables of the money-changers, and the seats of them that sold doves" (Matthew 21:12).

To really understand the situation one must know something about the character of the ancient Temple in Jerusalem and the purpose for which it was used. The Temple was not one but a series of buildings and courtyards. The actual place of worship was the inner court of the Temple where the sacrifices were offered. Within that inner Temple was the Holy of Holies which only the High Priest entered on special occasions.

Surrounding the inner Temple were many courts and wings housing the Supreme Court, quarters for the priests and Levites; and within the Temple area but far removed from the actual place of worship was the general courtyard where the multitudes gathered. In this general courtyard were the booths of the merchants who sold animals and birds for the sacrifices and also the banks where pilgrims might exchange their foreign courrency for Palestinian money in order to purchase these animals or birds. These were the money-changers and the sellers of doves of whom the New Testament speaks.

Actually these people were in a perfectly legitimate business performing an important function in the religious economy of ancient Judea. Three times a year, during the festivals of Passover, Shovuos, and Succos, Jews from all over the world made a pilgrimage to Jerusalem to bring their gifts and offerings to the Temple. Since many came from great distances they could not bring live animals or birds with them for the prescribed sacrifices. Therefore, they had to buy them in Jerusalem. These foreign pilgrims also brought with them their foreign money which they had to exchange for Palestinian currency just as we do today when we travel in a foreign country. It was for their convenience that the merchants and bankers (money-changers) were permitted to carry on their business in the outer Temple precincts.

That some of these merchants were dishonest is undoubtedly true. In that, they were no different from many today who abuse the privileges of our economic system. It is unfortunate, however, that a prejudiced account in the New Testament gives the impression that all of them were dishonest and that the Temple was "a den of thieves."

The condemnation which Jesus hurled at the sellers of doves and money-changers was in keeping with his whole attitude toward religion. Like the great Hebrew prophets, whose teachings he reiterated and emphasized, he, too, believed that religion is no mere routine of sacrifices and ceremonials but an experience and love of God expressed in personal integrity and social righteousness. In condemning the merchants and money-changers, he was condemning the overemphasis on the whole sacrificial system as a means of worshipping God even as the great prophets of the Jewish Bible had condemned it seven hundred years before he was born. It was their spirit and teachings he was trying to revive in his own generation.

Who Crucified Jesus?

There is a joke that goes the rounds, usually during the Easter season, that would have humorous overtones were it not for its unhappy implications. It seems that a Christian had just returned from church on Easter Sunday and met a Jew walking along the street. Without any warning he went up to the Jew and struck him. When asked the reason for this un-provoked assault the man replied, "You Jews killed Christ." "But that happened nineteen hundred years ago," the Jew protested. "Maybe so," was the reply, "but I just heard about it this morning."

The tragic story of the crucifixion has been the cause of im-measurable suffering for Jews across the centuries. Each generation of Christians in medieval Europe hearing the story anew turned in vengeance upon the Jews in their midst. And even in more enlightened centuries and lands the annual re-telling of the suffering of the Christ has often reawakened the slumbering prejudices against the Jews everywhere.

No Jew would expect nor even suggest that Christian reli-gious education and preaching should not dwell on the story of the passion and calvary, for we realize that it is the very essence of the Christian concept of salvation; but as a matter of simple justice it is not unreasonable to expect that the ac-count of the crucifixion should be told in relation to the time and circumstances when the tragedy occurred.

According to the New Testament Jesus was a Jew. All his disciples and followers were Jews. When Jesus was accused by the priests for what they believed was his dangerous claims that he was the Jewish Messiah, two false witnesses had to be bribed to testify against him. Apparently the Jews who knew of him were friendly to him. The Gospels tell us that when Jesus came to Jerusalem to celebrate the Passover crowds of Jews greeted him with the cry, "Hosannah" (Hebrew: *Ho-*

shee-a-nah, "save us"). Only the religious authorities seem to have been against him; and they were against him because they feared that anyone who claimed to be the Messiah was a danger to the status quo and would be a source of trouble for them from the Roman authorities. Let us not forget that Judea was then a Roman province and one of the things that Jews, restive under Roman domination, looked for in their Messiah was to liberate them from Rome.

The significant figure Jesus has become in Christian tradition and the role he now plays in Christian theology prevent us at times from realizing that to the people of his own time he was not so important. Jesus himself complains of the failure of the people to appreciate his ministry when he says: "A prophet is not without honor save in his own community." The people among whom he lived and taught regarded him as just another of the many popular teachers and preachers who traveled through ancient Judea in those turbulent times. The place that Jesus holds in Christian theology, which developed later, was unknown and would have been incomprehensible to most of the Jews of those days. Even his own disciples didn't understand the man in their midst. And to most of the Jews who were looking for a Messiah, Jesus did not fulfill their messianic expectations.

They looked for someone who would liberate them from Roman oppression, and Jesus told them: "Render unto Caesar that which is Caesar's." They looked for a Messiah who would miraculously usher in the golden age of justice, peace, and human brotherhood promised by the Hebrew prophets, and as far as they could see Jesus did not fulfill that hope. The world they lived in was no better than before. And the crowning disillusionment was that Jesus died at the hands of Roman executioners. The Messiah, who was to save his people, was himself crucified by the enemies of his people.

Jesus was crucified by the Romans. Hanging on an upright pole with a cross piece, the shape of a man stretched out, was a favorite Roman method of executing those condemned to death. We are told in the Gospels that when Jesus was hung on the cross, he was placed between two thieves who were crucified for the crimes they had committed.

To the Romans Jesus' crime was political. He claimed to be

the Jewish Messiah, the hoped-for redeemer of his people from Roman oppression. As one who claimed to be the Messiah he was regarded as a threat to Roman domination of Judea and was treated as such, with death by crucifixion as the penalty.

During this period the Jews had no power to execute. They could try and condemn, but the Roman authorities had to carry out sentence. In the case of Jesus we are told in the Gospels that he was tried by a priestly court, judged guilty of heresy, and turned over to Pilate, the Roman governor, for sentence. The Gospel account puts all the blame on the Jews and declares Pilate completely innocent of the judicial crime.

What actually happened no one really knows. But there are many reputable Christian biblical scholars who believe the Gospel account of the trial and the crucifixion to be biased against the Jews and in favor of the Romans, since it was among the Romans that the Gospels were actually written down and it was in the Roman world that Christianity hoped to achieve and did achieve its greatest success. There is good historical reason to believe that the Roman governor, Pontius Pilate, was anything but the kind and considerate man described in the Gospels. His lack of any regard for Jesus is indicated by the fact that he allowed his soldiers to maltreat Jesus; and when Jesus was nailed to the cross he let them place a crown of thorns on his head in mockery of Jesus as the Messiah, king of the Jews, and of all Jews who looked for a Messiah to free them from Rome.

But there is a much more significant implication in the whole tragedy of calvary which most of us often forget or ignore. According to Christian theology the death of Jesus was ordained by God Himself to fulfill His purpose for mankind. "God so loved the world" is the idea of this theology, "that He sacrificed His only begotten Son to atone for the sins of mankind." The death of Jesus was part of the divine plan for salvation. Both the Jewish authorities who judged Jesus guilty of heresy and the Romans who crucified him were instruments of God, fulfilling His will.

The New Testament writers all agree that Jesus could have saved himself had he wished, but he went to his death with complete acceptance of his fate out of his love for unredeemed humanity. "Forgive them, Father, for they know not what they do" were his last words. Of course they didn't know what they did. How could they have known when even Jesus' own disciples did not fully comprehend his role in the life of mankind? It required the experience and the insight of Saul of Tarsus (later known as Saint Paul) to make the world understand that the life and death of Jesus was God's plan for human redemption.

If only we could understand the life and death of Jesus in its historical setting, in the light of the religious, social, and political conditions of that time, the New Testament account of the crucifixion could be taught without continually reawakening the slumbering prejudices and hatred against Jews which, once aroused, are not easily laid to rest again. And this kind of understanding need not violate or jeopardize any important Christian dogma or principle. On the contrary, the essential message of the New Testament expressed in the teachings of Jesus, the Beatitudes, the Sermon on the Mount, and the Golden Rule would be immeasureably enhanced by a more understanding and more just interpretation of the Jew's role in the crucifixion story.

There is great hope for future happier relations between Christians and Jews, as Christians increasingly approach the last days of Jesus with greater understanding of what Christians at their best know is the true Christian spirit of love and forgiveness. More and more is the ancient tragedy of innocence crucified becoming the symbol of mankind's universal tragedy —man's inhumanity to man. Ever since his death Jesus—the symbol of love and human brotherhood—has been crucified again and again, often by those who profess to revere him as Lord and Master. He was crucified in the bigotry of the Middle Ages when Christian fought against Christian and both presecuted the Jew. He was crucified when six million Jews were done to death in Nazi concentration camps and crematoria. He is crucified every time brother slaughters brother in war, every time a man raises his hand against his brother man in hate whether he be white or black or yellow or brown, or denies him his unalienable human rights as a child of God.

This awareness, taking root and growing in the hearts of Christians and non-Christians, may yet fulfill the hope of the ages for the kingdom of God with peace on earth and good will to all men everywhere.

Why Do Christians Observe Sunday and Jews Saturday as the Sabbath?

The day of rest ordained in the Jewish Bible, Old Testament, is the seventh day of the week, which according to our reckoning is Saturday. The early followers of Jesus observed the Saturday Sabbath. Later, when Christianity became largely the religion of Greeks and Romans and the gulf between Judaism and its daughter religion widened, the Christians gave up the Saturday Sabbath and adopted Sunday because it was the day on which Jesus was believed to have risen from the dead. It is therefore called the Lord's Day and has become the Christian Sabbath, except for the Seventh Day Adventists, who observe the Saturday Sabbath.

May Jews Recite the "Lord's Prayer"?

Not in its present form. Jews do not regard the prayer (Matthew 6:7-13), which Jesus asked his disciples to use, as the "Lord's Prayer," for to Jews Jesus is not "the Lord." Only God is Lord, Therefore, Jews cannot recite the prayer in its present form. However, there is nothing in the prayer which is not consistent with basic Jewish teaching.

Our Father, Who art in Heaven, hallowed be Thy name. Thy kingdom come, Thy will be done on earth as it is in heaven. Give us this day our daily bread, and forgive us our debts (our sins) as we forgive our debtors (those who sin against us). And lead us not into temptation, but deliver us from evil. For Thine is the kingdom, the power, and the glory forever. Amen.

This prayer expresses ideas inherent in Judaism. But since the death of Jesus and the growth of Christianity this prayer has become so basically associated with the Christian religion that it is not used by Jews in this precise form.

If Jesus Was a Jew, Why Don't Jews Use the New Testament in Their Worship?

Although most of the moral, spiritual, and ethical teachings of Jesus are derived from his Jewish background, from the teachings of the Hebrew prophets and the rabbis, there is much in the New Testament that in contrary to Jewish religious beliefs. The teaching that Jesus is the son of God is foreign to Judaism. This and many other ideas and stories in the New Testament, which were written under the influence of Greek and Roman religious ideas, are not acceptable to Jews.

Moreover, since the New Testament has become the Bible of a different religion, it is not used by Jews any more than Christians would use the Koran, the Moslem Bible.

What Is the Relation of the Passover Meal to the Last Supper?

The Passover was one of the three great pilgrimage festivals in ancient Judea. The other two were Succos (Feast of Tabernacles in the autumn) and Shovuos (Feast of Weeks and Ripe Fruits in the summer). To celebrate these festivals Jews from all over the world considered it their duty to make a pilgrimage to Jerusalem to offer their sacrifices and to bring their free-will gifts to the Temple. It was to celebrate the Passover that Jesus and his disciples came to Jerusalem.

The Passover begins with a special meal on the eve of the first day of the seven days' (Orthodox and Conservative Jews observe eight days) observance of the festival. This meal is called the Seder, and as part of its ceremonial, matzah (unleavened bread) and wine are used. These are the two symbols to which the New Testament refers when it describes Jesus as telling his disciples that the wine is his blood and the unleavened bread his body. The "Last Supper" was, therefore, the Seder meal, and the wine and wafers used in the Christian Communion Service are symbolic of the wine and matzah used by Jesus and his disciples in the celebration of the ancient Passover.

What Is the Difference between Passover and Easter?

Passover is sometimes referred to as the Jewish Easter. This is a mistake that has arisen because the two holydays come about the same time, usually about April.

The Passover commemorates the deliverance of the ancient Hebrews from slavery in Egypt under the leadership of Moses. Easter commemorates the resurrection of Jesus on the third day after his death. He died on Friday and, according to Christian tradition, rose from his grave on Sunday, hence Easter Sunday.

The reason why the two holydays come about the same time is that the tragedy of Jesus' death occurred during the Passover season. It was during the Passover season, the traditional Jewish season of liberation, that the Jews looked for the coming of the Messiah who was to liberate the people from their oppressors and usher in God's kingdom on earth. That is why Jesus appeared in Jerusalem during this season, not only to celebrate the Passover but to fulfill the Jewish expectation of the Messiah's advent during this festival of freedom.

Does the Sermon on the Mount Express Ideals Not Found in Judaism?

The heart of the New Testament's ethical and spiritual ideals is found in the so-called Sermon on the Mount contained in Matthew 5-7, and in a shorter form in Luke 6. The account in Matthew tells us that the sermon was delivered by Jesus on a hill; in the Luke version the sermon is said to have been delivered in the plain. Most scholars believe that the beautiful sayings which constitute the sermon were not delivered at any one time, but were collected by the compilers of the New Testament from scattered sayings of Jesus on various occasions. But whether it is a single sermon or thoughts expressed at different times, the compilation does express some of the loftiest ideals which the spirit of man has produced, and it is often pointed to as evidence of the advance in ethical idealism and spiritual insight of the New Testament over the Jewish Bible (Old Testament).

In an excellent book, written in 1911 by Rabbi Gerald Friedlander, titled *The Jewish Sources of the Sermon on the Mount,* the author goes into great detail to point out that nearly every statement in the Sermon on the Mount is either a direct quotation from the Jewish Bible or a paraphrase of it; and that many of them were expressions of contemporary Jewish teaching which the rabbis, who lived prior to the birth of Jesus, had made part of developing Judaism.

The following is a very brief analysis of the Beatitudes and their parallels in the Jewish Bible from which Jesus drew much of his inspiration:

1. Blessed [Happy] are the poor in spirit for theirs is the kingdom of Heaven (Matthew 5:3).

Happy is the man that hath not walked in the way of the wicked (Psalm 1:1).

Happy is he that considereth the poor (Psalm 40:2).

2. Blessed [Happy] are they that mourn for they shall be comforted (Matthew 5:4).

They that sow in tears shall reap in joy (Psalm 126:5).

Happy is the man whom Thou chasteneth, O Lord . . . that Thou mayest give him rest from the days of adversity (Psalm 94:12, 13).

3. Blessed [Happy] are the meek for they shall inherit the earth (Matthew 5:5).

The meek shall inherit the earth (Psalm 37:11).

4. Blessed [Happy] are they who thirst after righteousness, for they shall be filled (Matthew 5:6).

My soul thirsteth for God, for the living God (Psalm 42:3).

And the effect of righteousness is quietness and confidence for ever (Isaiah 32:17).

He that followeth after righteousness and mercy findeth life, righteousness and honour (Proverbs 21:21).

5. Blessed [Happy] are the merciful for they shall obtain mercy (Matthew 5:7).

Happy is he that considereth the poor, the Lord will deliver him in the day of evil (Psalm 41:1).

He who has mercy on his fellow creatures shall obtain mercy from Heaven [God] (Talmud Sabbath 151 b).

6. Blessed [Happy] are the pure in heart, for they shall see God (Matthew 5:8).

For the Lord is righteous; He loveth righteousness; the upright [pure in heart] shall behold His face (Psalm 11:7. *see also* Psalm 17:15).

7. Blessed [Happy] are the peacemakers for they shall be called the children of God (Matthew 5:9).

These are the things that ye shall do, speak ye every man the truth with his neighbour, execute the judgment of truth and peace in your gates (Zechariah 8:16).

Keep thy tongue from evil and thy lips from speaking guile (Psalm 34:13).

Be of the disciples of Aaron; seek peace and pursue it (Abot 1:12).

8. Blessed [Happy] are they that are persecuted for righteousness' sake; for theirs is the kingdom of heaven (Matthew 5:10).

I gave my back to the smiters, and my cheeks to them that plucked off the hair. I hid not my face from shame and spitting, for the Lord God will help me (Isaiah 50:6-7).

Was Jesus the Originator of the Golden Rule?

The beautiful statement, often called the Golden Rule, "Whatsoever ye would that others do unto you do even so unto them," which Jesus laid down as the fundamental principle of the good life, is not original with him.

Hillel, one of the greatest of the ancient rabbis whose influence was widespread among Jews and whose every word was cherished and quoted, died when Jesus was still a child, perhaps a boy of ten. Hillel was once asked by a pagan to explain the whole of Judaism while the latter stood on one foot. He wanted the essence of Judaism in a sentence. The rabbi was equal to the challenge and said, "What is displeasing unto thee, do not unto another. That is the whole of Judaism. All the rest is commentary." Here we have the Golden Rule expressed in its original form in Judaism. Jesus was undoubtedly familiar with this statement of Rabbi Hillel.

Indeed, when Jesus was asked what one must do to inherit eternal life he said:

"What is written in the Law [Torah, first five books of the Jewish Bible]? How readest thou?" And the man answering said: "Thou shalt love the Lord they God with all thy heart, with all thy soul, and with all thy strength, and with all thy mind, and thy neighbor as thyself." And He [Jesus] said unto him: "Thou hast answered right; this do, and thou shalt live."

—Luke 10:25-28

The statement "to love God with heart and soul," and so on is taken from the Book of Deuteronomy 6:5, and the second part—"to love one's neighbor as oneself"—is taken from the Book of Leviticus 19:18.

To Jesus, as to the other great teachers in Judaism and in all great religions, the essence of religion was expressed in love of God and love for one's fellow men.

The following are expressions of the Golden Rule as found in the sacred books of some of the other great religions of the world:

Hinduism: Do not to others what ye would not wish done to yourself; and wish for others too what ye desire and long for yourself. This is the whole of Dharma. Heed it well.

—Mahabharata

Mohammedanism: Noblest religion this—that thou shouldst like for others what thou likest for thyself; and what thou feelest painful for thyself hold that as painful for all others too.

—Hadis

Confucianism: A disciple asked, "Is there one word which may serve as a rule of practice for all one's life?" Answer: Is "reciprocity" not such a word? Do not to others what you would not want done to yourself—this is what the word means. If you act thus your public life will not, nor will your private life, arouse ill will.

—Analects

Taoism: Pity the misfortunes of others; rejoice in the well being of others; help those who are in want; save men in danger; rejoice at the success of others and sympathize with their reverses even as though you were in their place.

—Taoist Writings

Zoroastrianism: That which is good for all and any one, for whomsoever—that is good for me. What I hold good for self I should for all. Only Law Universal is true Law.

—Zend Avesta

Jainism: Thus we enjoin on you, thus do we say, thus we believe, thus we proclaim to all: No living thing should be slain anywhere, nor ordered forcibly this way and that, nor put in bonds, nor tortured any way, nor treated violently otherwise; because you are that same which you would slay or order here and there against his will, or put in prison, or subject to pain or treat with violence; ye are that same, the self-same life doth circulate in all.

—Bhadra-bahu

Buddhism: Is there a deed, Rahula, thou dost wish to do? Then bethink thee thus: "Is this deed conducive to my own harm, or to that of both?" Then is this a bad deed entailing suffering? Such a deed must thou surely not do.

—Majjhima Nikaya

Note: The references are from Robert E. Hume, *The World's Living Religions,* Charles Scribner's Sons, New York, 1936, and from the *Essential Unity of All Religions,* Bhagavan Das.

Is It True That Judaism Is a Religion of Relentless Justice and Christianity a Religion of Love?

It is a popular pastime in which, I am happy to say, most modern Christian students of religion do not indulge, to contrast Judaism with Christianity to the disadvantage of the former, asserting that Judaism is a stern religion of strict justice and inexorable retribution whereas Christianity is a religion of mercy and love. They point to the Jewish Bible (Old Testament), Exodus 21:23, which reads: "But if any harm follow [the problem dealt with is a violent quarrel between two men] then thou shalt give life for life, eye for eye, tooth for tooth, burning for burning, wound for wound, stripe for stripe." In contrast they point to the New Testament, Matthew 5:43, in which Jesus says: "Love your enemies and pray for them that persecute you."

The first and obvious objection to such a contrast is that the statement from Exodus represents a code of laws that goes back fifteen hundred years and more before Jesus was born. It is the code of a primitive society, the *Lex Talionis* (law of retaliation), a practice which was not eradicated in some parts of Christian Europe until modern times, and which still exists in isolated parts of that continent and in some parts of our own country in the form of the vendetta or blood feud. Placed against the Exodus example of primitive Hebraic justice is the high spiritual attitude of Jesus, who, according to Christian teaching, is the perfect efflorescence and embodiment of divinity. No wonder the Jewish ethic comes out second best.

However, to really understand the Jewish ethic as contained in the Jewish Bible which, incidentally, has been amplified and heightened during the past twenty-four hundred years since the Bible was completed, one must take the Bible as a whole. The Jewish Bible is not one book; it is a library of books. These books cover more than fifteen hundred years of Jewish religious growth. They contain some of the earliest expressions of Hebraic quest for God as well as some of the deepest spiritual insights ever achieved by the mind and spirit of man. The statement from Exodus 21 represents one of the primitive concepts; yet primitive as it is, the concept of "an eye for an eye" was a great advance upon the codes of Israel's ancient neighbors who often permitted the injured person or his family to carry on a blood feud to the extermination of one or the other of the contending families. The statement in Exodus 21 puts an outside limit upon retaliation for injury. Vengeance may be meted out only to the extent of the injury, no more—"an eye for an eye, a tooth for a tooth, a life for a life," the last of which modern society still exacts in capital punishment. Moreover, very early in the process of Jewish Bible interpretations the sages explained the Exodus statement as meaning monetary compensation for the injury.

To understand the ethics of the Jewish Bible and to be fair in evaluating it, one must realize that although the Jewish Bible contains the statement from Exodus 21, it also contains the Ten Commandments in Exodus 20. It contains some primitive beliefs in the efficacy of animal sacrifices as a way of worshipping God; it also contains the glorious challenge of the prophet Micah:

> Wherewith shall I come before the Lord,
> And bow myself before God on High?
> Shall I come before Him with burnt offerings,
> With calves of a year old?
> Will the Lord be pleased with thousands of rams,
> With ten thousand rivers of oil? . . .
> It hath been told thee, O man, what is good,
> And what the Lord doth require of thee;
> Only to do justly, to love mercy
> And to walk humbly with thy God.
>
> —Micah 6:6-8

The Jewish Bible contains some attitudes which may be repugnant to the modern educated conscience; but it also contains unsurpassed ethical pronouncements such as these in the book of Leviticus 19:17-18: "*Thou shalt not hate thy brother in thy heart . . . Thou shalt not take vengeance . . . but thou shalt love thy neighbor as thyself: I am the Lord.*" And should one say that this refers only to love for one's Hebrew neighbor, let him read on in the same chapter, Leviticus 19:33-34: "*And if a stranger [a non-Hebrew] sojourn with you in your land ye shall not do him wrong. The stranger that sojourneth with you shall be unto you as the home born among you, and thou shalt love him as thyself for ye were strangers in the land of Egypt: I am the Lord your God*" [italics mine].

When Jesus said, "Love your enemies," he was not really saying anything which Jewish teaching before his time had not already expressed. In that same book of Exodus, to which we have already referred, Chapter 23:4-5, we are told, "*if thou meet thine enemy's ox or his ass going astray, thou shalt surely bring it back to him. If thou see the ass of him that hateth thee [thine enemy] lying under its burden thou shalt not pass by him; thou shall surely help him to release it.*"

The saintly Hillel, who died when Jesus was a boy of ten, and who shaped Jewish thought and tradition more than any single individual except Moses himself, was asked, "What is the essence of Judaism?" He replied: "What is displeasing unto thee, do not unto thy neighbor. That is the whole of Judaism. All the rest is commentary"—a thought which in diverse forms has been expressed by other great religions and has become the Golden Rule of life.

Does the New Testament's "Nonresistance" Doctrine Imply a Difference between the Christian and Jewish Ideal?

One of the assertions which Christians sometimes make to point out the supposed superiority of the New Testament ideal over that of the Jewish Bible is derived from a statement in the Sermon on the Mount:

> You have heard that it is said, "An eye for an eye and a tooth for a tooth." But I say unto you, do not resist one who is evil. But if any one strikes you on the right cheek, turn to him the other also; and if anyone would sue you and take your coat, let him have your cloak as well; and if anyone forces you to go one mile, go with him two miles.
>
> —Matthew 5:38-42

No one really knows what Jesus meant by this injunction, "not to resist evil." If he meant nonresistance to evil under any and all circumstances, if he meant to allow the evildoer to have his way without any attempt to stop him, then in this he suggested a way of life contrary to the main stream of Judaism. If, however, he meant, as many Christians today interpret it, that one should not return evil for evil, blow for blow, insult for insult, but that one should return good for evil in the hope that this might soften the evildoer and make him contrite and inspire him to turn away from his evil ways, then Jesus was in perfect harmony with Jewish teaching.

The Book of Proverbs in the Jewish Bible, a collection of Jewish wisdom centuries before Jesus was born, expresses Jewish teaching beautifully in these thoughts: *A soft answer turneth away wrath; but a grievous word stirreth up anger* (15:1); *Hatred stirreth up strife, but love covereth all transgressions* (10:12); *Answer not a fool according to his folly, lest thou also be like unto him* (26:4); *Rejoice not when thine enemy falleth, and let not thy heart be glad when he stum-bleth* (24:17).

The injunctions in Exodus 23:4-5, "If thou meet thine enemy's ox or his ass going astray, thou shalt surely bring it back to him. If thou seest the ass of him who hateth thee [thine enemy] lying under its burden thou shalt not pass by him; thou shalt surely help him to release it," are certainly no injunctions to return evil for evil. The Talmud tells us that when the Egyptians, who were pursuing the fleeing Israelites, were being drowned in the Red Sea the angels began to sing for joy. Whereupon God rebuked them saying: "How can you rejoice when these my children are perishing!" "Thou shalt not take vengeance" (Leviticus 19:17) is a commandment which goes to the heart of Jewish teaching. "Hate the sin, but not the sinner" is a basic precept which guided the rabbis of the Talmud.

But to return good for evil does not mean in every situation that one shall not resist evil and the evildoer. Nor do Christians today generally interpret the Matthew passage in that way. When an individual tries to take the words of Jesus literally even Christians regard him, if they are charitable, as an other-worldly saint; if they are not charitable they think of him as a psychological deviate who should not be permitted to be at large. The well-known jest of the preacher who turned the other cheek, and when it, too, was slapped, attacked his assailant, is indicative of the fact that the doctrine of nonresistance to evil is not taken literally even by Christians.

There is no difference between Judaism and Christianity in the profound insight that moral persuasion is infinitely better than the use of force both in individual and group relation, even on a national and international level. We all know, and the Jewish lawgivers, prophets, sages, and rabbis, as well as Jesus, knew that hatred only breeds hatred and ultimately destroys the hater himself; that anger and bitterness only inspire their counterpart and contribute to many illnesses through the mental and emotional tensions which they cause.

Jewish religious teachers fully realized, as did Jesus later on, that our human personality grows and flowers only as it allows the God-spirit in us to be expressed through kindness, sympathy, and outgoing love for all, even for one's enemy.

The Jewish sages may not have known the psychological vocabulary we use today; but they had most of the insights which modern psychology is only now discovering and labeling.

However, the rabbis differ from the absolute interpretation of the "nonresistance" doctrine in that they recognize that there are situations in which evil and the evildoer must be resisted, sometimes even with force. Judaism realizes that the power of moral example can be effectively used only when there is a moral conscience to which it may appeal. If individuals or nations do not possess a moral conscience consistent with our Judeo-Christian understanding of what a "moral conscience" implies, our efforts to persuade them by moral example alone will usually prove ineffective. "Turning the other cheek" may even encourage the evildoer to slap it harder—to further aggression and evil doing. He may interpret what we call "moral persuasion" as weakness to be exploited. That is exactly what happened in Nazi Germany.

Judaism recognized this limitation to moral persuasion from the beginning. The insights of the Hebrew lawgivers, prophets, sages, and rabbis enabled them to see realistically man's limitations. They knew that men are not and rarely can be angels. The writer of Psalm 8 reaches his highest estimate of man when he says: "Thou hast made him but little lower than the angels" (this is the Jewish Publication Society's version; the Christian revised standard version says: "Little lower than God"). Man is imperfect, says Judaism. He is torn by the demands of the flesh and the yearning of the spirit; and it is an eternal and very difficult conflict as every human being can testify. Therefore, Judaism hesitates to make demands beyond what mortals can fulfill. However, it does envisage a time when the highest attainable goals—love and human brotherhood—will be fulfilled right here on earth as the prophet Isaiah expressed it in his beautiful but somewhat extravagant imagery:

And the wolf shall dwell with the lamb,
And the leopard shall lie down with the kid;
And the calf and the young lion and the fatling together;
And a little child shall lead them.
And the cow and the bear shall feed;

Their young ones shall lie down together;
And the lion shall eat straw like the ox.
And the sucking child shall play on the hole of the asp,
And the weaned child shall put his hand on the
    basilisk's den.
They shall not hurt nor destroy
In all My holy mountain;
For the earth shall be full of the knowledge of the Lord,
As the waters cover the sea.

—Isaiah 11:6-9

That was a vision of the perfect world and an expression of a hope that man will some day achieve it by developing the God-spirit and potentials within him. It is a vision which Orthodox Jews believe will be fulfilled by the coming of the Messiah, which Orthodox Christians believe will be ushered in by the second coming of Christ, and which Liberal Jews and Christians believe man himself will achieve through a more perfect knowledge of God and with His help.

When this messianic hope shall have been fulfilled the whole problem of evil shall also have disappeared, for man will then be so imbued with the knowledge and love of God and his fellow men that he will have no need for the injunction "not to resist evil." There will be no evil to resist. But in the meantime Judaism realizes that imperfect man has to live with himself and his fellows, with his imperfections and his conflicts in an imperfect world. He has to face the problems of daily life in their competitive as well as their cooperative aspects. So Judaism, recognizing that so long as man and his world are imperfect and evil doing is not only possible but can become uncontrollable, urges us to resist evil and to overcome it both within ourselves and our world—all this with the ever present help of God.

However, even in this imperfect world, while we are striving for the messianic golden age, Judaism strongly emphasizes, as we have already seen, that in our efforts to establish happy human relations both on the individual and group level, love is more effective than hate. In achieving our desired goals, moral force is in the long run more effective than armaments; and human brotherhood and all the blessings that could flow from it to enrich our individual lives can be realized more surely through mutual understanding, respect, cooperation, and good will than through mutual suspicion, distrust, antagonism, and war. It is only in evil situations in which force becomes necessary as a last resort that Judaism reluctantly counsels us to resist the evil by what means we can most effectively remove it from our midst.

Can Jews Ever Accept Jesus?

That depends on what Jews are expected to accept about Jesus. No Jew can ever accept Jesus as the Christ, the uniquely divine son of God who was sacrificed to atone for the sins of mankind, and still remain a Jew. For the many reasons already given in answer to other questions on Judaism in this book, it is impossible for a Jew, whether he is Orthodox or Reform, to accept the historic Christian dogmas about Jesus and still continue to be a member of the Jewish faith. However, many Jews can and do recognize the greatness of Jesus, the Jewish moral and ethical teacher who tried to revitalize the essential spirit of prophetic Judaism in his day and generation.

Many Jews can and do accept the deep spiritual insights of Jesus revealed in many beautiful statements in the New Testament expressing some of the high ideals and values of Judaism. In these ethical and moral ideals and spiritual values Jews see a restatement by Jesus of what the great Hebrew prophets and sages had taught. The man Jesus who made these statements, whose life embodied them and whose suffering glorified them—that man many Jews can and do accept as one whose life and work enriched the spiritual tradition which Judaism gave to the world.

In this sense do Jews speak of the Judeo-Christian tradition and heritage—a tradition of moral, ethical, and spiritual ideals and values which Jews and Christians share through Jesus the man, the rabbi, the great religious teacher. Jews can never accept the divinity of Jesus as Christians understand that concept, but they can and do accept the divine character of his inspired moral and ethical teachings, even as they accept the divine character of all teachings which bear the stamp of true divine inspiration whether they are uttered by Jews or by the great religious teachers of other faiths. As our prayerbook so beautifully expresses it: "O Lord, open our eyes that we may see and welcome all truth, whether shining from the annals of ancient revelations or reaching us through the seers of our own time; for Thou hidest not Thy light from any generation of Thy children that yearn for Thee and seek Thy guidance" (*Union Prayerbook,* Vol 1, newly revised edition, p. 35).

Unity in Diversity

Since time began men searched for God
  To give them faith for life;
A meaning and a purpose high
  Transcending pain and strife.

They looked for Him in sun and star,
  But found Him not in these;
Nor on the peaks of mountains high,
  Nor in the seven seas.

They probed the mysteries of earth;
  They reached unto the sky;
The God they sought eluded them;
  They knew no reason why.

At last their vision inward turned;
  Their hearts they probed and found
That when man sought his brother man
  His life with God was bound.

Raphael H. Levine

How good and how pleasant it is
For brothers to dwell together in unity.
—Psalm 133

At a brotherhood service in our temple I began my part of our Jewish-Christian witness to the unity in the midst of our diversity by trying to explain why I am a Jew. "I am a Jew," I said, "first of all because I was born of Jewish parents; because I was reared in the synagogue and was indoctrinated into our Jewish faith and traditions. From childhood I rejoiced in the celebration of our Jewish festivals and was inspired by the awesome majesty and beauty of our high holydays. When I grew toward maturity I learned about other great religions and found them noble in concept and rich in the beauty of their traditions; but there was nothing in any of them so unique and challenging as to overmaster the years of beautiful and wholly satisfying experience I had found in my own. My faith as a Jew makes every possible demand upon my intellect and spirit so that even if I were to achieve the highest degree of maturity possible for me I could not fulfill all its challenge to what is potentially deepest and best in me. That is why I am a Jew. I shall live and die a Jew, for through Judaism I can express my most far-reaching spiritual goals and highest aspirations as a child of God for myself and for my fellow men."

I dare to suggest that many Christians, if they were to make a confession as to why they are Christians, might say something similar. It is first of all the accident of birth and rearing that makes us Christians or Jews. It is only as we grow to maturity that we make a conscious choice either to remain in the faith into which we were born or to adopt some other faith more in harmony with our adult insights and needs. But in either event it is in the diversity of belief, forms of worship, rituals and ceremonies in the traditions of Christians and Jews in which we make our choices. The things that unite us as religious people derive from our faith in God, the Creator and Ruler of the universe and Father of all mankind. As the prophet Malachi so eloquently pleaded: " Have we not all one Father; hath not one God created us all?" (Malachi 2:10). God is One, but the ways of knowing Him are infinite in their variety. Most great mountain peaks can be reached by diverse trails, but when climbers reach the summit they stand on common ground. So also in the ascent to the mountain of God. Because of our diverse historical, educational, and traditional backgrounds each of us takes the trail to God's holy mountain best suited to his needs; but when we catch a glimpse of its topmost height we see the resplendent vision of the Father of us all.

I recall an experience during my ministry in England which deeply impressed me. A dear friend, a Christian minister, in appreciation of our friendship and mutual regard, once said to me in a moment of outgoing good will: "Levine, you are a real Christian." I was touched by his tribute and I replied, "P——, you have a Jewish heart." That exchange of mutual respect and understanding goes to the heart of the fundamental unity of our two faiths, which we express in our diverse theologies and dramatize in our diverse forms of worship, holydays, rituals, and traditions.

When my friend called me a "real Christian" there was no implication that I subscribed or was ready to subscribe to his unique Christian beliefs and worship; nor was there any implication in my phrase of tribute, "Jewish heart," that he would abandon his faith for mine, or that one was better than the other. Both of us were merely trying to express our deep regard for the other's spiritual insight and character, and we were both using language sanctified by our respective religious traditions. But though we used different idioms we were clasping hands in the deepest understanding and love for one another. And why not? Was not the spirit of Christianity born of the body and soul of Judaism?

In trying to express the essential teachings of Jesus, the New Testament records:

> And behold one came and said unto him, "Good Master, what good things shall I do that I may have eternal life?" And Jesus said unto him, "Why callest thou me good? There is none good but one, that is God; but if thou wilt enter into life, keep the commandments." And the man said unto him "Which?" And Jesus replied, "Thou shalt do no murder. Thou shalt not commit adultery. Thou shalt not steal. Thou shalt not bear false witness. Honor thy father and thy mother, and thou shalt love thy neighbor as thyself."

—Matthew 19:16-20

On another occasion the New Testament records:

> Then one of them that was a lawyer asked him [Jesus]
> a question, tempting him and saying, "Master [Rabbi],
> which is the great commandment in the law [the Torah]?"
> And Jesus said unto him, "You shall love the Lord your
> God with all your heart and with all your mind. This is
> the first and great commandment. And the second is like
> it, You shall love your neighbor as yourself. On these two
> commandments hang all the law and the prophets."
>
> —Matthew 22:35-40

In both these records of the nub and core of Jesus' ethical
and moral teaching, the New Testament tries to state the
essence of the Christian way of life. Thus when my friend
called me a "real Christian" he was trying to say what any
Christian today who uses that phrase would say in tribute to
one of another faith—that he loves him for the high quality
of his character and soul. And so the Jew when he uses the
phrase "Jewish heart" expresses the best a Jew can say of
him whom he loves. For what Jesus said in answer to both
men in Matthew 19 and 22 were words taken from the Jewish
Bible, which Jesus was taught as a Jewish child and which he
embodied in life as a man. The answer in Matthew 19 is
from the Ten Commandments, Exodus 20 and Deuteronomy
5. The second answer, Matthew 22, is from the *Sh'mah*,
the affirmation of God's oneness which is the rallying cry of
Judaism: "Hear, O Israel, the Lord our God is one God;
and thou shalt love the Lord thy God with all thy heart, and
with all thy soul and with all thy might" (Deuteronomy 6:4);
and from Leviticus 19:18, "But thou shalt love thy neighbor
as thyself, I am the Lord."

These great commandments from the Jewish Bible quoted
by Jesus express the overarching and undergirding unity
which binds Christians and Jews together as brothers in the
Fatherhood of God in spite of our differences in creed,
rituals, and traditions. They challenge us to explore within
ourselves and to bring into active living on every level of our
relation to God and to our fellow men those qualities of
character and soul which, if really expressed in the lives of

Christians and Jews, could and would glorify God in the eyes of all the family of man.

> It hath been told thee, O man, what is good,
> And what the Lord doth require of thee,
> Only to do justly, to love mercy
> And to walk humbly with thy God.
>
> —Micha 6:8

What Are the Areas of Agreement between Jews and Christians?

Perhaps the best summary of the areas of agreement between most Christians and most Jews is embodied in a joint statement prepared by the British Council of Christians and Jews, an affiliate of the World Conference of Christians and Jews, which is an outgrowth of the National Conference of Christians and Jews organized in America in 1928. The statement, endorsed by Protestants, Catholics, and Jews, is as follows:

As Christians and Jews, while recognizing the important religious differences between us, we affirm on the basis of divine revelation that the dignity, rights and duties of man derive from his creation by God and his relation to God.

We acknowledge God as the Creator and Lord of the universe, and as the Father of all human beings: we see in their relation to God the bond which unites them, even amid division and conflict, and in Him the authority to which all are subject. Moreover, we find the basic motive for ethical conduct in man's response to God as He makes Himself known in His wisdom and goodness.

By the Will of God in creation man is both an individual and a member of society, so that both individuals and communities owe obedience to His rule. Moreover, there is true community only where there is full personal life, and vice versa.

Therefore:

We acknowledge the authority of the moral principles

which are implicit in the nature of man by virtue of his relation to God and of his qualities as a rational, moral and social being. From these it follows that it is the duty of men to respect in others the right to:

(1) Life. Since each human being is the child of God and has special value in His sight as an individual, his life must be respected and preserved. At the same time, he must similarly respect the life of his fellow man and is under obligation to promote his good.

(2) Liberty. The responsibility which falls upon man as a child and servant of God involves the necessity for freedom. He must therefore be given opportunity for the free exercise of the spiritual and moral powers entrusted to him. Life in organized society makes demands and entails restrictions upon the individual, but the fundamental principles of liberty alike for the individual and communities may never be sacrificed.

(3) Personal dignity. Each individual possesses worth as a person and must treat others as such, while other persons and the community must accord similar treatment to him. This principle involves recognition of his status as a member of society with a contribution to make to the whole, and is opposed to discrimination on grounds of color, race or creed.

We repudiate both the individualism which would make a man a law unto himself and the totalitarianism which would subordinate and sacrifice all other values to race, nation, state, class or party. Against the first, we claim that only as a man accepts himself from God and all his life as under God can he truly live. Against the second, we affirm that all human institutions stand under God's rule and judgment and none may usurp the loyalty which is due to Him alone.

Rights are exercised and duties discharged in a world which includes things as well as persons. Here we would maintain the followng principles:

(1) Things must be subordinated to persons, and the property rights should always be secondary to considerations of human welfare and social justice.

(2) Nature is to be respected and not merely exploited. It is a revelation of God and a sphere of His purpose: man may not squander its bounty and must show due regard for its beauty.

The right attitude of a community to its members, of persons to persons, and of persons to things, cannot be fully achieved without the recognition, alike by the individual and by the community, of God and of the relation of man and nature to him." (Fundamental postulates of *Christianity and Judaism in Relation to the Human Order*.)

Does the Recognition of the Common Elements in All Great Religions Imply Indifferentism?

There is a fear among some religious individuals and churches that to participate in interfaith cooperation may give the impression that one faith is as good as another and may thereby develop an attitude often referred to as "indifferentism." There is, undoubtedly, a basis for this apprehension. Unthinking people may draw unwarranted inferences from such interfaith relationships. But the danger of such possible inferences is more than compensated by the increased understanding and good will interfaith activities often can accomplish. If such cooperation leads to better understanding between members of the diverse faiths and helps them realize that they are basically the children of one Father, and that it is the will of that Father that members of all faiths should live and work together to promote justice, peace, and brotherhood in the world; and if this interfaith cooperation helps them toward that goal by even so much as the proverbial hair's breadth, the possible risk of "indifferentism" is worth taking.

One can understand that when a religion claims to be the only true way to God it may be confusing to the members of that faith to discover that there are other paths leading to God's holy mountain. But if the members of that faith are taught that although there is only one God, the ways of worshipping Him may be many and diverse, there cannot be any serious danger that indifferentism will result. This very problem was presented to a medieval Jewish philosopher in the question: "If there is only one God why are there so many religions?" to which the rabbi replied: "God is One, but his children because of their diversity in race, language, culture and tradition see the reflection of God's glory in their own unique and diverse ways."

This is the basic attitude of Judaism voiced by a great rabbi nearly two thousand years ago when he said: "The righteous among all people shall have a share in the world to come." The Talmud amplifies and substantiates this attitude in the following dicta:

The just among the Gentiles are priests of God.

Deeds of mercy are the Gentiles' offering reconciling them with God.

When God created Adam He took earth from the site of the Sanctuary, and from the four corners of the earth, and breathed into his nostrils the breath of life. Hence all men are equal in the sight of God.

These statements from the Talmud and the basic Jewish attitude of tolerance and respect for other faiths do not imply that Judaism regards all faiths as equal in the sense that they are on the same spiritual level. Judaism recognizes that there are degrees of spiritual maturity in the diverse religious creeds and ways of worship. Some are of a higher, others of a lower order of spiritual insight and understanding of God. By his cooperation with other faiths the Jew does not say that your religion is as good as his. *He does say that your religion, if it helps you to know and love God and your fellow men, can do for you what his religion does for him, not necessarily in a better or worse way, but in a different way, because your background and training makes your religious needs different from his, and therefore your way of finding religious satisfaction is different from his.*

This is a recognition of a basic psychological fact. People are different; they see things from different points of view. It is these differences which make for religious diversity. If God had intended us to worship Him in a uniform manner He would have created us in one mental pattern. But in His infinite wisdom He created us with the capacity to develop diverse patterns of life and thought, insights and behavior.

This capacity to be different is the very glory of our manhood. That is why I have no fears of "indifferentism" because of interfaith cooperation. I see in it only the potentials of a greater understanding and respect for the other man's faith while cherishing my own. As our Jewish prayerbook states: "Almighty and merciful God. Thou hast called Israel to Thy service and found him worthy to bear witness unto Thy truth among the peoples of earth. Give us grace to fulfill this mission with zeal tempered by wisdom and guided by regard for other men's faith" (*Union Prayerbook*, Vol. I, newly revised edition, p. 34).

THE RABBI AND THE BISHOP: WHERE JEWS AND CHRISTIANS AGREE AND DIFFER

THE RABBI: Bishop, the more I study our two religions, the more I am convinced that the things that unite us as Jews and Christians are much more significant than the things that divide us. I recall an experience during my ministry in England which I cherish. A dear friend, a Christian minister, in appreciation of our friendship and mutual regard, once said to me, "Levine, you are a real Christian." I was deeply touched by his tribute and I replied, "P——, you have a Jewish heart." That exchange of mutual respect and understanding goes to the heart of the fundamental unity of our two faiths. The quality of life expressed in the phrases "real Christian" and "Jew at heart" I think is essentially the same.

THE BISHOP: In a sense you are right, Rabbi. A great Pope said, speaking to Christians, that we must remember, "we are all spiritually Semites." By which he meant no doubt many things; but certainly this, that Christians share a common inheritance with their Jewish brothers which is a determining and commanding element in Christianity. A passionate loyalty to God Whose will is known and to be obeyed; a certainty that history is a sure theater of God's provident action; an assurance that God takes the initiative in human affairs—that He reigns on earth as in heaven; a granite faith in the reality of human freedom under God and of human responsibility to God for one's brother man —these are some of the imperative elements in our blood, Jew and Christian together, and they are ties which bind us together far more than we realize. But there are differences, differences that are deep, maybe not in essence but certainly in emphasis. I am afraid, Rabbi, that there are many theological bones in Christianity which as a Jew you wouldn't be able to digest.

THE RABBI: I agree. For example the doctrine of the Trinity. As a Jew reared in the traditions of the *Sh'mah* which has become the watchword of our faith: "Hear, O Israel, the Lord our God, the Lord is One," I find it difficult to understand the Christian conception of the Triune God.

THE BISHOP: You are not the only one. We Christians do not pretend fully to understand the mystery either. However, we try to explain it by saying that it represents God in three persons. Early Christian theologians borrowed the word "person" from the Greek word *persona*, which means a mask and describes the masks used by ancient Greek actors to depict the various emotion and roles they played. Thus tragedy was depicted by the actor wearing a sad-faced mask, comedy and joy by a comic mask. The doctrine of the Trinity tries to describe God in three aspects or roles. God the Father describes God as the creator of the universe; God the Holy Ghost describes His activity in the universe, His all-pervading spirit; God the son describes an aspect of Him which human beings can best understand, God in the form of a human being, in the Christ.

However, to speak of these activities of God as "roles" or "parts" which God plays is not fair to the doctrine of the Trinity; for this would imply that the Father, the Son, and the Holy Spirit were really only one mind, or being, doing different things. Yet, on the other hand, to say that the three are really three separate Gods would make Christians polytheists, which of course we aren't and couldn't be. So, in trying to borrow or coin words to describe our beliefs, Christians had to make the words carry new meanings. The "person" of God the Father is as much separated from the Son as, say, a man as an author is separate from the same man as a husband, or the hero of a great novel is separate from the man who writes it. The "Deity" or "Godhead" is one—the centers of thought and consciousness and purpose are three. Does this help?

THE RABBI: Yes, but I see what you mean by the theological bones which as a Jew I would find difficult to digest. To us Jews God is one and indivisible. To be sure God has many attributes; He plays many roles as we see His power and His love manifested in the universe, in our human life and history. The finite human mind catches glimpses of only a small portion of the attributes or "roles" of God. But we do not personify them. For us Jews any personification of the attributes or "roles" of God, even in the sense you describe would be a limitation upon His Oneness. That is one of the theological differences that separates us.

THE BISHOP: There is another even more difficult one, I fear, for you as a Jew to digest, the doctrine of salvation through Christ.

THE RABBI: I'm glad you mentioned it because this is one of the Christian dogmas which Jews find very difficult to understand. What do Christians mean by "salvation through Christ"?

THE BISHOP: That is a very complicated problem. And I suppose that not all Christians would answer it the same way; but substantially I think most Christians would agree. The Christian goes back, as you know, to your own Jewish Bible, to the story of creation and the fall of man. Adam and Eve, the first man and woman, were created by God perfect in their innocence and goodness. They were also endowed by God with the divine gift of freedom, a glorious but very dangerous gift. For freedom implies the freedom to choose the evil as well as the good. It also implies the acceptance of responsibility for one's choice. Adam and Eve misused that freedom. They ate from the fruit of the tree of knowledge which God had forbidden them to touch. They disobeyed God. As a result, they fell from the state of grace and innocence in which they had been created. And since then, all their descendents, all human beings are tainted with that original sin.

But, Rabbi, it is not quite so simple as I stated it. Most Christians probably would not accept the story of the Garden of Eden as literal, historical truth. They would understand it—no doubt as Jews do too—as a story symbolizing a basic human predicament, the problem of Man's persistent misuse of the freedom God gave him. St. Paul stated it when he said "that good which I would I do not; the evil which I wouldn't I do."

I am sure you have experienced or have seen this kind of inner conflict going on in all of us—this struggle between what we are and what we ought to be—this seemingly irresistible and inevitable compulsion to sin. St. Paul was confronted with this conflict in himself. He also saw it in others. And in spite of the Torah, the Jewish moral and ethical disciplines which he knew and tried to live by, he couldn't resolve this conflict. That is why he was driven to seek a solution in a power outside himself—in the supernatural power of God—which he found in the sacrifice which God made out of His love for man by allowing Himself, in the person of Christ, to die on the cross as the great atonement by which man might be freed from the taint of the original sin; in a word, to give man a chance to start clean all over again, to begin a new kind of manhood personified in Christ. That is what Christians mean by "salvation through Christ" and that "Christ died for our sins." When a person becomes a Christian—not merely accepts Christ with his lips, but surrenders his life to Christ, tries to live the Christlike life, loving God and his fellow men as Jesus said—then God's promise of salvation is fulfilled in and for that person.

THE RABBI: We Jews, too, recognize this inner conflict between what we are and what we ought to be. But Judaism explains it differently and solves it differently. Judaism rejects the doctrine of "original sin." We do not believe that the sin of Adam and Eve put an ineradicable taint in all human beings after them, from which the individual cannot free himself. Every human being, because of his great and dangerous gift of freedom, as you put it, is born with the capacity to learn to choose between good and evil. Man, say the rabbis, is born with a *yetzer Tov,* an inclination to good, and a *yetzer Ra,* an inclination to evil. But he is also given the power by God to suppress the one by developing the other.

Here, Bishop, I think is the basic difference between

Christianity and Judaism in their evaluation of man. We do not believe that man was created perfect and fell from grace. The rabbis were struck by the fact that in the story of creation in the Book of Genesis, after every act of creation the Bible says "and God saw that it was good," but after man was created the phrase, "and it was good" was omitted. They wondered why, and this was their explanation. All nature was created perfect and complete—each thing after its kind—each creature according to its nature. Only man was left unfinished; but above all other creatures man was endowed with the power to improve and perfect himself. He was made in the image of God; that is, he was endowed with a portion of God's own creative power which God intended him to use to perfect himself.

That is why God gave man moral freedom, freedom to make moral choices. Without such freedom man's moral and spiritual strivings and achievements would have no meaning or value. But freedom can be dangerous if misused. So God gave man the Torah, His revealed will in the Ten Commandments, in the teachings of the prophets, in the commandment to "love his neighbor as himself," in all the moral, ethical, and spiritual disciplines which flow from God's revealed will; and it is man's responsibility to live by the will of God—and if he does he attains that self-fulfillment as a child of God which Jews understand by the word "salvation." I think we Jews are more optimistic about man and his future here on earth than you Christians are.

THE BISHOP: I think you are right. We are frankly more pessimistic about man's capacities for perfection than you are. We cannot escape the tragic dilemma of the human conflict as we Christians see it. The best human intentions go astray. The best of God's gifts are misused. The old devil in us—what St. Paul called "the old Adam"—refuses to die in spite of everything we do.

St. Augustine has defined it as a "defect of will," the impotence of man to free himself from this devil in us. That is why we Christians feel compelled to seek a solution in the supernatural power and love of God. That is why we see in Christ's agony and death our redemption and our salvation.

THE RABBI: I must confess that it is difficult for me to understand how Christ's agony and death free man from this "defect of will," from the dilemma of the human conflict.

THE BISHOP: You have touched on a fundamental difference between the Christian and the Jewish attitudes toward man's relation with God, perhaps the most basic difference of all, and a most difficult one to explain. The author of St. John's Gospel says, "The law was given by Moses but grace and truth came through Jesus Christ." I may begin by saying that to the Christian "grace" means the power which God's love gives man, like the confidence one friend gives another except it is infinitely greater. This love of God was demonstrated dramatically in the sacrifice which He made as the Christ in atonement for our sins. Since we feel secure through our faith in God's love through Christ's sacrifice for us, we believe that through faith in Christ, we can rise above the tensions, anxieties, and frustrations of earthly life and imperfect human relationships. This faith and the security that comes from it, we believe, give the Christian a power to live in a way which those who do not possess that faith can never know.

Perhaps I ought to add that Christians feel that God is so infinitely closer to us than even an intimate friend or husband or wife could be, that the loving grace of God expresses itself in a real, although mystical, unity with Him. Even a devoted husband and wife are two separate people. But the God in Whom we live and move and have our being is not so separated from us (except by our own wills); and grace is then—at least potentially—more close in us and a part of us then even the deepest human love could be.

THE RABBI: I can see how the possession of faith in God, or in Christ as you put it, can give a person that security which is a release of power within us. But it must be a faith possessed, not a belief professed. There is a vast difference between believing in God and professing to believe in Him. It was Jesus Himself who said, "Not everyone who says to me, 'Lord, Lord,' shall enter the kingdom of heaven, but who does the will of my Father in heaven" (Matthew 7:21). To say that one has faith in Christ is not enough, is it? One must demonstrate it by one's every thought and word and deed. Our possession of faith and of the grace of God can be known only by the fruit we produce, by the kind of life we live. If that is true, Bishop, I see little difference in the quality of life expressed by a Christian who has the "grace of God" and the quality of life of the Jew who lives by the Torah, the divine discipline which is so often misinterpreted as law.

St. John's interpretation of Torah as law is entirely misleading. Torah, as we Jews understand it, is much more than laws and statutes. It is the embodiment of the word of God, the expression of the Divine Will for mankind. It is the law of God in the hearts of men; as the Prophet Jeremiah expressed it: "I shall put My law (Torah) into their inward parts; and in their hearts will I write it" (Jeremiah 31:33). And every Jew who lives by the Torah is a person whose life is an expression of the love of God and of his fellow men. Such a Jew has faith and grace and power.

THE BISHOP: I would go along with that, Rabbi. But we Christians believe that faith and grace and power can come to us not through our own efforts, however heroic and dedicated, and disciplined even by your conception of Torah, but through God's initiative and His supernatural power. We Christians cannot escape our diagnosis of the human situation; and what we see of human nature and man's misuse of his freedom makes us pessimistic about his capacities for self-perfection. I admit that we Christians do not have the same faith in man alone as you Jews, certainly not in his capacity to build God's kingdom on earth.

THE RABBI: We Jews do have faith in man's capacity to build a world of justice, freedom, love, and brotherhood, which we call God's kingdom on earth. *But not by himself. He does need the help and guidance of God*; and we believe that he gets both through Torah. The man who lives by Torah does not rely upon his own unaided human power.

He lives according to God's will. He ceases to be self-centered and lives a God-centered life, even as you say the Christian does who possesses power through the grace of God. But here is the difference. The Christian lives the God-centered and God-directed life only as God gives him "grace" to do so, through his faith in Christ. The initiative is entirely with God. Man himself cannot exercise his will to attain "grace." He can only receive it as a free gift from God.

Judaism teaches us that man can and must exercise his will in order to live by Torah—the God-guided life. Man, say the rabbis, is co-worker with God. He is God's partner in the creative process, at least in the creation of his own character, in the fulfillment of his potentials as a human being created in God's image.

God gives us our life, our body, mind and heart. He gives us the measureless resources of the universe to work with. He gives us teachers to guide us, and the Torah to live by. Also, he has given us freedom to choose between good and evil. "I set before you this day life and good, death and evil, in that I command you this day to love the Lord your God, to walk in His ways . . . I call heaven and earth to witness that I have set before you this day life and death, the blessing and the curse; therefore choose life" (Deuteronomy 30:15-19). That is God's part in this divine-human enterprise, and in this God has and still does exercise the initiative. Man's part is to accept the responsibilities implicit in his moral freedom and to choose God's way and to live by it.

This acceptance of responsibility man must do for himself. God cannot do it for him. "Everything is ordained by God," say the rabbis, "except the fear of God." God does help those who try to help themselves. God is always present, and everywhere; but men must make the effort to make contact. The relation between God and man as Judaism sees it is a two-way street—it is an interrelatedness—in which the initiative is both with God and man. In the beginning of creation the initiative was all with God. But once man was created and was given freedom, the relationship between God and man became a partnership, with God the senior partner to be sure.

THE BISHOP: Let me interrupt a moment, Rabbi. One of the things which confuses me about Jewish-Christian relationships is what you have just said. I think a Christian would agree with every word you have spoken. Certainly I would —the gift of freedom, the privilege of partnership with God, even the Torah—Jews don't have any monopoly on those things. After all, St. Paul said, "The law is holy, and the commandment holy, and just, and good." And Jesus said, "Think not that I am come to destroy the law, or the prophets; I am not come to destroy, but to fulfill."

The differences between us are not in any lack of respect among Christians for God's law or for human freedom and responsibility to work together with God. These things are shared by Jews and Christians alike. The differences between us, I think, lie chiefly in two areas we have only touched on briefly.

One area is the relative importance each of us attaches to *this* world and to *this* history. Both of us agree that God created this universe, and that it is good, and that man has the most serious responsibilities to live in it and use it as a child of God should. But we differ, I think, in what the ultimate future will be. You said to me one time, "Judaism is optimistic about man's future on earth."

THE RABBI: I did, because man was created in the image of God; because God gave him a portion of His own creative power and the freedom to use it; because God *is*; all may not be right with the world, as Browning said, but Judaism believes all will *become* right with the world. That is also why we Jews seem to emphasize life here on earth.

THE BISHOP: I think this may be characteristic of Judaism, Rabbi. But Christians do not feel that God's will can or will ever be perfectly expressed on earth. The kingdom of God, as we understand it, can only come after history is done, outside this creation—at least in any final sense. Therefore, we are less optimistic than Jews are about the possibility of an earthly paradise.

More than that, Christians frankly do not believe that

man can hoist himself by his own bootstraps. To keep God's law is a duty for us as for you. But the danger of a false complacency, of self-righteousness, of self-deception and a misuse of our freedom which turns even man's best acts into something hateful and destructive—this danger, which is the danger of what Christians call "pride," is so great that we frankly do not feel that man alone can overcome it.

Christ said to us once, "When you have done all that is required of you, then say 'I am an unprofitable servant.'" This means, to us, not that we should not keep Torah, but that, when we have kept it, we should still recognize that God alone is good, and that whatever hope there may be for mankind must lie in God and not in us. Are not these differences the really significant ones?

THE RABBI: Not really, Bishop, Judaism recognizes that perfection is only with God; that man can only approximate the Godlike life, never achieve the perfection of the Divine. Nor does the Jew think that man by making the effort to live the good life and even succeeding need necessarily grow proud and arrogant because of his achievement. Indeed the sin of "pride" is as abhorrent to the Jew as to the Christian. The Prophet Micah stresses as one of the three greatest virtues "to walk humbly with God."

At every Sabbath Service we say, "Lord of all worlds, not in reliance upon our own merit do we lay our supplications before Thee, but trusting in Thine infinite mercy alone. For what are we, what is our life, what our goodness, what our power?"

The difference between us is not in our attitude towards pride and humility, but in our *emphasis* upon man's capacity for exploring within himself and developing the qualities of soul and spirit which reflect his kinship with God.

We Jews do not believe that "man can hoist himself by his own bootstraps." We believe that he needs the help of God, and we believe that God is ever present, "nearer to us than breathing and closer than hands and feet" as Tennyson said, but only those whose hearts are open can experience that Presence and be strengthened by it. God has already taken the initiative in human affairs. After all, He created us. But while to be sure man cannot "hoist himself by his own bootstraps," he can make the initial effort. He can at least have a desire to know God, And if he has that desire he has already taken the first step and from then on God is always by his side. The rabbis put it in this way, "God says, 'open the door of repentance if only the width of the eye of a needle, and I will open it for you wide enough for a wagon to pass through!' "

As for our emphasis upon God's kingdom on earth, it does not mean that we Jews believe that God's kingdom ends on earth, nor does our life end here. We believe in immortality. The fact is, as you know, the concept of life after death so important in Christianity was derived from Judaism. We Jews believe in life after death. But what happens to us after death we do not know, nor does the best Jewish tradition try to imagine or to describe it.

All we know is that in God's world there is the fullness of life, and His world encompasses *not merely the physical universe and life on earth but all eternity*. So we leave the immortal future to God's mercy and love. But what happens to us here on earth is something over which Judaism teaches us that we have a large measure of control. That's the real difference between us, as I see it.

Actually it is a difference in our interpretation of man's relation to God, a difference in judgment as to how man lives, grows, develops his potentials as a human being created in the image of God. It is a difference of understanding as to how a human being develops character and achieves fulfillment—whether it comes to him as a gift of God or whether he can participate creatively in becoming the kind of person God wants him to be.

THE BISHOP: Perhaps that is where our paths diverge. It is a matter of interpretation and emphasis. That is why conversation—the meeting and sharing of people together—is so important in reaching understanding. Understanding can never be built on either arrogance or soft-headedness. Christ, speaking to Christians out of the Judaism into which He came, really can teach us both, if we will only respect our differences, talk together about them, recognize them honestly and clearly, and let God guide our thoughts so that in the end both sides are richer because of having known the other. To stay smugly within our own walls will lead to nothing but emptiness and pride. But to differ, honestly, and then to talk together about our differences; and then to ask God to lead us to learn what the differences have to teach each one of us—this is the way of understanding and brotherhood.

THE RABBI: It is indeed—the only way. My path to God through Judaism is the best for me, born and reared as I have been in the tradition of Jewish faith and practice. It is the religious pattern through which I can express what is deepest and best in me as a child of God. It may not be the best for you, Bishop, or for members of your Church reared in the tradition of historic Christian faith and practice. Indeed, even within the framework of Christianity itself there are many diverse paths to God.

I believe that diversity of religious faith and practice is inherent in the very nature of human life. Even in experiences that can be verified objectively different people interpret them differently. Witness the conflicting testimony of people who see the same traffic accident. If differences of interpretation can rise out of people seeing the same physical situation and fact, how much more diverse are the possibilities of interpretation of such an intimately personal experience as man's endeavor to understand and to experience the unfathomable majesty and mystery of God!

For any religion to claim an exclusive knowledge of God and man's relation to Him is, in my opinion, to limit the majesty and greatness of God, not to glorify Him. If God had intended that all His children should seek Him by one and the same path He would have made us all of one mold, thinking the same, feeling the same, doing the same. But He didn't. He made us in His image—each a unique personality reflecting in our diverse theologies like a diamond reflects the colors of the rainbow in the sunlight, fleeting glimpses of His infinite and incomprehensible Personality.

THE BISHOP: I like the way you expressed what we have tried to do in this dialogue. It has been our hope that unprejudiced people reading it might come to a better understanding of our two great faiths, which have molded the spiritual life of our world and so immeasureably enriched it —what we call our Judeo-Christian tradition, both in its fundamental differences and its even more meaningful unity. I sincerely hope that in this talking together many others—both Jews and Christians—who will share our conversation through this discussion will come to a more genuine respect for one another's faith and a recognition of the common quest for the life God intended for us.

I hope none of our readers will get the impression that we are comparing our two faiths to determine superiority of the one over the other. Our only purpose, as I see it, is to bring knowledge where there has been ignorance; understanding where there has been prejudice; respect where too often there has been tolerant contempt. It was our Lord and Master, Jesus, born in the tradition of Judaism, who said, "Ye shall know the truth; and the truth shall make you free." I hope that we have helped to bring a little more of truth about Judaism to Christians and to Jews about Christianity; and, through this better understanding between us, helped us both, Christian and Jew, to live and work together in the spirit of the brotherhood God intended for us.

THE RABBI: I say a fervent "amen" to that.

Appendix A: A Space Ship's View of Jews in America

> Give me your tired, your poor,
> Your huddled masses yearning to breathe free, . . .
> Send these, the homeless, tempest tost to me,
> I lift my lamp beside the golden door.
> —Emma Lazarus (inscription on the
> Statue of Liberty)

THE SETTLEMENT OF the Jews in America follows the pattern of Jewish migration established by them in ancient times when Abraham, the first ancestor of the Hebrews, left his native city of Ur in the Chaldees in quest of a better way of life impelled by the will of his invisible God. Early in their history Jews ventured across perilous seas and into the far corners of the then known world to establish their spiritual and commercial centers. Their migrations were motivated by many drives. Among them were the spirit of adventure, creative urge to build in virgin fields, the flight from presecution, and the quest for freedom of conscience and freedom of opportunity.

These motivations stimulated the earliest Jewish arrivals to the new world; and they came with Columbus. Records of Columbus' voyages of discovery list among his associates a number of Marrano Jews (Jews forced into Christianity by the Spanish Church) including Roderigo de Triana, Alonso de la Roderigo Sanchez, and Luis de Torres, the interpreter. Luis de Torres was the first white man to set foot on American soil.

Before the Pilgrims landed on Plymouth Rock, Jews settled in the Western Hemisphere in Spanish America, fleeing from the Spanish and Portugese Inquisition and seeking to worship their God in freedom. The earliest records we have of Jewish settlement in what is now the United States tells of Elias Lagado in Virginia in 1621, Mathias de Sousa in Maryland in 1634, and Jacob Barsimeon in New Amsterdam (New York) in 1654. In that same year a group of twenty-three

Dutch Jews from Recife (Pernambuco), fleeing from the Inquisition which the Portuguese instituted when they conquered that Dutch colony, arrived in New Amsterdam and sought refuge from Governor Peter Stuyvesant. He refused. But upon the insistence of the Dutch West India Company he grudgingly agreed to allow them to land on condition that the "poor among them shall be supported by their own people." To this the refugees gladly agreed; and how well they carried out their promise is attested by the great philanthropic institutions which the Jews of New York pioneered and which have become the pattern of social service throughout the country during the nineteenth and twentieth centuries.

At first the tiny Jewish community of New Amsterdam was not permitted to build any synagogue nor to make themselves felt as a religious community. They were allowed, however, to worship in private homes. In 1728 the community grew large enough, and encouraged by the more tolerant rule of the British, who conquered the colony, the Jews of New York, as it came to be known, erected the first synagogue building in the colonies in 1728. A second group of Jews came to Newport, Rhode Island, in 1657 and built their synagogue which is still standing and has recently been made a national shrine. Jews settled in Philadelphia in 1703 and established their first congregation in 1745. In Savannah, Georgia, Jews came in 1732 and built a synagogue two years later. One of the Savannah Jews, David Emanuel, became the governor of Georgia in 1801, the first Jew of a long line who since then served with distinction in the civic life of their respective communities and on the national scene whenever they were given the opportunity. Charleston, South Carolina was the fifth Jewish settlement in 1741.

From the eastern seaboard, Jews together with other American pioneers followed in the wake of the explorers, pushing westward across the uncharted wilderness to build our American civilization out of the virgin forest. They were among the earliest pioneers who blazed trails to the Pacific coast. They were with the forty-niners in California. They were among the first white men to pierce the wilds of the Pacific Northwest. Wherever they went they brought with them the refinements of civilization to the rough pioneer camps in their pedlar's packs. Their general stores grew into many of the large mercantile establishments in which America today takes such legitimate pride. Side by side with their non-Jewish neighbors the Jews worked to build their small communities into the flourishing cities of today. They accepted their share of all civic responsibilities wherever and whenever they were given the opportunity. They served on city councils. They became city and state executives. They helped to establish chambers of commerce. They were pioneers in the establishment of community social agencies and community fund-raising programs. They served, some with distinction, as national legislators, as jurists, as diplomats, as soldiers and officers in every war from the War of Independence and throughout American history. Their part in the educational life in America is a most honorable one, producing Nobel Prize winners in many fields and pioneering in the advancement of science, technology, and medicine.

To make a roll of honor of Jews who made outstanding individual contributions to the upbuilding of America would take more space than this space ship's view would permit. But a few names stand out in such bold relief against the background of our country's growth that they must be mentioned. Among them are Judah Touro who was born in Newport, Rhode Island, in 1775, the son of a rabbi. His contribution to the early economic life of America is so significant and his philanthrophies so outstanding that his name has come down among the great in American history. The Newport synagogue was subsequently named after him and was made a national shrine by our federal government.

Hayum Solomon is another worthy of mention. It was his personal financial sacrifice which helped save the Continental Army in its darkest hour. It is estimated that Solomon, whose official title was Broker to the Office of Finance, gave $200,000 of his own money to the cause of the American Revolution. He died penniless. His descendants have never been reimbursed although Congressional Committees have investigated their claims and recommended repayment.

Uriah P. Levy, a commodore of the United States Navy in the War of 1812, was responsible for the law abolishing corporal punishment in the U. S. Navy. During the Civil War

Jews fought on both sides together with their non-Jewish fellow citizens. The vice president of the Confederacy was Judah P. Benjamin.

In the development of industry and commerce the name of Julius Rosenwald, guiding genius behind the gigantic Sears, Roebuck organization, is outstanding. He used the millions he accumulated to establish the Rosenwald Foundation for the education and uplift of the Negroes in this country. Another name that comes easily to mind is that of David Lubin, an immigrant from Poland, who devoted his life to aiding farmers both in this country and throughout the world.

In the entertainment world the unparalleled role which Jews have played is universally recognized. Such names as Al Jolson, Eddie Cantor, George Jessel, David Belasco, Oscar Hammerstein, Irving Berlin, Yehudi Menuhin, Jascha Heifetz, Arthur Rubinstein, George Gershwin, and many more, which movie, radio, and television fans and concert goers could easily mention, have become part of America's entertainment vocabulary.

In the field of jurisprudence the names of three Jews stand out among the great of the American Bench and Bar. One is Justice Louis D. Brandeis who with Justice Holmes did more than any other men since Justice Marshall to shape the character of American law. Justice Cardozo of the Supreme Court and Justice Felix Frankfurter are the two others.

The American labor movement owes an immeasurable debt to Samuel Gompers who founded and was the first president of the American Federation of Labor. Others who rank high among labor's statesmen during the present century are David Dubinsky and Sidney Hillman, whose leadership of the International Ladies' Garment Workers has established patterns which other labor unions have since adopted.

Among the immortals of the American press the name of Joseph Pulitzer holds a unique place in Journalism's Hall of Fame. The Pulitzer Prize which he established has become the hallmark for outstanding achievement in the field of journalism, literature, and allied arts. Another name to conjure with is that of Adolph Ochs, until his death publisher of the New York *Times*, universally recognized as one of the world's greatest newspapers.

But a mere catalogue of great Jewish names cannot adequately indicate the impact which the Jew and Judaism have had upon the upbuilding of our country. Indeed the very foundations of our American Way were undergirded by the ideals and values which Judaism first conceived and proclaimed and which through Christianity spread in all the world. The Judeo-Christian tradition is the very heart and soul of the American Dream. It is not mere rhetoric which the non-Jewish historian Lecky used when he said: "Hebraic mortar cemented the foundations of American Democracy."

It is a matter of common knowledge how much the founding fathers of our country drew for their inspiration upon the Jewish Bible. The Puritans who came to Plymouth in 1620 patterned their new commonwealth upon the commonwealth of ancient Judea. The code of the Plymouth Colony established in 1636 stated that:

It was the great privilege of Israel of old and so was acknowledged by them, Nehemiah 9th and 10th, that God gave them right judgments and true Lawes. They are for they mayne so exemplary, being grounded on principles of moral equitie as that all Christians especially ought always to have an eye thereunto into the framing of their politique constitutions. We can safely say both for ourselves and for them that we have had an eye principally unto the aforesaid platforme in the framing of this small bodies of lawes.

In seeking a fitting inscription for the Liberty Bell a verse was taken from the Jewish Bible, Leviticus 25:10: "Proclaim liberty throughout the land unto all the inhabitants thereof."

Since those early days the basic ideals of the Juedo-Christian tradition have been woven into the pattern of our American institutions. We are deeply conscious that it is under God that our country has become great among the nations of the world; and it is with the guidance of God that our country will continue great, fulfilling its destiny into the unforseen future.

Appendix B: Important Events in Jewish History

> When thou passeth through the waters,
>   I will be with thee,
> And through the rivers, they shall not overflow thee...
> For I am the Lord thy God,
> The Holy one of Israel, thy Savior. . . .
>
> —Isaiah 43:2-3

B.C.E. *is Before the Christian Era.*

C.E. *is Christian Era (our modern reckoning).*

Most of the B.C.E. *dates are approximate.*

1800 B.C.E.—Abraham leaves Ur in the Chaldees to migrate to Canaan (*see* Genesis 12).

1600 B.C.E.—The Hebrew clans enter Egypt. Story of Joseph and his brethren.

1300-1220 B.C.E.—Life and activity of Moses; the exodus from Egypt; giving of the Ten Commandments and beginnings of Jewish religion under Moses.

1220-1050 B.C.E.—Conquest of Canaan; period of the Judges; stories of Samson, Gideon, Deborah, Jeptha, and so on.

1050-973 B.C.E.—Hebrew tribes united under Kings Saul and David. The prophet Samuel plays an important role during this period.

973-933 B.C.E.—The reign of King Solomon—a period of peace and prosperity, when the Temple is built in Jerusalem and the religion is centralized.

933 B.C.E.—Secession of the ten northern tribes; division of Palestine into two kingdoms, the Kingdom of Israel in the north and the Kingdom of Judah in the south.

887-851 B.C.E.—Period of Elijah, champion of *Yhvh*, against the encroachment of Baal worship under the influence of Jezebel, the Phoenician wife of Ahab. Elijah has become the great legendary hero of Jewish history believed to have been transported to heaven in a fiery chariot. In Jewish folklore Elijah is believed to roam the earth righting wrongs, helping the deserving in their need, and performing miracles when the occasion requires. He is also believed to be the one who will precede the *Messiah* and announce his coming.

750-400 B.C.E.—Period of Hebrew prophecy during which the literary prophets lived and preached and wrote their messages now contained in the Bible under their names. Their teaching was revolutionary in its concept of God and man's relation to Him. Their emphasis upon justice, righteousness, and love as the only way to worship God gave to the world much of its ethical and moral ideals and values. Their insistence that God was creator of the universe, father of all mankind, and director of the great movements in history gave us our ideas of monotheism, the belief in one God, and all the values that flow from that concept (*see* "What Is the Bible?").

750-730 B.C.E.—Amos and Hosea.

738-700 B.C.E.—Isaiah.

730-722 B.C.E.—Micha.

722 B.C.E.—Destruction of Samaria (capital of the northern kingdom) by the Assyrians. Influential people were deported and the country was colonized by non-Israelites who intermarried with the remaining inhabitants forming the Samaritan people, named for the capital, Samaria. The legend of the ten lost tribes began at this time. The tribes were not actually lost; only the important people had been exiled. The masses remained and became known as Samaritans, a remnant of whom still exists in Palestine.

625-580 B.C.E.—Jeremiah (early part of this period also Nahum, Zephaniah, Habakkuk).

597-580 B.C.E.—Ezekiel.

550-538 B.C.E.—Deutero-Isaiah (second Isaiah).

520 B.C.E.—Haggai and Zechariah, also Trito-Isaiah (third Isaiah: Isaiah 56-66).

460 B.C.E.—Malachi.

450 B.C.E.—Joel.

400 B.C.E.—Jonah.

586 B.C.E.—The kingdom of Judah conquered by the Babylonians. The Temple at Jerusalem is destroyed and the important people are exiled to Babylon, beginning the Baby-

Ionian exile which plays such a significant part in Jewish history.

538 B.C.E.—Jews, exiled to Babylonia, permitted to return to Palestine to rebuild their country. Permission granted by Cyrus the Great of Persia after he conquered Babylonia.

580-530 B.C.E.—Beginnings of the synagogue, meeting place for worship.

500-300 B.C.E.—Editorial revision of the Bible manuscripts and beginnings of the Bible arrangement.

300 B.C.E.—Beginning of Bible interpretation by the sages laying foundation for the Mishnah (*see Talmud*).

250 B.C.E.—Bible translated into Greek, The *Septuagint*.

168-165 B.C.E.—The Maccabean War, the first war for religious freedom. The Jews rebelled against an attempt to destroy their religion. Under the leadership of a priest, Mattathias and his sons, especially Judah, a successful war was fought against heavy odds culminating in Jewish independence and saving of Judaism. The *Hanukah* festival commemorates this event.

4 B.C.E.—Birth of Jesus of Nazareth.

27-30 C.E.—Activities of Jesus of Nazareth.

67-70 C.E.—War with Rome ending in the destruction of Jerusalem, the Temple, and the Jewish State. Beginning of the Diaspora, the dispersion of the Jews throughout the world.

60-80 C.E.—Activities of Saul (St. Paul) and the beginnings of Christianity.

132-135 C.E.—Ill-fated Bar Kokhba rebellion against Rome.

200 C.E.—Compilation of the *Mishnah* by Judah Ha Nasi (Judah the Prince), head of the Jewish community.

250-850 C.E.—Development of Jewish communities in Babylonia. It was during this period that great Talmudic schools were established and the *Talmud* was organized and completed about 500. The Babylonian Jewish communities took over the leadership in Jewish life after Palestinian Jewry had lost its leadership about 250 C.E. due to the growing power of Christianity and the restrictions imposed by the Church.

622 C.E.—Rise of Mohammedanism. The *Hegira*, flight of Mohammed from Mecca to Medina; beginning of the Moslem era.

767-900 C.E.—The Karaite Schism. During the eighth century a revolt against the rabbinic method of interpreting the Bible was inaugurated by a scholar, Anan ben David, in Babylonia. His followers founded the schismatic movement called *Karaism* from the Hebrew word *karah*, "to read." The Karaites insisted upon a literal interpretation of the Bible without the elaborate hermeneutic expedients to which the rabbis resorted in their endeavor to make the Bible applicable to the changing needs of Jewish life. The sect still survives, mostly in Egypt.

740-1016 C.E.—Kingdom of the *Khazars*, a pagan people living in the Crimea who were converted to Judaism. Their king, Bulan, invited Christian, Mohammedan, and Jewish teachers to explain their respective religions. He was impressed by the fact that both Christianity and Mohammedanism derived their inspiration from Judaism. So he adopted the Jewish faith and his people followed him. For nearly three hundred years this Jewish kingdom lived its isolated existence until it was conquered by the Muscovites and disappeared from history.

943-1030 C.E.—Decline of the Babylonian centers of Jewish life which had maintained world Jewish leadership for nearly eight hundred years. The decline was occasioned by the growing influence of the Jews of Spain and the turbulent world conditions which prevented the Babylonian schools from obtaining funds from the scattered Jewish communities of Europe.

900-1200 C.E.—Golden Age of Spanish Jewry; a period of tolerance under the Moors in Spain giving rise to a flourishing Jewish life. Great rabbis, poets, philosophers, merchants, and statesmen flourished during this period. Some of the outstanding among the Jews of this period were Hasdai Ibn Shaprut, Samuel Ibn Nagdela, Solomon Ibn Gabirol, Judah Halevi, and Abraham Ibn Ezra.

1040-1105 C.E.—Age of *Rashi*, Rabbi Solomon ben Isaac. *Rashi* is the abbreviation of his name made up of his initials. He lived in France and became the greatest Bible commentator of his age. His influence on Jewish thought and on the understanding of the Bible was so profound that to this day every Hebrew Bible is published with a *Rashi* commentary.

1135-1204 c.e.—Age of Maimonides, the greatest rabbi and philosopher of medieval Jewish life. He was a great physician also and exerted a profound influence upon Jewish, Moslem, and Christian thought.

1100-1700 c.e.—Period of darkness for European Jews. Persecutions, restrictions, and segregation marked this unhappy period.

1000-1300 c.e.—The Crusades with their persecutions and expulsions of Jews.

1290 c.e.—Jews expelled from England (readmitted in 1656 under Cromwell).

1349-1350 c.e.—The Black Death taking heavy toll among Europe's people. Jews blamed for Black Death and accused of poisoning the wells.

1450-1492 c.e.—Persecution of the *Marranos* in Spain. The *Marranos* were Jews who were forced into Christianity during the religious persecutions at the end of the fourteenth and the beginning of the fifteenth centuries. They continued to practice Judaism in secret and the Holy Inquisition was instituted largely to ferret out and punish these "heretics."

1492-1671 c.e.—Jews expelled from Spain. Some flee to Amsterdam. Age of Menasseh Ben Israel, famous Dutch Jewish scholar, who influenced Cromwell to permit the Jews to return to England, from which they had been expelled in 1290.

1400-1800 c.e.—Period of the ghetto. Jews segregated into separate quarters in many large cities, restricted in their movements and in their occupations.

1565 c.e.—Publication of the *Shulchan Arukh* (arranged table) by Joseph Caro. This monumental work is a complete codification of Jewish law, custom, and practice developed up to that time. This code is authoritative for all Orthodox Jews to this day.

1626-1676 c.e.—*Sabbatai Zevi*, a pseudo-Messiah, who misled thousands of Jews throughout Europe with his messianic pretensions. He was finally imprisoned by the Turks, and to save his life became a Mohammedan. Some of his followers also became converted and founded a Judeo-Mohammedan sect known as the *Donmeh*.

1632-1677 c.e.—Age of *Spinoza*, one of the greatest philosophers of all time. Baruch (Benedict) Spinoza was the son of a Marrano family that fled from Portugal in the first quarter of the seventeenth century. His philosophical system, a mystical pantheism equating God with the universe and the universe with God, has profoundly influenced all thought since his day.

1660-1797 C.E.—Rise of *Hasidism,* a Jewish religious movement emphasizing the emotional element in religion with stress on prayer, ecstasy in worship, and humility as the prime virtue. It was founded by Israel Baal Shem Tov (*see Hasidism*).

1776 C.E.—Declaration of American Independence.

1806 C.E.—Napoleon Bonaparte called Jewish leaders of France to a meeting. He promised the Jews equal civil and political rights if they would pledge undivided allegiance to France—if they regard themselves in all respects as Frenchmen, differing from their fellow citizens only in religion. Beginning of modern nationalism; also of Jewish emancipation from the ghettoes and their entrance into the modern world.

1801-1811 C.E.—Beginning of the Reform movement in Judaism. Inspired by the emancipation edict of Bonaparte, Jews entered the world and began to feel the need of adapting their religious life to the new circumstances. Israel Jacobson, a German Jewish merchant, began the movement by establishing a school on modern lines in Westphalia and also by introducing certain reforms in the synagogue worship, such as sermons in German, German hymns, and confirmation for boys and girls.

1814 C.E.—The Hamburg Temple organized as the first Reform congregation.

1815-1855 C.E.—*Haskalah* (enlightenment), a literary renaissance in Poland and Russia which revived Hebrew as a spoken and written language and also emphasized secular scholarship at a time when religious studies were the chief and often the only subjects taught in Jewish schools.

1894 C.E.—The infamous Dreyfus trial in France. Dreyfus, a Jewish army captain, falsely accused of betraying his country. Much anti-Jewish feeling aroused. Theodore Herzl, deeply chagrined at the growth of anti-Semitism, wrote his *Jewish State* as a solution to the Jewish problem.

1896 C.E.—The first Zionist Congress called by Herzl, at Basle, Switzerland. The Zionist movement was organized with the objective of securing Palestine as the legally recognized homeland of the Jewish people.

1914-1918 C.E.—World War I.

1917 C.E.—Bolshevist Revolution in Russia, beginning of Soviet Communism.

1917 C.E.—Balfour Declaration issued by Great Britain, saying that Britain looks with favor upon the establishment in Palestine of a Jewish national home.

1922 C.E.—Britain given mandate over Palestine to implement Balfour Declaration.

1922-1929 C.E.—Large-scale immigration of Jews from Europe to Palestine.

1923 C.E.—Nazi party founded by Hitler.

1932 C.E.—Hitler "elected" chancellor of Germany. Rise of Nazism and beginnings of Jewish persecution, which ended with the expulsion of Jews from Germany by 1939.

1939 C.E.—Beginning of World War II; also the systematic destruction of Jews in the Nazi invaded countries until six million were put to death in concentration camps, gas chambers, and crematoria by 1945.

1945 C.E.—Hitler and Nazism destroyed in Germany by the victorious United Nations.

1948 C.E.—Israel's independence recognized and war between Israel and Arab States.

1949 C.E.—Israel a member of the United Nations.

1949-1962—More than one million Jewish immigrants settled in Israel.

1956—Sinai campaign, in which Israel, Britain, and France invaded Egypt to redress the seizure of the Suez Canal and the interference by Egypt of shipping through that great waterway contrary to treaty agreements. The invasion was stopped by the pressure of the United States and the United Nations.

1961—The Eichmann trial in Jerusalem, which focused

world attention on Adolph Eichmann, Hitler's appointee to preside over the destruction of the Jews of Europe. Eichmann was found guilty of masterminding the program by which six million Jews were destroyed in concentration camps, gas chambers and crematoria from 1940 to 1945.

Appendix C: Important Events in American Jewish History

1492 C.E.—Discovery of America by Columbus in the same year the Jews are expelled from Spain. Jews help Columbus. Several Marranos (Jews who adopted Christianity under compulsion) played an important part: Luis de Santangel, chancellor of the royal household; Gabriel Sanchez, treasurer of Aragon; Luis de Torres, an interpreter; and Rodrigo de Triana, sailor who first sighted land.

1631 C.E.—Recife, capital of Brazil (now called Pernambuco), captured by Dutch. Many Marranos living there return to Judaism, thus establishing first really Jewish community in Western Hemisphere.

1654 C.E.—Recife captured by Portuguese. Inquisition restored. Jews had to flee. Twenty-three men, women, and children sought refuge in the Dutch colony of New Amsterdam (New York). Allowed to settle after some argument on condition they take care of their own poor. They were allowed to worship privately but not to build a synagogue.

1682 C.E.—A synagogue established in a rented house in New York.

1728 C.E.—First synagogue built in New York, called Shearith Israel; still in existence.

1763 C.E.—Synagogue built in Newport, Rhode Island. Later called Touro synagogue after great Jewish merchant and philanthropist, Judah Turo. Synagogue still stands and has been made a national shrine.

1776 C.E.—Declaration of Independence written.

1776 C.E.—War for independence. Activities of Hayyum Salomon who helped finance the war of independence, friend of Robert Morris, colonial treasurer.

1789 C.E.—The Constitution of the United States adopted. Bill of Rights embodied in first ten amendments guaranteeing religious freedom to all.

1776-1789 C.E.—Jewish population in United States estimated at three thousand, mostly Sephardic Jews from Holland, British colonies, and escaped Marranos.

1840 C.E.—Jewish population estimated at fifteen thousand, mostly Sephardic Jews.

1840-1880 C.E.—Great German Jewish immigration raising Jewish population from fifteen thousand to a quarter of a million. Polish, English, and some Russian Jews also came during this period, but most of them were German Jews seeking religious and political freedom.

1846 C.E.—Beginning of Reform Judaism in America with the coming of Rabbi Isaac Mayer Wise from Bohemia.

1880-1924 C.E.—Great wave of East European immigration stimulated by the persecution of Jews in Russia and Eastern Europe. Population increases through immigration and natural birth rate from a quarter of a million to three and a half million. Since then the growth from further immigration and natural increase made the Jewish population in the U. S. approximately six million by 1962.

1917 C.E.—Entrance of America in World War I.

1918 C.E.—Beginnings of large-scale philanthropy for relief and rehabilitation of East European Jews in Europe and in Palestine.

1942-1945 C.E.—World War II.

1932-1962 C.E.—Period of large scale philanthropy. Development of Federated Funds and United Appeals reaching into hundreds of millions for relief and rehabilitation. This period also a time of community organization with the development of federations and community councils.

Bibliography

Books for Further Reading

The following list of books recommended for further reading is by no means either the most complete or the best available. However, the present writer had to choose from a vast library of worthwhile works touching every question mentioned in this book. He chose those with which he is most familiar and which he feels are best suited to the ordinary reader. The books listed below are merely suggestions.

THE BIBLE

The Holy Scriptures, Jewish Publication Society, 1939, authorized Jewish version.

The Holy Bible, revised standard edition, Thomas Nelson and Sons, 1952. The latest revised Protestant version of the Old and New Testaments.

"*The Legacy of the Prophets*," by Raphael H. Levine. A pamphlet published by the National Federation of Temple Brotherhoods.

The Bible for Home Reading, by Claude G. Montefiore, 2 vols.

The Literature of the Old Testament, by J. A. Bewer, Columbia University Press, 1922.

Pathways Through the Bible, by Mortimer Cohen, Jewish Publication Society.

The Prophets, Their Personalities and Teaching, by Beryl D. Cohon, Charles Scribner's Sons.

The Story of the Prophets, Isaac Landman.

THE TALMUD

Everyman's Talmud, A. Cohen.

A Rabbinic Anthology, Claude Montefiore and James H. Lowe.

The Talmudic Anthology, Louis I. Newman, Behrman House.

The Talmud, H. Polano, 1878.

The Wisdom of Israel, Lewis Browne, Random House.

JUDAISM

Judaism as Creed and Life, by Morris Joseph, London, 1925 (Reform).

Basic Judaism, by Milton Steinberg, Harcourt, Brace & Co., 1947.

The Jewish Religion, by M. Friedlander (Orthodox).

Jewish Theology, by K. Kohler (Reform).

247

The Essence of Judaism, by Leo Baeck.
Judaism as a Way of Life, by S. S. Cohon, Union of American Hebrew Congregations (Reform).
Judaism in Theory and Practice, by Beryl D. Cohon, Bloch Pub. Co., 1948.
What Jews Believe, by S. S. Cohon, U. A. H. C. (Reform)
What Jews Believe, by Phillip Bernstein, 1951.
What is a Jew?, by Morris Kertzer, Collier Books, 1961.
Judaism, by George Foot Moore, 2 vols.

JEWISH HISTORY

A History of the Jews, Solomon Grayzel, Jewish Publication Society, 1947.
A History of the Jews, A. L. Sachar, Alfred Knopf and Co., revised in 1951.
Stranger than Fiction, Lewis Browne, 1925.
History of the Jews, H. Graetz, 1891, 6 vols.
A History of the Jews in the U. S., Lee J. Levinger, U.A.H.C., 1935.

ANTI-SEMITISM

Must Men Hate?, Sigmund Livingstone, 1944.
"The Resolution of Intergroup Tensions," Gordon W. Allport, pamphlet of National Conference of Christians and Jews, 1952.
Living Without Hate, A. J. Murrow, Harper Bros., 1951.
Anti-Semitism Yesterday and Tomorrow, Lee J. Levinger, Macmillan Co., 1936.

JEWISH CUSTOMS AND PRACTICES

The Jewish Festivals, H. Schauss, Union American Hebrew Congs.
The Lifetime of the Jew, H. Schauss, Union American Hebrew Congs.

GENERAL

The Universal Jewish Encyclopedia, 10 vols.
The Jews, Their History, Culture and Religion, edited by Louis Finkelstein.
A Social and Religious History of the Jew, Salo W. Baron, 3 vols.

CHRISTIANITY AND JUDAISM

Judaism and Christianity Compare Notes. Rall and Cohon.
A Catechism of Christian Doctrine (Catholic), revised edition of the Baltimore Catechism.
Year Book of Christian Churches. 1952.
One God, Fitch, Lothron Stoddard Co.
Jewish Sources of the Sermon on the Mount, Gerald Friedlander, 1911.

A Jewish View of Jesus, H. Enelow.
Jesus of Nazareth, Joseph Klausner.
Why Jesus Died, Pierre Van Passen.
Jesus in the Jewish Tradition, Morris Goldstein, 1950.

Index

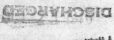